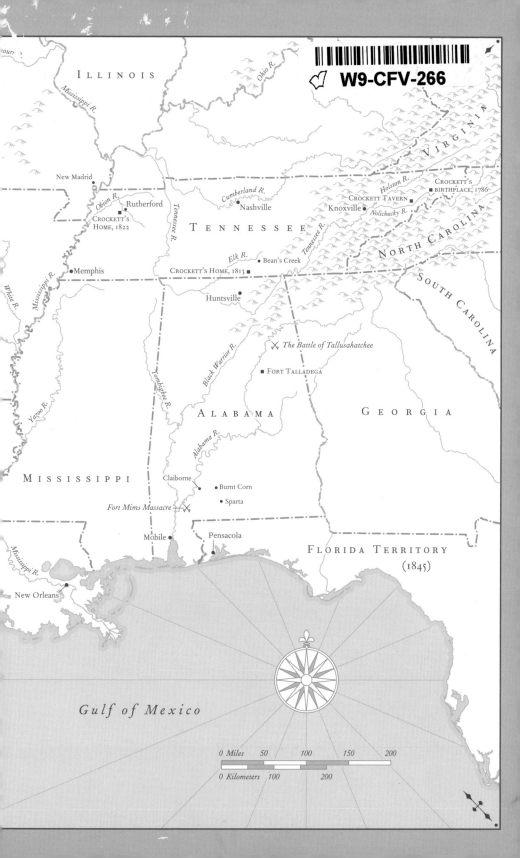

ILLINOIS

Mississippi R.

Ohio R.

VIRGINIA

New Madrid

Cumberland R.

Holston R.

CROCKETT'S
BIRTHPLACE, 1786

•Rutherford

CROCKETT TAVERN

Obion R.

Nashville•

Knoxville•

Nolichucky R.

CROCKETT'S
HOME, 1822

Tennessee R.

TENNESSEE

Tennessee R.

NORTH CAROLINA

Elk R.

•Memphis

CROCKETT'S HOME, 1813 ■ •Bean's Creek

SOUTH CAROLINA

White R.

Mississippi R.

Huntsville•

The Battle of Tallusahatchee

■ FORT TALLADEGA

Black Warrior R.

ALABAMA

GEORGIA

Yazoo R.

Tombigbee R.

Alabama R.

MISSISSIPPI

Claiborne•

•Burnt Corn

• Sparta

Fort Mims Massacre

Mobile•

•Pensacola

FLORIDA TERRITORY
(1845)

Mississippi R.

New Orleans•

Gulf of Mexico

0 Miles   50   100   150   200

0 Kilometers   100   200

American Legend

Also by Buddy Levy

Echoes on Rimrock:
In Pursuit of the Chukar Partridge

American Legend

The

REAL-LIFE ADVENTURES

of

DAVID CROCKETT

Buddy Levy

G. P. Putnam's Sons

New York

G. P. PUTNAM'S SONS
Publishers Since 1838
Published by the Penguin Group
Penguin Group (USA) Inc., 375 Hudson Street, New York, New York 10014, USA * Penguin Group (Canada),
90 Eglinton Avenue East, Suite 700, Toronto, Ontario M4P 2Y3, Canada (a division of Pearson Penguin
Canada Inc.) * Penguin Books Ltd, 80 Strand, London WC2R 0RL, England * Penguin Ireland, 25 St
Stephen's Green, Dublin 2, Ireland (a division of Penguin Books Ltd) * Penguin Group (Australia),
250 Camberwell Road, Camberwell, Victoria 3124, Australia (a division of Pearson Australia
Group Pty Ltd) * Penguin Books India Pvt Ltd, 11 Community Centre, Panchsheel Park,
New Delhi–110 017, India * Penguin Group (NZ), Cnr Airborne and Rosedale Roads,
Albany, Auckland 1310, New Zealand (a division of Pearson New Zealand
Ltd) * Penguin Books (South Africa) (Pty) Ltd, 24 Sturdee Avenue,
Rosebank, Johannesburg 2196, South Africa

Penguin Books Ltd, Registered Offices:
80 Strand, London WC2R 0RL, England

Library of Congress Cataloging-in-Publication Data

Levy, Buddy, date.
American legend : the real-life adventures of David Crockett / Buddy Levy.
p.   cm.
Includes bibliographical references.
ISBN 0-399-15278-4
1. Crockett, Davy, 1786–1836.   2. Pioneers—Tennessee—Biography.   3. Frontier and pioneer life—Tennessee.
4. Tennessee—Biography.   5. Legislators—United States—Biography.   6. United States. Congress. House—
Biography.   7. Alamo (San Antonio, Tex.)—Siege, 1836.   8. Soldiers—United States—Biography.   I. Title.
F436.C95L48   2005   2005053472
976.8'04'092—dc22

Printed in the United States of America
3   5   7   9   10   8   6   4   2

Book design by Stephanie Huntwork
Endpaper map by Jeffrey L. Ward

While the author has made every effort to provide accurate telephone numbers and Internet addresses at the time of publication, neither the publisher nor the author assumes any responsibility for errors, or for changes that occur after publication. Further, the publisher does not have any control over and does not assume any responsibility for author or third-party websites or their content.

No man can make his name known to the forty millions of this great and busy republic who has not something very remarkable in his character or in his career. But there is probably not an adult American, in all these widespread States, who has not heard of David Crockett. His life is a veritable romance, with the additional charm of unquestionable truth. . . . As such, his wild and wondrous life is worthy of the study of every patriot.

JOHN S. C. ABBOTT, 1874

CONTENTS

ACKNOWLEDGMENTS

Many people deserve thanks for their assistance at various levels in the creation of this book. My core group of writing colleagues, the Free Range Writers, has been supportive and constructively critical throughout the entire process of this book and during all my writing endeavors since the late 1980s, and my appreciation of their support is deep and abiding. They are Collin Hughes, Kim Barnes, Jane Varley, and Lisa Norris. My agent, Scott Waxman, was instrumental in the conception of this work, and he provided sage counsel during the proposal phase, offering a shrewd editorial eye and positive vision for what the book could become. He is creative, attentive, exceptional. Thanks also to his colleague Sally Wofford-Girand for recognizing that Scott and I would be a good fit and for introducing us, and to Rob Buchanan for first taking an interest in the book. Chris Pepe, my editor at Putnam, offered excellent advice and keen insight throughout, her wealth of experience showing in her deft sense of pacing and brevity. Working with her has been a genuine pleasure.

Four noted (and oft-quoted) scholars quickly responded to a barrage of unsolicited e-mail queries, and I very much appreciate their passion, their scholarship, their forthcoming and candid responses, their depth of knowledge. Thanks to William C. Davis, Michael Lofaro, Andrew Burstein, and H. W. Brands.

I am indebted to a number of archivists and librarians for their good-spirited assistance as I researched this book. Notably, the entire staff at the Tennessee State Library and Archives in Nashville was extremely helpful, immensely knowledgeable, and always professional. Thanks especially to archivists Susan Gordon and Darla Brock, as well as Marylin Bell Hughes. At the Smithsonian National Portrait Gallery, Lizanne Garrett was cheerful, expeditious, and efficient in helping me with images and portraits.

The Center for American History at the University of Texas in Austin was an invaluable resource, and their entire staff made my visit and work enjoyable and efficient. The Daughters of the Republic of Texas Library at the Alamo is a remarkable place, and one senses the history all around those hallowed grounds. The folks there are friendly, detail-oriented, and passionate about Texas history. Warren Stricker, archivist, was particularly helpful and provided me with timely assistance and ideas. At my own institution, Washington State University, I have benefited immensely from interlibrary loans in Holland New Library. The fine, hardworking staff, especially David Smestad, Nancy Beebe, Bob Davis, Shirley Giden, and Kay Vyhnanek, have allowed me to obtain a wide array of materials from a web of libraries and research institutions around the nation, with impressive speed and efficiency.

My early readers included dear friends John Larkin and Kim Barnes, whose sharp eyes and attentive scrutiny I need and greatly appreciate. Longtime friend and muse Sara Aglietti provided spirit, affirmation, and sense of humor. Computer guru Sharon Harris kept me from blowing up my computer. I value her kind patience.

Thanks, finally, to my entire family, immediate and extended, whose support is unequivocal and deeply appreciated. To my lovely children, Logan and Hunter, who endured my absences, and to my wife and partner, Camie, who has always believed in me: you give me more than you will ever know.

Prologue

THERE ARE MEN, and there are legends, and in rare instances the two converge.

On a late December evening in 1833, a weather-worn but well-dressed man of forty-seven heads down the blustery Washington City (present-day Washington, DC) streets toward the Washington Theatre. There is a distinct swagger in his gait, a cockiness and confidence in his purposeful stride and compact, stocky frame. His angular face and aquiline nose are ruddy and wind-scoured, betraying a life outdoors, and his hands, though they have not felt the sure tug of reins or the smooth stock of a hunting rifle in quite some time, are still calloused and craggy.

As he walks, people call out, and some crane their necks as he passes, hoping to get a better look. When they do, their faces brighten with recognition. He smiles and walks on, nodding and waving as he goes.

He has plenty to smile about, and much on his mind as he nears the theater.

He has just begun a new book, a memoir, one he has determined will be "truly the very thing itself, the exact image of its author,"[1] though he knows there is a bit of tongue-in-cheek to that claim. The book will contain politics, too, and if he plays it right, the book might just make him some money and keep him in Congress for another term or two. Better yet, it could set him up for a run at an even bigger prize—the presidency of the United States of America. Only a few years earlier the very notion would have been preposterous. But now? Nothing seems unattainable.

He is pleased with his recent victory in a hard-fought congressional race, yet it is not so much the political victory as the attendant notoriety that has him practically giddy. More and more his name has started to appear in newspapers across the nation, stories and anecdotes about him (many of them spurious, but that does not stop them from being published), and there is even a well-known writer in Maine, one Seba Smith, who has created a character patterned after him and an ongoing dialogue in the Portland, Maine, *Daily Courier* that has begun to circulate widely across the eastern seaboard and beyond. It is hard to imagine all this hullabaloo over a man from the brambly canebrakes, a squatter from the sticks.

Even more astounding, an unauthorized biography of his life entitled *Life and Adventures* appeared early in the year, and it flew off the shelves so quickly that it was later rereleased in New York and London under the revised title *Sketches and Eccentricities*. Enthusiastic sales firmly ensconced his name and image in the public dialogue and imagination.

And now this play, *The Lion of the West*. It had originally opened in New York two years prior, in 1831, and even then there was widespread agreement that the play's central character, Nimrod Wildfire, was patterned after him. The connections and parallels were close enough that the author, James Kirke Paulding, wrote to him before the play's original release requesting assurances that the play would not be injurious to his character. The play's success simply assured his international fame.

The crowds arrive at the theater and are quickly ushered into the waiting area, men and women dispersing to take their seats. The man, the celebrity, waits restlessly until the entire theater has filled and goes silent, with just the whispery murmur of expectation coursing through the room.

Then he and the usher start down the aisle, and as they move all heads turn to him and applause begins, slowly at first, then building until everyone is clapping loudly. The man, unaccustomed to such attention and a little embarrassed, bows slightly and gives a quick wave as he takes his reserved seat at the very front and center of the theater.

Finally the curtain rises slowly and out leaps the star of the show, actor

The actor James Henry Hackett as Nimrod Wildfire,
"The Lion of the West." The character was based largely
on David Crockett, and contributed significantly to
Crockett's celebrity. (James Henry Hackett. Lithograph by
Edward Williams Clay, print 1830–1857? Smithsonian
National Portrait Gallery, Washington, DC.)

James Hackett in the role of Nimrod Wildfire. Clad in backwoods hunting regalia, in leather leggings and a woodsy buckskin hunting shirt and toting a long rifle in his arms, his head is adorned with a furry wildcat-skin hat. He steps to the front of the stage, pauses, then smiles before bowing appreciatively to the man sitting front and center, the man on whom his character, and the play he is about to perform, are based. The man rises from his seat, grinning broadly, and returns the bow, and in that moment pays homage to his very own growing legend, to the myth he is destined to become. The poignancy of this moment, the odd mirroring image, captivates the audience and they erupt in a frenzy of cheers and applause.

The man they cheer is Colonel David Crockett of the state of Tennessee, and the scene is a remarkable and powerful confluence of fiction and fact, of legend and man.

The ovation roars on, and as Crockett finally bows to the audience and takes his seat, he must understand that his present situation is unique—for the man, alive and in the flesh, has just met his own myth.

Origins

B EFORE THE MYTH AND LEGEND of Davy Crockett surfaced there lived the real man, David Crockett, born August 17, 1786, "at the mouth of Lime Stone on the Nola-chucky river" in present-day Greene County, east of Knoxville, Tennessee. A lone marble slab now overlooks the stream, marking his likely birth site. He inherited hard times and the brutal realities of pioneer life, when families could never consider themselves safe, not even in their own homes. Theirs was a self-inflicted insecurity, wrought from squatting on Indian land, a consequence of thousands upon thousands of impoverished British "frontiersmen" departing their own green shores beginning in the 1700s and swarming over what they perceived as new and open land. David Crockett's ancestors were among those hopeful nomads from Ireland and Scotland who came to the idea of America with the promise of a better and more prosperous life and then met with unexpected challenges, including coexisting with native people. The fight for this land defined nearly every aspect of the early American experience, and it was into this embattled climate that young David was born.[1]

The earliest pioneer settlers elbowed one another and the native inhabitants for the best land available. Crockett's grandfather's name (also David) appears in the court records of Lincolnton, North Carolina, for 1771, when deed records show that he purchased a 250-acre plot of ground along the Catawba River.[2] Four years later he packed up his family and scrabbled across the flinty Appalachians, descending into the verdant northeastern end of what would eventually be Tennessee.[3] The region turned out to be a contentious grid of land, with squatters and speculators believing it to be reserved for North Carolina. Simultaneously, it was among the last areas allocated by treaty to the Creek and Cherokee nations.[4] In 1776, members of the Watauga Settlement or Association, a loosely self-governed community in the heart of disputed land along the Holston River valley, engaged in a series of clashes with the Indians. Ironically, on July 5, 1776, just a day after the historic events taking place in Philadelphia, David Crockett and his son William Crockett signed a petition asking the legislature of North Carolina to annex, and thereby control, the region.[5]

Speaking of his namesake grandfather during these perilous early days, David Crockett later remarked in his narrative, "He settled there under dangerous circumstances, both to himself and his family, as the country was full of Indians, who were at that time very troublesome."

The Indians had reason to be "troublesome." The onslaught of settlers seemed unceasing, and though the local tribes (Chickamauga, Creek, and Cherokee) had signed treaties assuring them of these lands, the voracious settlers and land speculators ignored them. By 1778, North Carolina had set up laws forbidding whites to survey, or even trespass upon, Indian lands, but shrewd entrepreneurs had already set up land-purchase offices in North Carolina, claiming more than a million acres inside the Indian country.[6] Fed up and hostile, the Indians began engaging in attacks on settlers wherever and whenever they happened upon them. The Indians' only hope was to intercept the settlements head-on, attempting to continuously dislodge or dismantle existing outposts and keep the pioneers always moving, in a state of trepidation and displacement.

One day in 1778 a small band of marauding Creeks happened upon the first David Crockett's homestead in Carter's Valley. As Crockett wrote in his *Narrative,* "By the Creeks my grandfather and grandmother Crockett were both murdered, in their own house" (near present-day Rogersville, Hawkins County, Tennessee). David and his wife were at home, along with boys Joseph and their youngest, James, and all were unprepared for the stealth and speed of the attack.

A rifle shot shattered Joseph's arm, and James, who was deaf and mute and less able to flee or defend himself, was abducted. James lived with the Indians for nearly twenty years until he was, according to Crockett, discovered by brothers William and John and subsequently "delivered up" from his bondage and "purchased from an Indian trader." Having spent nearly two decades with the Indians, for years afterward James attempted, without luck, to relocate gold and silver mines he had visited while blindfolded. Brother John Crockett was away at the time of the attack, working as a backwoods ranger scouting frontier outposts. He later fathered David Crockett.[7]

For his part, John Crockett's life was marred by failed attempts and tough luck, land speculation that garnered him nothing, and, more than once, bankruptcy. Some of his tendencies—recurring poverty among them—he would pass to his son, David. But the elder Crockett was a man of solid character and an honest, hardworking nature. In 1780 he married Rebecca Hawkins, a young Maryland woman who came to the Holston Valley with her father, Nathan.[8] Almost immediately the Revolution took him away from home; he joined up with the Lincoln County militia to serve as a frontier ranger. By October 1780 he returned in time to join a group called the "over-mountain men." In his *Narrative* David Crockett remembers it this way: "I have learned that he was a soldier in the revolutionary war, and took part in that bloody struggle . . . in the battle at King's Mountain against the British and the tories."

These brave men slung their muskets over their shoulders and struck out into the mountains, joining army regulars to contest a force of nearly 1,100 soldiers under the command of British Major Robert Ferguson, who had selected the high promontory of King's Mountain for protection. The "over-mountain men" stormed in, trouncing Ferguson's force, slaughtering 150 and holding 810 captives. The defeat proved a turning point, undermining British efforts to control the Carolinas and scuttling a plan to attack Virginia.[9]

The war subsided, and in the next few years John Crockett remained near home, focusing on his family and a variety of jobs in addition to farming, including serving as a magistrate or constable in Greene County. Unlike many backwoodsmen inhabiting the territories, both John and Rebecca could read and write at least rudimentarily, an advantage in signing documents and keeping the legal details involved in court or office work in order.[10] And they concentrated, as most pioneer families did of necessity, on growing their family. By 1786 they had moved to a homestead at the confluence of the Nolichucky River and Limestone Creek, a plot of ground and dreams called "Brown's Purchase," originally "bought from the Indians by Colonel Jacob Brown of South Carolina for as much merchandise as a single pack-horse could carry."[11] They grew patchy parcels of corn, raised a few cattle and the odd hog, hoping in this way to eke out subsistence in relative safety, the continuing Indian attacks and skirmishes taking place more to the north and east of them, at least for the time being. There was also the comfort of a few friendly neighbors, their cabins and outbuildings flanking Limestone Creek and the meandering Nolichucky. The makeshift community included former Wataugans who had relocated there in a defiant act of self-government, untrusting of the far-off seats over the mountains in Pennsylvania, North Carolina, and Virginia.[12] The Crocketts and their neighbors were cash-poor and frayed from warring with Indians and the British, but they remained guardedly optimistic that their tenuous land claims and speculations would yield wealth and prosperity if they could hold on to them long enough. The Land Ordinance of 1785, which was intended to create new states from the western lands while simultaneously eradicating its indigenous populations, would allow the claimholders to resell and profit from the land.[13] In fact, the ambitious group went so far as to write a temporary constitution for a state they named Franklin, but this dream dissolved in 1789, when North Carolina resumed control, ceding its western territories to the centralized government.[14] By the time Tennessee finally became a state in 1796, John Crockett had suffered a host of troubling debts and setbacks, including a failed gristmill venture he'd entered into with a man named Thomas Galbreath. They built the mill on adjacent Cove Creek and had high hopes for its success—only to see worse luck follow bad: a violent flash flood washed the entire project downriver before it was finished. David Crockett later recalled, "They went on very well with their work until it was done, when there came the second epistle to Noah's fresh, and away went their mill, shot, lock, and barrel. I remember the water rose so high that it got up into the house we lived in, and my father moved us out of it, to keep us from being drowned."

Two other significant recollections of David Crockett's early home life underscore his fledgling fascination with the potential disaster that loomed just off the front porch of any farmstead. His earliest remembrance was of a near-death experience involving water, perhaps in part explaining what became a lifetime ambivalence toward the element. Crockett was just a toddler when he and his four older brothers were out playing along the stream; the older boys then hopped into John Crockett's canoe and pushed out into the current. Perhaps because he was so small, they left David on shore and paddled away. David realized immediately that none of them knew how to handle a boat, for it was headed backward toward a raging waterfall. A local field worker noticed their predicament and sprinted downstream after them, tearing off his clothes as he went. "When he came to the water he plunged in, and where it was too deep to wade he would swim, and where it was shallow enough he went bolting on; and by such exertion as I never saw at any other time in my life, he reached the canoe, when it was within twenty or thirty feet of the falls." The man managed to pull the boat ashore, doubtless saving the boys' lives.

Not long after this experience, another incident occurred that impressed itself indelibly into the young boy's memory. His uncle Joseph Hawkins (his mother's brother) was out deer hunting during the autumn when he saw movement in the brush. Hawkins turned, watched quietly, and when it moved again he leveled and fired into the grape bushes. As it turned out, the movement had been of an unfortunate neighbor out picking grapes, and Hawkins had shot him right through the body. "I saw my father draw a silk handkerchief through the bullet hole, and entirely through his body; yet after awhile he got well, as little as any one would have thought it. What become of him . . . I don't know; but I reckon he did'ent fancy the business of gathering grapes in an out-of-the-way thicket soon again."

His prospects flushed downstream in the flood, resilient John Crockett moved again, this time about thirty miles away to a 300-acre plot of ground on the main wagon road between Abington, Virginia, and Knoxville. It was time to try his hand at yet another opportunity: running a roadhouse/tavern. A good deal of foot and wagon traffic passed through, and it seemed potentially profitable. So, working tirelessly, John Crockett (with help from his ever-expanding family, which would eventually total six sons and three daughters, in that order) dug himself a foundation into the banks near a small spring and erected a six-room, rough-hewn log building that would be both the Crockett home and an accommodation for weary travelers.[15] It was subsistence living at best, with outdoor privies, the tavern itself weather-beaten, leaking both air and water, the in-sides musty and smoky and filled day and night with a rough lot of crude, hard men, drovers and their bedraggled families. Oxen, mules, and horses milled about, snorting, standing or shifting in their own leavings. The road accommodated a constant stream of teams traversing the frontier from east to west and back again, taking livestock, animal skins, and hard-wrought produce to market in the east, and returning with more refined goods like rugs and furnishings. The Crocketts would run this roadhouse for over two decades, finally following David's trail heading west. According to Crockett, his father's tavern

was on a small scale, as he was poor; and the principle accommoda-tions which he kept were for waggoners who travelled the road. Here I remained until I was twelve years old; and about that time, you may guess, if you belong to Yankee land or reckon, if like me you belong to the back-woods, that I began to make up my acquaintance with hard times, and a plenty of them.[16]

Even with grown sons pitching in, making ends meet proved impossi-ble for John Crockett, who had recently lost his 300-acre parcel to a 400-dollar debt and was forced to sell out at public auction for a paltry forty dollars.[17] William Line, who bought him out, apparently allowed John Crockett to retain his tavern, but the setback forced the elder Crockett to begin the rather common practice of hiring out his sons as "bound boys" to teamsters moving along the busy overland supply line. Benjamin Franklin was bound out to service at the age of twelve to an older brother, an unsuccessful venture that led to his eventually setting off on his trav-els alone.[18] On the frontier the arrangement served a dual purpose—a family could rid themselves of one hungry mouth while also garnering the scant wages of the bound boy on his return. So it was that John

Crockett struck up just such a deal with a Dutchman named Jacob Siler, who was driving a herd of cattle to Rockbridge, Virginia, and needed an assistant.

Young David Crockett headed north in his new capacity as servant boy, scared and homesick, having never been away from home before, just twelve years old, and accompanied only by a complete stranger he'd never laid eyes on until the evening before. It was winter, deathly cold, with snow swirling and drifting across the road. They straggled along for what seemed endless days, traveling by foot more than 200 miles in two weeks, the young boy trudging along with a heavy heart but duty bound to his father and his new Dutch master. Siler paid him five or six dollars for his work, which Crockett would later describe as "bait" to get him to stay on. He also assumed it would be his father's bidding:

> I had been taught so many lessons of obedience by my father, that I at
> first supposed I was bound to obey this man, or at least I was afraid to
> openly disobey him; and I therefore staid with him and tried to put on
> a look of perfect contentment until I got the family all to believe I was
> fully satisfied.[19]

Crockett illustrated his ability to play a role, and also that his charisma, if still unpolished, could work to his advantage. For weeks he assumed the guise of contented servant, convincing the family that he was happy, while planning to steal away, knowing that Siler had taken advantage of him by forcing him to stay on against his will after they'd successfully delivered the cattle. Crockett seemed to grasp intuitively that he would need to be industrious and manipulative to survive on the road.[20] One day, while playing with some other local boys along the roadside some distance from Siler's house, Crockett recognized a group of passing wagoners as friends who sometimes stopped by his father's tavern. He made himself known to an older gentleman, told him of his forced predicament, and begged to return to his own family. The wagoner, a Mr. Dunn, agreed to take Crockett along as well as protect him if the youngster would meet them down the road the next morning.

Crockett rolled up his scant belongings, tucked them under his head, and attempted to sleep, but slumber proved evasive:

> For though I was a wild boy, yet I dearly loved my father and mother, and their images appeared to be so deeply fixed in my mind, that I could not sleep for thinking of them. And then the fear that when I should attempt to go out, I should be discovered and called to a halt, filled me with anxiety; and between my childish love of home on the one hand, and the fears of which I have spoken, on the other, I felt mighty queer.[21]

Finally he could stand it no longer and rose, slinking into the darkness hours before sunrise. He broke a trail through eight inches of new snow, guessing his way to the main road as he fought a blinding blizzard. "I had not even the advantage of moonlight, and the whole sky was hid by the falling snow, so that I had to guess at my way to the big road, which was about a half-mile from the house." He endured seven freezing miles through knee-high drifts, but he was comforted by the snowfall: "My tracks filled so briskly after me, that by daylight, my Dutch master could have seen no trace which I left."

Crockett eventually stumbled upon the wagoners, who appeared as a blurry mirage, feeding their horses and preparing for the journey. The horses huffed thick plumes of steam, their nostrils edged with frost. The young boy went inside, warmed himself by the fire, ate a hearty breakfast, and departed with the wagoners and his savior, Mr. Dunn. Crockett began to dream again of home, poor as it was, and his family. The wagoners plodded slowly along the road and he "numbered the sluggish turns of the wheels, and much more certainly the miles of travel," until he determined to set out on his own on foot, for he believed he could travel twice as fast as the wagons. Crockett continued, gaunt and famished, for days until he was finally overtaken by a man leading a horse, who kindly offered him a ride. The man chaperoned him to within fifteen miles of his home. After crossing the Roanoke, they parted ways and Crockett trudged the final fifteen miles home, arriving by evening, frail and shivering, but happy to be among his own folk after nearly two months. As it turned out, the homecoming was short-lived, and little did he know that his time on the road was its own kind of learning that would come to serve him well.

Crockett settled into a fairly routine life—playing along the riverbanks and in the woods with local children and his siblings, getting his first taste of hunting as he pegged squirrels and foxes with rocks or slingshots. A hard worker, he would split wood rails for fences, swinging a hefty ax or wedge and maul, and help around the tavern in whatever way his father asked. He helped build things, repaired broken wagon wheels and buggies, and learned to work with leather and wood and steel. After work and supper he would sometimes steal into the shadowy corners of the tavern and listen to the brawling, hard-drinking teamsters tell tall tales of life on the road. He observed real, raw human behavior. Such storytelling, coupled with his time outside and out on the trail, was his earliest education in managing the unrelenting fact of frontier life.[22]

The following fall his father arranged for David and his brothers Wilson, William, Joseph, and John to enroll in a small country school. David's parents, having the bare bones of learning, understood that a formal education offered a chance for their children to succeed beyond their current station, even though enrolling more than one would have come at some financial cost, or at the very least, trade in board and lodging.[23]

But the sedentary world of the schoolroom never sat well with David, whose personality drew him outside toward the next adventure. Like his father, who occasionally used canings to solve disciplinary transgressions, young David was hot-tempered. His first stint at formal schooling proved brief and volatile:

> I went four days, and had just began to learn my letters a little, when I had an unfortunate falling out with one of the scholars—a boy much larger and older than myself. I knew well enough that though a school-house might do for a still hunt, it wouldn't do for a drive, and so I concluded to wait until I could get him out, and then I was determined to give him salt and vinegar.[24]

Young Crockett lay in wait for him by the roadside. When the boy wandered along, Crockett bushwhacked him, scratching his face and tearing at him "like a wild cat." Fearing the repercussions from an angry schoolmaster, Crockett hid out for days, pretending to go off to school each morning, then lying out in the woods all day until school was over. Then he would return home with his brothers, who agreed to keep his hooky-playing a secret from their father. Eventually, the schoolmaster sent a note home to John Crockett inquiring why David was absent. Crockett's father read the note and, as he had been "taking a few horns" of whiskey, "and was in good condition to make the fur fly," he broke into a rage, lighting after young Crockett with a hard length of old hickory. Crockett recalled:

> We had a tolerable tough race for about a mile; but mind me, not on the school-house road, for I was trying to get as far t'other way as possible. And I yet believe if my father and the schoolmaster could have both levied on me about that time, I should never have been called on to sit in the councils of the nation, for I think they would have used me up.[25]

Never before had he seen his father so angry, "puffing and blowing as though his steam was high enough to burst his boilers."

After narrowly escaping his father, Crockett sneaked to a house of an acquaintance, Jesse Cheek. Here he hired on, along with one of his brothers, to help Cheek as he headed out on a cattle drive. Crockett figured both home and school were too hot to return to for some time, so off he went on the excruciatingly long "drove," passing through Abingdon, and then through Lynchburg and Charlottesville, until they arrived in a town called Fort Royal, nearly 400 miles away, where Cheek sold his cattle. Crockett started homeward again with a new companion, and they alternately rode and tied a single horse, but Crockett soon found that this man did far too much riding and not enough walking, leaving him impatient to cut out on his own. The man gave him four dollars for his expenses on the 400-mile journey, with which Crockett bought some provisions and hoofed along the road, tired and lonely, part of him thinking that enough time had passed to allow his father's (and the schoolmaster's) rage to cool, part of him still not certain.

He soon fell in with a wagoner named Adam Myers, heading north toward Geraldstown. It was the wrong direction, but the man assured Crockett that after he finished his business he would return south to Tennessee. Within a couple of days they met up with his brother again, who pleaded with Crockett to head back home immediately. Crockett pondered this, but soon thought better of it:

> I thought of the schoolmaster and the race with my father, and the big hickory he carried, and of the fierceness of the storm of wrath that I had left him in, and I was afraid to venture back; for I knew my father's nature so well, that I was certain his anger would hang on him like a turtle does to a fisherman's toe, and that, if I went back in a hurry, he would give me the devil in three or four ways.... That

promised whipping, it came right slap down on every thought of home. I finally determined that make or break, hit or miss, I would just hang on to my journey.[26]

So began Crockett's earliest tendencies to light out, to keep moving, to live by his own devices in the woods from day to day. It may well have been at this early juncture that his famed motto began to form in his head. "Be always sure you're right—then go ahead!"

Runaway

FEAR OF PARENTAL AND SCHOOLMASTER WRATH led Crockett on a two-year odyssey and rite of passage into adulthood. By accident, circumstance, and providence, young David Crockett had found relative independence on the open road. The period conjures Mark Twain's unforgettable characters Huckleberry Finn and Tom Sawyer; Crockett relied on his guile and savvy to survive alone, living from one adventure to the next. He was also beginning to understand how to use his burgeoning charisma and personality to influence people and orchestrate their feelings toward him. To survive the rigors of the road, a young boy needed to be smart, industrious, resilient, and something of an actor, and all these traits—plus others like ambition and pride—began to germinate in the youngster.[1] Though he started for home, little did he realize how many adventures, miles, and years lay between his wandering feet and the home in Tennessee that was never far from his mind and heart.

He hired on with a man named John Gray, for whom he labored in the fields, planting grain, plowing and assisting in various chores around the farm for twenty-five cents a day.[2] He liked the feeling of freedom and independence that having his own money gave him, and he saved all he could for the next three years as he toiled the road like a grown-up teamster, but he was often duped or cheated by older and more authoritarian men, and the pay never amounted to much. The work began to strengthen him physically and mentally, giving him the taut and sinewy limbs and powerful torso that he would later use to his advantage hunting for food and furs and fighting in the military.

As it happened, Adam Myers began making pretty regular runs between Baltimore and Geraldstown, and more than once Myers asked young David Crockett if he would like to come along. At last, having earned enough money for some decent clothes, Crockett determined that a trip to an exotic place might be interesting, "to see what sort of place it was, and what sort of folks lived there."[3] It was the spring of 1800, and Crockett had never been to a real city in his life, or to the seaside. Before they departed, Crockett squared with Gray, then handed over to Myers his only seven dollars, what amounted to his entire life savings, a risky but not uncommon means of banking for a lad unaccustomed to carrying his own money around.

They obtained a wagonload of flour and proceeded on the road, Crockett anxious and excited to be going somewhere new but also busy at his tasks tending horses and stock. At Ellicott City, a mill town on the outskirts of Baltimore, a noisy roadside work crew spooked Myers's team. The horses reared, kicking and neighing, breaking the wagon-tongue off and galloping down the road, the flour barrels bouncing and exploding into a cloud of fine powdery dust. Amazingly, when all the dust and flour had settled, Crockett stood unhurt on the roadside comprehending how close he had just come to being dragged behind the wagon and "ground fine as ginger." He understood at that moment the fickle nature of providence, and he recalled it with playful metaphor: "This proved to me," he later mused, "that if a fellow is born to be hung he will never be drowned; and, further, if he is born for a seat in Congress, even flour barrels can't make a mash of him."[4]

They managed to locate another wagon and salvage the rest of their load, and Crockett and the disgruntled wagoner limped on to Baltimore. While Myers had the runaway wagon repaired, Crockett walked down to the wharf. For the first time in his life he gazed on great merchant ships, their sails flapping in the briny sea breeze, and heard the eerie creaking of the massive wooden hulls and salty ropes as thick as his waist lashed to the docks. Crockett must have faced the ocean in disbelief, for he had never conceived such things to be found in nature, or to be made by man. His imagination leapt at the possibilities, and he became so curious that he stepped aboard the nearest ship, marveling at the slow sway underfoot. An old and wizened captain met him and inquired whether he wished to accompany the ship to London, for the captain could use a boy like him, with his chipper, easygoing nature and road-hardened toughness. Though he possessed no nautical experience, the adventurous young Crockett delighted at the chance, for by now he was "pretty well weaned from home"[5] and open to the idea of new adventure.

He set off to gather his clothes, provisions, and money from Myers, but enthusiasm turned to fear when Myers flatly refused to let him have any of them, threatening to whip him and confine him if Crockett did not obey. The stern and tyrannical wagoner thus changed the course of Crockett's history, for the boy had been only minutes away from becoming a mariner bound for England. At the same time Crockett learned that trust is illusory on the frontier. Looking over his shoulder at the magnificent ships bound for faraway lands, Crockett could only do as he was told and bide his time until another opportunity presented itself. He put it like this: "I determined to throw myself on Providence, and see how that would use me."[6]

Back on the road with the wagoner, Crockett "resolved to leave him at all hazards," and before dawn one morning he rounded up what few clothes he had and took off on foot, hungry and penniless, toward Tennessee. He wandered for days, sleeping in vacant barns and hay sheds, under the eaves of outbuildings, always slinking out before dawn, afraid of being caught by the owners or overtaken by Adam Myers himself. One day he happened on another wagoner, a man named (by absolute coincidence) Henry Myers. He appeared kind, and inquired about Crockett's situation, which brought the tough youngster to tears despite his attempts to shore up. The weight of his loneliness and all his troubles bore down on him. "For if the world had been given to me, I could not, at that moment, have helped crying."[7] Through a storm of sobs Crockett told the kind Henry Myers about being deceived and ill treated in Baltimore, and how he had been left "without a copper to buy even a morsel of food."[8]

The tale enraged Henry Myers, who swore loud at the scoundrel for mistreating a young boy in this way, and he vowed to backtrack, find Adam Myers, and force him to return Crockett's money. Though he feared the eventual run-in, Crockett was bolstered by his new ally's size and passion: "My new friend was very large, stout-looking, and resolute as a tiger . . . and swore he would have my money, or whip it out of the wretch who had it."[9] They did confront Adam Myers, who blamed Crockett for attempting to shirk his duties and run off with a ship's captain bound for London. Then he admitted, reluctantly, that he had spent all of Crockett's hard-earned seven dollars. Pressed by the large and angry man, Adam Myers offered to pay Crockett back when they returned to Tennessee, and at this promise Crockett felt reconciled.

Crockett left with his new ally Henry Myers, and they traveled south together for several days. Crockett again became impatient at their progress and determined to strike out alone, on foot. But before he left, while they were all convened at a roadhouse, Myers told a small assemblage of men Crockett's tale, how he had recently been treated, and how he would be passing penniless through "a land of strangers, where it was not even a wilderness."[10] They passed around a money purse and handed Crockett the collection of three dollars.

That sum held out as far as Montgomery, Virginia, where he worked for a month for a man named James Caldwell at a shilling a day. Crockett then hired on with a hatter, Elijah Griffith, agreeing to work four years for him. After eighteen long months, Griffith fell deep into debt and fled the region, leaving Crockett broke and destitute once more.[11] A grim pattern seemed to be developing, and the perceptive youngster knew he had to break the cycle. Life on the road had taught him much, but it was not a life he wished to live permanently. Crockett worked as he could to properly clothe himself and garner a small purse, and then, weary and lonely, he cut out for home.

He arrived finally at the banks of the New River and found the water roiling with whitecaps, the froth so high that no one would risk taking him across by boat. He persuaded some folks to let him borrow a canoe, which he claimed he could navigate. Lashing his bundle of clothes firmly to the seat, he put in to the roaring, churning river, which "was a mighty ticklish business."[12] Crockett turned the canoe into the wind and waves, breakers flooding over the bow, and fought upstream nearly two miles before he could land. By the time he struck shore he was soaked to the core, the canoe half-filled with water, his hands nearly frozen to the paddle. He was so overjoyed at having made the crossing alive that he scarcely felt the cold. He plodded along for three miles until he found a house and a fire to warm him, and took "a leetle of the creater, that warmer of the cold, and cooler of the hot." It was perhaps the young man's first taste of spirits, and he did not find unfavorable the taste and effect.[13]

Warmed and fed, the pleasant burn of whiskey in his belly, he slogged on until he reached the home of his uncle Joseph in Sullivan County, Tennessee. Ironically he happened across the same brother who had accompanied him on the cattle drive of three years before.[14] After they had spent a few weeks together, David Crockett struck out for home, alone once more.

Crockett kept on until he reached his father's tavern late in the evening.[15] He humbly inquired whether he might stay the night, and as it was a roadhouse, he was allowed. Then, much like Huck Finn, he decided to play a trick on his family, keeping his identity hidden to see if anyone would know him. He had been gone for so long and had grown so much that his family did not recognize him at first, partly because Crockett remained in the dimly lit corners and hardly spoke to anyone. When they were all called to supper and seated at the table, Crockett's eldest sister finally recognized him. She sprang up, seized him around his neck, and exclaimed, "Here is my lost brother!" Crockett's own response had a Huck Finn–like sheepishness: "The joy of my sisters and my mother, and indeed of all the family, was such that it humbled me, and made me sorry that I hadn't submitted to a hundred whippings sooner than cause so much affliction as they had suffered on my account."[16]

Crockett was now sixteen, and his increase in size and age, coupled with his father's elation at his unexpected return, safeguarded him against his "long dreaded whipping." Crockett would later recall in his *Narrative*, "But it will be a source of astonishment to many, who reflect that I am now a member of Congress—the most enlightened body of men in the world—that at so advanced an age . . . I did not know the first letter in the book." With all his travel and work experiences, by pioneer standards he was already a man, yet he couldn't even write his own name.[17]

THREE

The Dutiful Son
Becomes a Man

D AVID CROCKETT'S HOMECOMING heralded growth and change, the arrival of a more devoted and responsible, even dutiful, son, a young man with a budding sense of self and an understanding of the importance of how others perceived him. He viewed his father as an honest if unlucky man and endeavored to help him as much as he could. A strict paternal system of order by necessity ruled the frontier, and although by most measures David Crockett was already himself a man, he would remain under his father's command and tutelage until he moved out and started his own family. Also, throughout his life David Crockett illustrated judiciousness, a fair-minded personality reflected in his decision making. Arriving home after such a long absence, he still felt duty-bound to his father.

During David's years away his father had continued to buy on credit, ending up indebted to others more frugal or fortunate. As a result, he had creditors all over the county. John Crockett viewed his son's return as an opportunity to help him repay at least a couple of these debts, after which time he would consider them even and turn his son loose. David remembers the deal they struck: "He informed me that he owed a man, whose name was Abraham Wilson, the sum of thirty-six dollars and that if I would set in and work out the note, so as to lift it for him, he would discharge me from his service, and I might go free."[1]

Crockett tore into this new responsibility with tenacity and the vigor he had learned in all his odd jobs away from home. He toiled tirelessly, working every single day straight for the entire half-year period. Impressed by this work ethic, Wilson asked Crockett to stay on, but Crockett declined, finding Wilson's place and company shady. "It was a place where a heap of bad company met to drink and gamble, and I know'd very well if I staid I should get a bad name, as nobody could be respectable that would live there."[2] Already he was concerned with his reputation, and was developing a sense of what others thought of him and his associates, and how this reflected on one's character. He had seen and heard things on the road, in the dark and musty taverns and seedy roadhouses from Tennessee to Baltimore and back again, that none of his brothers or friends had witnessed—tough characters and rude talk, boozing and carousing and brawling—and he understood already, if only viscerally, that he was destined for much more.

Instead of taking the offered job, he hired on with an honest Quaker farmer named John Kennedy to eradicate another debt of his father's, this one for forty dollars. Crockett seemed bent on making up for any anguish or trouble caused by his running away, and showed an inclination to better himself. He finished the work, then borrowed one of his employer's horses and rode the fifteen miles to his father's place to deliver the paid note to him. At first John Crockett grew shamed and confused, assuming that it was the debt he still owed Mr. Kennedy being presented to him for collection, and he explained that, as usual, he hadn't the money to pay. David then told his father that the note was not a debt, but rather the amount paid in full, and that he offered it as a present to him. "At this, he shed a heap of tears; and as soon as he got a little over it, he said he was sorry he couldn't give me any thing, but he was not able, he was too poor."[3]

But there was one thing that his father could give him, and had already promised him, and that was his freedom. David Crockett recollects no words that passed between them on the subject, but with his father's debt paid he turned proudly away from his house and boyhood home and went back to the Kennedy place. A transformation had occurred: David Crockett had grown up, a rite of passage he earned by facing rather than running from hardships and oppression. He was now free to do as he pleased, to go wherever he wanted. His inquisitive mind longed for more than the open road. But he needed to get himself flush, having spent the last year or so working off his father's debts. "I went back to my old friend the Quaker, and set in to work for him for some clothes . . . my clothes were nearly all worn out, and what few I had left were mighty indifferent."[4]

Crockett understood that to improve himself he needed to look respectable, and that the young ladies around the county would not be interested in a threadbare ragamuffin. He had seen enough girls and women in his travels, plenty to have piqued his natural curiosities. During Crockett's two-month tenure at the Quaker's farm, Kennedy's niece, a young woman from North Carolina, came to visit. Crockett was immediately smitten, and his first crush gave way to full-fledged infatuation, such that he recalled it with a heightened sense of melodrama: "And now I am just getting on a part of my history that I know I can never forget. For though I have heard people talk about hard loving, yet I reckon no poor devil in this world was ever cursed with such hard love as mine has always been, when it came on me." After several stammering attempts he managed to speak to the Quaker's niece, and she was at least momentarily willing to listen to the stuttering young man. The hyperbole of young love was evident in Crockett's dire assessment of the situation: "I told her that she was the darling object of my soul and body; and I must have her, or else I should pine down to nothing, and just die away with the consumption."[5]

The girl was honest, and informed the poor lovesick suitor that she was already engaged to her cousin, one of the Quaker's sons. Crockett was devastated, his response typical of a youth's first love affliction. "This news was worse to me than war, pestilence, or famine." But the insightful young man determined something else at this moment of defeat. He somehow likened his failure to win her heart the result of his own character flaw, and knew he had to make something of himself in the world, but he felt inadequately prepared. He mused, "All my misfortunes growed out of my want of learning." By luck, Kennedy had a married son, a schoolteacher, who lived but a mile away, and Crockett struck a deal to go to school four days a week and work two to pay for his learning and boarding. He applied himself for six months, "learning and working back and forwards," until he could read in his primer, write his own name, "and cypher some in the three first rules in figures."[6] This was all the formal schooling Crockett ever had in his life, though he remained an astute student of human nature and would continue to improve his reading and writing by himself. He grew restless and desirous of the opposite sex, reasoning that a spouse would somehow complete his metamorphosis into manhood. As he put it, "I concluded I couldn't do any longer without a wife; and so I cut out to hunt me one."

Soon enough, Crockett met and took a shine to Margaret Elder, one of three eligible and attractive sisters who lived in the neighborhood. Margaret was coy and evasive and Crockett was stricken with longing. "I would have agreed to fight a whole regiment of wild cats if she would only have said she would have me." He persisted, giving her very little peace until she broke down and consented, and they set a wedding day. Crockett even went so far as to obtain a marriage license on October 21, 1805, in Dandridge, Tennessee.[7] One Saturday, just a few days before the appointed nuptials, Crockett went to see his fiancée. He had a brand-new long rifle, which he carried to hunt the woods for deer, and he planned to stop along the way to participate in a shooting competition. At just nineteen, Crockett was already a deadeye marksman, and he won a whole beef in the contest, then sold it for five dollars "in the real grit," hard currency rather than banknotes. Winning the contest and the cash put Crockett in "a flow of good humour," which translated to carousing and backwoods frolic that took him and the other contestants through the night and well into Sunday. Drunk and dirty, reeking of booze and tavern smoke, Crockett stumbled to Margaret's uncle's house, where he met her sister, who blubbered that Margaret had deceived him; she was already promised to another man, and they were to wed on the following day. Crockett's tardiness and tendency toward debauchery certainly hadn't helped his cause.[8] Though the sister urged him on, claiming her mother preferred Crockett, he stopped in his tracks, devastated again. "My heart was bruised, and my spirits were broken down . . . so I bid her farewell, and turned my lonesome and miserable steps back again homeward, concluding that I was born only for hardships, misery, and disappointment."

The rejection put Crockett in "the worst kind of sickness—a sickness of the heart and all the tender parts," and he moped about, twice heartbroken and utterly dejected. When it came to love, he appeared only destined for heartache. "I now began to think, that in making me, it was entirely forgotten to make my mate; that I was born odd, and should always remain so, and that nobody would have me."

Evenings, after long and arduous days of work, Crockett would sling his rifle over his shoulder and head out into the dense forests to hunt, and the time afield, kicking along through the soft ferns and grasses, crawling along fresh game traces, took his mind off his suffering. On one such evening Crockett came to a clearing and the house of a Dutch widow and her daughter, a girl with whom he was acquainted but for whom he had no amorous intentions. He referred to her as being "well enough to smartness, but ugly as a stone fence." She was also loquacious and amusing, free to poke fun. She jibed at Crockett for his recent disappointments with women, reminding him of the old aphorism that "there was as good a fish in the sea as had ever been caught out of it." His heart still ailing, Crockett doubted this adage very much, and at any rate, whether it were true or not, looking upon her homely visage he concluded that she was not one of the good fish. The girl must have felt sorry for him, because she invited him to their family's reaping, where she promised to introduce him to one of the prettiest girls in the entire region. Reapings were multiday community frolics, or "stomp downs," that included some work in the form of harvest, but were primarily social events complete with music, dancing, games and competitions, and skits and plays for the children. Crockett enjoyed a good time as much as the next fellow, and he was already starting to sharpen his bragging and storytelling skills. He had learned that a tale improves with the telling, until he even believed some of his fabrications himself. He agreed to invite as many friends along as he could find, and he would come to the reaping.

Almost as soon as he arrived he blended in well, his gregarious nature at home meeting new people. Among the large assemblage there was a particular "old Irish woman" who immediately accosted Crockett and, as he put it, "had a lot to say." She turned out to be the mother of the girl he had come to meet, had been informed of his business there, and teased him, praising his "red cheeks" and promising she had a sweetheart for him. Crockett had been jilted enough to remain wary of his prospects, but later that evening he was introduced to the Irishwoman's daughter, Polly Finley, and he was not disappointed. "I must confess," he said, "I was . . . well pleased with her from the word go. She had a good countenance, and was very pretty, and I was full bent on making up an acquaintance with her."

As the sun set, lively music started up and with it people began pairing up and dancing, swinging and knee-slapping to the fiddle tunes. Crockett asked Polly to dance, and they took "a reel" together, then sat down and conversed throughout the remainder of the evening, dancing when the mood struck them or others prompted them. The competitive and persistent young man may even have tried his hand at the fiddle. Polly's mother, Jean Kennedy Finley, came around periodically, which did not go unnoticed by Crockett, who even became a bit nervous and confused when she jokingly referred to him as her "son-in-law." Already a shrewd student of human nature, Crockett understood the importance of gaining Polly's mother as an ally, and he treated her with great politeness, giving her much more attention than he would have otherwise. He looked at it this way: "I went on the old saying of salting the cow to catch the calf."

The frolic continued all through the night, right on until sunrise and the first chirpings of birds. In the dawn twilight they engaged in a series of plays to entertain the youngsters, and Crockett reckoned he had "not often spent a more agreeable night." Youthful heartache often mends with subsequent infatuation, and Crockett's recent maladies of the spirit were assuaged by his new prospects. He found that his "mind had become much better reconciled than it had been for a long time," and he immediately returned home to the Quaker's and struck a deal to work six months straight for a fair-priced horse. Proper courtship of the Finley girl would require transportation and money, so he put in hard at work for the next six weeks until her image and his memories of her so clouded his thoughts and daydreams that he simply had to go see her and meet the rest of her family. He mounted his new horse and rode off to her house, where he finally met her father, a man he immediately found amiable. Mrs. Finley proved "as talkative as ever," and inquired all about Crockett, trying to assess his potential as a husband and son-in-law. Manipulative, pushy, and opportunistic, she failed to tell him that there was a rival suitor in the mix. Crockett figured that out soon enough when Polly arrived home with the rival at her side.

"There was a young man with her, who I soon found was disposed to set up claim to her, as he was so attentive to her that I could hardly get to slip in a word edgeways." But the sting he still felt fanned a competitive flame in him: "I was determined to stand up to my rack, fodder or no fodder." Crockett feigned departure to see if Polly might give him some indication as to her desires, and sure enough, she suggested that as Crockett had just arrived, and lived fifteen miles off, that he should stay and the other fellow might depart. Crockett quickly took advantage of the situation, culling Polly from "her old beau" like a cutting horse, and eyeballing him now and again "fierce as a wild-cat" until the rival begged off. Pleased with his progress, Crockett soon discovered that he had yet another complication—Polly's mother favored the rival. Crockett remained undaunted, managing to stay through supper and the rest of the night, departing the next morning for home.

Crockett applied himself to work and some hunting in the evenings, all the while thinking of Polly. A few weeks later, he was invited to participate in a wolf hunt. Wolves were plentiful in the area, and farmers viewed them as predators against their fowl and young livestock. Counties began to offer cash bounties for the hides of mature wolves, and Crockett would join up with other men and dogs and strike out into the woods.[9] On this occasion, while he was hunting in unfamiliar forests, the skies began to darken and thunder rumbled on the horizon. Crockett became disoriented, and against his own good judgment kept going, becoming completely lost as night fell. He had wandered six or seven miles into the woods and had not a clue which way to go, when suddenly he noticed "a little woman streaking it along through the woods like all wrath," and he hurried after her, figuring she would lead him to some form of shelter. He soon overtook her and to his great surprise and delight, it was Polly, also lost in the woods and running frantically to try to get home. She had been sent out to find her father's missing horses, but lost her way. She shivered, cold and scared, as lightning began to flare overhead. Crockett comforted her and suggested that they slow down. Finding a path that looked more worn than a game trace, he figured it would lead them somewhere. As blackness closed around them they came to a house, where they took shelter. "Here we staid all night. I set up all night courting; and in the morning we parted." Reoriented in daylight, they headed off to their homes, his ten miles off, hers about seven.

Crockett now grew fixated on Polly, and he turned hard to his work, adding his own rifle to his labor and paying off the bartered-for horse in only four weeks. The couple met and privately set a date for their wedding, and Crockett then embarked on the elaborate and highly ordered country customs required to gain her parents' final consent. When he arrived to ask for her hand, he found the father once again congenial, but "the old lady appeared to be mighty wrathy," Crockett noted, and when he brought up the subject of marriage, she glared at him "as savage as a meat axe." She raged loudly and ordered Crockett out of her house, even against her husband's protestations. Hoping to cool her down, Crockett reminded her that she'd called him "son-in-law" quite early in the proceedings, "but her Irish was up too high to do anything with her," so he arranged secretly with Polly that he would return the next Thursday and they would elope if they had to. He would arrive with a horse, bridle, and saddle for her, "and she must be ready to go" one way or the other, parental consent or no.

Crockett decided there was no time to dally. He'd been thwarted before, so he took out a marriage license on August 12, 1806. A friend, Thomas Doggett, cosigned the required $1,250 bond providing that no cause existed "to obstruct the marriage."[10] Then, following custom, Crockett gathered with an entourage including his eldest brother and his wife, another brother, a sister, and two other friends, and off they trotted toward Polly's house. Two miles from the house they converged with "a large company that had heard of the wedding, and were waiting." From there, Crockett sent his best man ahead as envoy, his flagon empty, to see whether he would be well-received by the father. His consent would be confirmed if he filled the flagon with liquor.

Crockett waited impatiently for the news. His recent bad luck with women and marriage, and the mother's scorn, gave him good cause for concern. Finally he heard the hooves of his envoy's horses trotting up, and he craned forward to know the answer. As he feared, Polly's mother was "as wrathy as ever," but the father had complied willingly, filling their flagon until it spilled over. Crockett responded to this good omen by hurrying to the house, leading a horse for Polly as he had promised. Crockett asked Polly if she was ready, and she nodded, then mounted her horse. Crockett commenced to depart with his bride, but Polly's father stood at the entrance to the property, barring the gate, hoping to convince the two to stay and marry right there on the premises.

He said that he was "entirely willing to the match, and that his wife, like most women, had entirely too much tongue." The fair-minded Crockett wanted to do what was right, and was willing to listen, so he whoa'd the horses and waited while William Finley took private counsel with his wife. Polly's father could be convincing when needed, because Jean Finley emerged altered, softening to Crockett right there, and asking his forgiveness for the way she had been behaving. She explained that Polly was her first child to marry, and she just wanted it to be right and proper. She promised to do the best they could by the couple if Crockett would simply agree to have the wedding at the Finley place. By this time Crockett had experienced all the wedding drama and complication he could stomach, so he consented immediately and sent for the parson. With what must have been great relief, on August 16, 1806, just a day short of David's twentieth birthday, he and Polly were wed.[11]

The rest of the evening went off without a hitch, and the next day they headed back to the Crockett Tavern. On the road they met a great company of people who had been waiting for their arrival. With all his family looking on, Crockett beamed with pride but also swallowed deeply with the responsibilities he had now brought upon himself: "And having gotten my wife, I thought I was completely made up, and needed nothing more in the world. But I soon found this was all a mistake—for now having a wife, I wanted everything else; and worse than all, I had nothing to give for it."

Polly's parents were as generous as they could be, given their own meager circumstances, but the dowry of his new wife did not amount to much—though the humble Crockett hadn't expected anything. The newlyweds received two healthy cows with calves, and immediately Crockett "rented a small farm and went to work." The farm was in close proximity to Polly's parents' place, on Bay's Mountain near Finley Springs (in present-day Jefferson County), and the two set in hard to make a home for themselves. Crockett's former employer, John Kennedy, offered a wedding gift of fifteen dollars' store credit, which Polly used for housewares and fabrics, and with this their humble cabin was soon "fixed up pretty grand." Right from the outset Polly pulled her weight, impressing Crockett with her skill and ingenuity:

> My wife had a good wheel, and knowed exactly how to use it. She was also a good weaver, as most of the Irish are, whether men or women; and being very industrious with her wheel, she had, in little or no time, a fine web of cloth, ready to make up; and she was good at that too, and at almost anything else that a woman could do.[12]

The sharecropping proved more difficult than Crockett had figured, if he had figured ahead at all, and likely hastened his developing disdain for farming. High rents and low yields on mediocre land conspired against them, and they had no profits to show after five years of continuous labor. Crockett later mused: "In this time we had two sons, and I found that I was better at increasing my family than my fortune." His first son, John Wesley, was born on July 10, 1807.[13] His second son, William, arrived sometime in 1809. With two new mouths to feed, Crockett acted in the tradition of many downtrodden yet hopeful frontiersmen: he packed up and headed out to new ground. As he put it, "I couldn't make my fortune at all . . . so I concluded to quit it, and cut out for some new country."

With the assistance of Polly's father, the young Crockett family moved nearly 150 miles in October 1811 to a five-acre patch of land near the headwaters of the Elk River's Mulberry Creek. Here, on state land, Crockett built a cabin and received a warrant for title of the property. He proudly carved his initials in a towering beech tree, like a bear marking his territory.[14] Crockett now had an old horse, a couple of colts, and woods and streams filled with game. Needing to feed and clothe his family, he began to spend more and more time out hunting, and his proficiency quickly became true expertise. Deer and small game were abundant. Crockett reflected on this time: "It was here that I began to distinguish myself as a hunter, and to lay the foundation for all my future greatness; but mighty little did I know of what sort it was going to be."

He had no understanding of the difficult trail to this "future greatness." As long as the hunting was good he kept at it, always preferring the chase and the solitary time stalking through the woods to the doldrums of farm labor. Though he tried to make a go of it by staying put on a farm, David Crockett simply was not meant for the plow, instead forever called to the unknown mysteries of the wilds. And that call would cost him. Though he entered a claim for fifteen additional acres to add to his place on the Elk River, he eventually lost the entire tract when he could not afford to pay his taxes.[15]

The Crocketts were forced to pack up once again, bearing all their belongings, which still did not amount to much, by horse and wagon to the Rattlesnake Branch of Bean's Creek, just north of the Alabama border. Crockett dubbed this home "Kentuck," perhaps presaging a future move to Kentucky, or possibly in allusion to the great hunter from there, Daniel Boone, whose legend Crockett would surely have known and admired. Though Crockett was too busy simply trying to survive from one day to the next, he was now a vital part of what would come to be known as the frontier and all that entailed, including the continued exodus westward and the sustained pressure that drove native populations farther and farther from their lands.[16] Crockett, by necessity, would have been too myopic to understand his part in this, but all around him white settlers were breaking treaties and encroaching dangerously onto land that was not rightfully theirs. Out hunting along the riverside, listening to Bean's Creek rolling gently over smooth stones, Crockett had no way of knowing that his life was about to alter dramatically, and that his skills with a rifle and as a game hunter would very soon be called upon in ways he had not anticipated, in hunting of a sort he could not have imagined.

FOUR

"My Dander Was Up"

FOR MOST OF THE FIRST HALF OF HIS LIFE David Crockett had lived from day to day, driven by the barest necessities of food, clothing, and shelter. His connection to the outside world, to the affairs of the nation or state, or even political circumstances affecting his own region, mattered little to him until his family had settled tenuously on Bean's Creek and a grave situation of immediate concern arrived smack on his doorstep.[1]

Crockett well knew that his own country was technically at war, since even the semiliterate would have seen the regional papers on June 4, 1812, announcing that the House of Representatives had voted a declaration of war against Great Britain. The British had persisted in seizing American sailing vessels, refusing to vacate forts and outposts on American territory.[2] Within a week, President James Madison had signed the bill and the nation was officially at war. But this meant effectively little to the lives of struggling frontier families who viewed the war as the government's problem. However, the British soon managed to bring the matter closer to home when they began to coerce Indian allies from as far north as the Canadian boundaries to the southern reaches of the Gulf Coast,[3] convincing them (with money, goods, and weaponry) to resist the settler's en-croachment by any means possible. Crockett remembered the stories of the attacks by rampaging Indians on his own parents and grandparents, and he was aware of the dangers they presented, but his was generally a noncombative nature, unless he was provoked. Though his temper was short, Crockett was more of a prankster who liked a good time. While he wasn't opposed to a little playful scuffling among the boys, actual war was another matter entirely. "I, for one, had often thought about war, and had often heard it described; and I did verily believe in my own mind, that I couldn't fight in that way at all."

Just as the young Crockett family was settling in on Bean's Creek, re-lations between settlers and the native population stretched perilously, then finally snapped. The whites continued their ceaseless pouring in and scattering out to the west and south, pushing populations of the Creek Nation to frustration and anguish as whites squatted on and acquired dis-puted lands. By circumstance, Crockett and his family were part of this exodus, and they dwelt on the cusp of what would come to be known as the War of 1812, and its bloody offshoot, the Creek War.

Due south, around the gulf port of Pensacola, tensions were high and the political situation was complicated. In addition to the growing English and Indian alliance, the Spanish, having yet to agree that West Florida had been annexed by the Louisiana Purchase, created a thorny problem by supplying Gulf Coast Indians with arms and hard goods, even food.[4] In July 1813, an armed band of Indians were moving north to their Upper Creek villages along the Pensacola Road when they were surprise-attacked by a party of 180 soldiers. The Creek band, numbering between sixty and ninety,[5] were resting in the south Alabama shade after a noon meal when the first volleys sprayed down upon them. The Indians scattered into the woods, dispersing but remaining quiet and on guard. Relishing the easy victory, the soldiers moved quickly in and began to loot the stores, supplies, and gunpowder abandoned by the Creeks. The greed proved a tactical mistake. Outnumbered by more than two to one but emboldened with anger, the band of Red Sticks (so named for their practice of painting their war clubs bright red to symbolize the blood of their fallen enemies), led by mystics Peter McQueen and High Head Jim, erupted screaming from the woods and violently drove away the numerically superior force.[6]

They had also managed to shame and enrage the whites, who took shelter and nursed their wounds at Fort Mims, a temporary installment erected around the home of Georgia trader Samuel Mims. The structure, about forty miles north of Mobile near the Alabama River, served as a safe haven and way station for troops moving through the region. As it turned out, their security at this outpost was more perceived than real.

The Creeks were ripe for retaliation. For some time they had been rallying behind the emotional and spiritual guidance of the great Shawnee chief, Tecumseh, whose name, legend, and uncompromising beliefs still echoed across the Appalachians. Tecumseh's resonating oratory had inflamed and inspired the Creek Nation. He had witnessed and endured enough displacement, enough broken treaties, enough illegal ransacking of Indian land. He raged and railed, inciting his people to action:

> Let the white race perish. Back whence they came, upon a trail of blood, they must be driven. Back! Back into the water whose accursed waves brought them to our shores! Burn their dwelling—destroy their stock—slay their wives and children, that the very breed may perish. War now! War always! War on the living! War on the dead![7]

Tecumseh's agenda had been bold, unwavering, and visionary—he would lead a confederacy of Indian tribes, stretching from the St. Lawrence River near the Canadian border and sweeping through the mountains and seaboard all the way south to the Gulf of Mexico, in a sustained attack

against the violating white settlements. Only such a determined and organized cooperation among native people would realize his dream, "to
sweep the white devils back into the ocean whence they had come and re-
store the continent to its rightful owners."[8]

Such was the sustained wrath that the Red Sticks brought to Fort Mims
on August 30, 1813. With the memory of the brutal surprise attack at
Burnt Corn still fresh and the wrath inspired by Tecumseh coursing
through the Red Sticks' warring veins, Chief Red Eagle (William Weath-
erford) led a stealthy attack on the encampment. The Red Sticks were
soon amazed to find the gates normally barring entry to Fort Mims wide
open—and unguarded! At high noon the Indians streamed into the defenseless fort, striking down a Major Beasley, who at last and too late had
arrived to defend the gates. War whoops wailed across the grounds and
soon Creeks overwhelmed the garrison in what would later be described
as among the more shocking and barbarous massacres in the annals of
frontier history. Dreadful carnage continued for the next few horrific
hours. "The bullets, the knives, the war clubs, the tomahawks, the flames
did their work, and more than half a thousand human beings in a few
hours perished."[9]

Though the attack was in fact retaliation, the grotesque nature of the
slayings would be most remembered among settlers. Women and children
were corralled, then butchered and scalped. Young children were held by
their legs and flung, their heads battered against the stockade walls. Women
were tackled and bludgeoned, and the pregnant women were eviscerated,
their unborn infants ripped from their wombs. Blood lust consumed the
marauding Creeks, and though Chief Red Eagle later claimed he wanted
no part of the massacre and had only intended to fire warning shots, once
it started he was helpless to stop the revenge. In the end, 275 settlers,
friendly Indians and mixed-bloods lay dead; only a small and terrified
number escaped the smoldering fort to tell their harrowing tale.[10]

News of the massacre traveled like wildfire across the frontier settlements, arriving even to quiet and pastoral Bean's Creek, where Crockett would have been out hunting along the banks, watching snapping turtles sunning on rocks, listening to the rising of trout in the slow-moving water. When he got word of the attacks, Crockett's normally congenial nature shifted and he determined that it was time to fight, perhaps as he remembered what had happened to his own family:

> For when I heard of the mischief which was done at the fort, I instantly felt like going, and I had none of the dread of dying that I expected to feel . . . I knew that the next thing would be, that the Indians would be scalping the women and children all about there, if we didn't put a stop to it.[11]

But packing up and running off to fight would come at a significant familial cost, and Polly begged Crockett not to go, arguing that she was in a strange land, and remaining alone raising two young boys was a frightening prospect for her, as fit and able as she was. In his absence, who would work what little ground they were attempting to farm? Who would provide them with meat? Her arguments impressed him, and he thought carefully about the consequences, and about her desires. Finally, the general call to arms, prompted by Tennessee Governor Willie Blount, and an innate patriotism, made up Crockett's mind. "I reasoned the case with her as well as I could, and told her, that if every man would wait till his wife got willing for him to go to war, there would be no fighting done, until we would all be killed in our own houses . . . and I believed it was a duty I owed to my country."[12]

Though Polly fought his decision with pleading and tears, she ultimately turned back to her weaving and the duties of the farm as he rode off to fight the Indians. "I was bent on it," Crockett later admitted. "The truth is, my dander was up, and nothing but war would bring it right again."

What Crockett would come to understand soon enough was that political machinations of national import were already at work, and that the muster to which he was responding was part of a broader movement generated from Washington itself. The Madison administration understood that these skirmishes and uprisings, incited by Tecumseh, needed to be thwarted before they gained momentum and spread to many tribes. The plan was to muster and send four armies—from Georgia, the Mississippi Territory, and Tennessee—into the heart of the Creek Nation, and convene their forces at the confluence of the Tallapoosa and Coosa rivers. The commander of the army from West Tennessee was General Andrew Jackson, a fierce, ambitious, and disputatious man with a penchant for dueling. Jackson had earned a reputation as a man not to be trifled with, an intimidating and unreasonable grudge-holder. He had killed Charles Dickenson in a duel in 1806, and was later embroiled in a scandal that threatened to tarnish his growing political reputation when he became involved in another duel between one of his young officers, William Carroll, and Jesse Benton. At the City Hotel in Nashville, tempers flared and four guns were fired, and though there remains disagreement about who fired first, Jackson took a bullet in the shoulder and was badly injured.[13] The incident cemented his image as a man with a hair-trigger temper. Jackson's shrewd political mind also understood that military fame and glory were absolute necessities for professional political advancement, and he had long champed at the bit to go fight Indians. By his early teens he had already developed deep and unwavering prejudices against the native people. Like many migratory whites, Jackson "accepted as indisputable fact that Indians had to be shunted to one side or removed to make the land safe for white people to settle and cultivate. The removal, if not the elimination of the Indian from civilized society, became ingrained in the culture."[14]

What Crockett did not know was that the army he was about to join and the battles he was soon to fight would help deliver Andrew Jackson, the man who would eventually become his nemesis, straight to the steps of the White House.

Polly had packed him down with as much dried and salted meat as he could possibly carry. He then mounted and waved good-bye to her and the boys as he rode off to Beaty's Spring, south of Huntsville, Alabama, where troops were gathering. "At last we mustered about thirteen hundred strong, all mounted volunteers, and all determined to fight, judging for myself, for I felt wolfish all over. I verily believe the whole army was of the real grit."[15] Most men, like Crockett, had left their women and children at home alone, or with relatives and neighbors, to fight a nebulous enemy, and the fear and uncertainty moved through the camp. Commanders reminded the men of the dangers they were to encounter, offering any who wished to leave the chance, before they were officially signed on for service. Crockett noted with pride that none took up the offer. Crockett himself signed on for a ninety-day enlistment.[16]

Word went round the spring that General Andrew Jackson was on his way south from Nashville with a horde of foot soldiers and mounted men, and fear grew into excitement. While they waited, Major John Gibson arrived, seeking volunteers to go with him into Creek country on a scouting mission. He wanted two of the most experienced woodsmen and marksmen available. David Crockett was immediately selected, proudly asserting that he would "go as far as the major would himself, or any other man," providing that he could select his own partner. Crockett selected a young man named George Russell, a son of old Major Russell, also of Tennessee. When Major Gibson saw Crockett's choice, he balked, claiming the stripling hadn't beard enough—he sought men, not mere boys. Crockett later confessed he was "nettled" at the major's doubt in his choice, for he valued Russell's pluck, and did not believe that age determined bravery: "I didn't think that courage ought to be measured by the

"Old Hickory." Andrew Jackson as he might have
appeared when Crockett first met him during the
Creek War. (Andrew Jackson. Hand-colored stipple
engraving by James Barton Longacre, copy after
Thomas Sully, 1820. Smithsonian National
Portrait Gallery, Washington, DC.)

beard, for fear a goat would have the preference over a man."[17] After some argument on the matter, Crockett held firm to his convictions, explaining that he had more knowledge of Russell's abilities, and eventually Gibson acquiesced.

David Crockett had entered the fray.[18] Major Gibson, Crockett, George Russell, and ten others headed out, crossing the Tennessee River at Ditto's Landing, then moving slowly and quietly due south about seven miles, making camp at nightfall. The next morning, Gibson and Crockett agreed that they would cover more ground, and more stealthily, if they split up, so Gibson took seven men and Crockett was placed in charge of five, and they agreed on a rendezvous point that evening some fifteen miles away. The loose plan was for Gibson to pass by the home of a "friendly" Cherokee named Dick Brown (who would later become a colonel and serve under Jackson), and Crockett to go by Brown's father's place, each to obtain all the intelligence they could to share when they met up. Crockett made it to the elder Brown's place, then enlisted a half-blood Cherokee named Jack Thompson to serve as a sentry. They agreed to communicate using owl hoots to avoid detection by hostiles. Crockett got to the rendezvous point that evening, and waited until nearly dark, but still Major Gibson failed to arrive. Knowing the road to be unsafe, Crockett took his men away from the well-used "Indian trace" and found a secluded hollow where they struck camp.

Deep in the night Crockett heard the screechy hoot of an owl, and he called back, and Jack Thompson emerged from the woods to report no sign of Gibson in the vicinity. They rested there until morning, but still Major Gibson failed to arrive. Here Crockett made his first significant military decision. Some of the men wished to return, spooked by the prospect that Gibson and his men had been butchered, but Crockett reminded them of their duty, that they had "set out to hunt a fight," and that they were bound to "go ahead, and see where the red men were at."

Moving quietly and carefully, they proceeded to a Cherokee town some twenty miles distant. At midafternoon of the second day they came to the home of a man named Radcliffe, who had married a Creek woman, had two sons, and was living in relative harmony on the edge of the Creek Nation. Radcliffe was well stocked, and he fed Crockett's company and their horses, providing the hungry men with "a great deal of potatoes and corn, and indeed, almost everything else to go on." But Radcliffe himself was "bad scared all the time," noting that just an hour earlier there had been "ten painted warriors at his house," and if Crockett and his boys were discovered there, the whole lot of them would be killed for harboring the soldiers. Again Crockett's men voiced their concerns and suggested they leave, but Crockett scoffed that his business had been to hunt "just such fellows," so they saddled up and readied to ride on. Crockett also understood that under such circumstances, it would be cowardly to return to camp.

They rode into the night, their shadows passing through the trees under brilliant moonglow, all of them afraid to talk for fear of the "painted warriors." They moved this way, sometimes riding and sometimes leading their horses through slanting moonlight and dark shadow, across creeks and ponds, until they came upon "two negroes, well mounted on Indian ponies and each with a good rifle." Ironically, the men were slaves who had been stolen from their owners by the Indians, and had fled them, and were now attempting to get back to their white masters. The two were brothers, big friendly fellows, and each could speak in Creek dialect as well as in English. Crockett convinced one to continue on to Ditto's Landing, the other he adopted as a guide and translator. Eventually they heard voices and discerned the flickering of firelight through the trees, and arrived at the encampment of a group of friendly Creeks.

Some of the boys had bows and were firing arrows into the trees by the fire and moonlight, and Crockett, playful and inquisitive even under the dangerous conditions, proceeded to join in, amusing himself and "shooting with their boys by pine light." Finally the newly enlisted slave guide returned from speaking with some of the Indian elders, his face grim. He told Crockett that the friendly Indians were concerned, and if the Red Sticks found them there they would all be killed. Crockett relayed the following message back through his translator: "If one would come that night, I would carry the skin of his head home to make me a mockasin." The friendly natives laughed aloud at the correspondence, admiring Crockett's nerve and humor, but unease spread across the camp, and the men left their horses saddled for a speedy departure, and they lay down, attempting to get what little rest they might with their rifles clutched across their chests.

Crockett lay dozing fitfully when he was startled awake by "the sharpest scream that ever escaped the throat of a human creature." An Indian runner arrived in camp and reported that the Red Sticks were coming, and that a large war party had been "crossing the Coosa River all day at Ten Islands, and were going to meet Jackson." Crockett believed he finally had some useful intelligence, and he felt compelled to convey the news quickly. News of Red Sticks on the warpath sent the friendly Indians into a frenzy, and they packed up and scattered in a matter of minutes. Crockett gathered his men and they quickly mounted up, knowing they had a long and dangerous ride ahead. By now, they were some sixty-five miles from the landing. They stopped only to water and feed their horses, riding through soreness and hunger and fear, until they came once more to the friendly Indian community where they had met Radcliffe, now vacated and ablaze. Crockett later boasted that they could easily have taken on a force of five to one, then mused wryly: "But we expected the whole nation would be on us, and against such fearful odds we were not so rampant for a fight."

The torched town at their backs, they rode by moonlight through the night, and stopped at daybreak at the Brown residence, to feed their horses and eat a hurried meal themselves. At about ten o'clock the next morning they straggled into the main camp, their horses limping and foaming, the men hunched, saddle-sore. Crockett dismounted and reported immediately to Colonel John Coffee the news from the front. Coffee took in the information but seemed to pay little attention to it, practically ignoring Crockett, who fumed quietly, not wishing to offend a superior: "I was so mad that I was burning inside like a tarkiln, and I wonder that the smoke hadn't been pouring out of me at all points." His rightful anger at being disregarded would shortly turn to real bitterness. Major

Gibson, who had been presumed dead, emerged the next day, and when with great histrionics and embellishments he relayed nearly the identical information that Crockett had previously brought to Colonel Coffee's attention, the Colonel acted immediately. Many years later Crockett would still remember that feeling of disparity, of being ignored simply because he was a common foot soldier and not an officer. It convinced him that the world could be hierarchical and unfair. "When I made my report, it wasn't believed, because I was no officer; I was no great man, just a poor soldier. But when the same thing was reported by Major Gibson!! Why, then, it was all as true as preaching, and the colonel believed it every word."

This perceived betrayal would be the seed of a growing distrust in Crockett, a deep suspicion of rank and privilege that would eventually fester into near-hatred.[19] At the time, Crockett simply took the insult quietly and went about his business, as immediate action was called for. Under orders, the troops erected breastworks nearly a quarter-mile long around the camp, and Colonel Coffee dispatched news of the developments via Indian runner to General Jackson, now stationed at Fayetteville.

Jackson was in no mood for the information. He had only arrived the previous day, and his arm was bound and useless, injured by gunshots in the aftermath of the duel between Carroll and Benton. The wounds had been very serious, a bullet having pierced, and remaining lodged in, his upper left arm, another slug having shattered his shoulder. Using "poultices of elm and other wood cuttings as prescribed by Indians,"[20] a doctor staunched the blood flow that might have killed him; it took Jackson almost a month before he was fit to rise from bed. But Jackson, as his men were coming to understand, was no ordinary man, and it would take more than a shattered arm to sideline him. As it turned out, he would carry that bullet with him through the Creek War, the Battle of New Orleans, and right into the White House, where it would finally be removed in 1832, in an operation without anesthesia, by a prominent Philadelphia surgeon.[21]

So it was that Jackson mounted up and drove a furious forced march from Fayetteville, arriving at Crockett's camp in some discomfort, his men's feet raw and blistered from the speed of their journey. Already, for the last six months or so, Jackson's men had privately been calling him by a nickname. Noting his toughness, willpower, and refusal to yield to anything, they dubbed him "Old Hickory," and the name stuck.[22] On October 10, 1813, acting on news conveyed to him by Colonel John Coffee but first iterated by David Crockett, an able volunteer of the Tennessee Mounted Militia, Old Hickory, his left arm slung tight to his body and his face stern and narrow but betraying no sign of pain, rode into camp and dismounted. The fight with the Indians he had longed for was about to begin in earnest.

The breastworks that the troops had erected were never put to use in defense, for Jackson's ire was up, and he quickly determined that the best tactic was to go on the offensive, to intercept the mobilizing Creeks to the south. Fatigued and hungry but now driven by the possessed Old Hickory—"Sharp Knife" to the Indians who faced his blade—the Tennessee Volunteers marched and rode for Creek country, essentially retracing Crockett's reconnaissance by crossing the Tennessee River, moving through Huntsville, then fording the river again where it passed Muscle Shoals. Jackson had split his forces, sending about 800, Crockett among them, under Colonel Coffee. The river at Muscle Shoals was dangerous, nearly two miles wide, with a bottom so rough and rocky that a number of horses' hooves became lodged between submerged stones. The riders leapt from them into the water and sloshed along on foot, leaving the panicked animals to founder, topple, and eventually drown in the muddy roil. The men drove on to the headwaters of the Black Warrior River, very near the present-day location of Tuscaloosa, and moved as quietly as a troop of 800 could into what was known as Black Warrior Town. It had recently been vacated, and the hungry soldiers proceeded to loot what stores remained, securing "a fine quantity" of beans and corn. Content with new food supplies, they then torched the town down to ash.

Crockett noted that the fields surrounding the town were pocked with very fresh Indian tracks, and he surmised that the Indians had anticipated their arrival and fled not long before. They pressed on, a number of the men now gaunt and haggard, heading to meet Jackson's main army at the fork where Crockett was originally to have made rendezvous with Major Gibson. The forces convened and reassessed the situation, realizing by the next day that they were completely out of meat. Jackson's army had originally assembled and moved so fast that they had arrived insufficiently supplied, and Crockett's division had used up all the provisions they had brought. Crockett took the opportunity to approach Major Gibson and ask him whether he might venture afield to hunt as they marched along, and Gibson consented, perhaps wishing to confirm the rumors of Crockett's hunting skills and marksmanship. They certainly needed the food.

Crockett left the main and had gone only a short distance when he came across a fresh-killed deer carcass, so recently dropped that the flesh was "still warm and smoking." Crockett surmised that the Indian who had killed the deer would be very close at hand, perhaps still in shooting range, and though, as he put it, "I was never much in favor of one hunter stealing from another, yet meat was so scarce in the camp, that I thought I must go in for it." Without hesitation he slung the bloody carcass in front of him across his horse and rode with his spoils until nightfall.

Returning to camp, he distributed the deer among the men, keeping a small portion for his immediate group, and they gorged themselves on the venison and gnawed on small rations of parched corn. The next day Crockett hunted again, this time flushing a pack of hogs from a canebrake and shooting one, and in moments gunfire erupted all around, sounding like battle fire. When Crockett arrived back with his hog he happily discovered that the hogs had broken from the cane toward the camp, and the soldiers had harvested a good number of them, and a hefty beef cow as well. They were temporarily sated, but things would soon get worse again. "The next day we met the main army, having had, as we thought, hard times and a plenty of them, though we had yet seen hardly the beginning of trouble."

Crockett's foreshadowing would prove accurate, as the men would soon face hardships so severe as to test their tenacity and patriotism and result in a famous mutiny. The convened armies plodded on, arriving back at Radcliffe's place, only to find that Radcliffe had stashed and hidden all his provisions. Even more remarkable was the revelation that the runner who'd screamed in the night and claimed that the "Red Sticks" were on the move had actually been an elaborate and successful ruse by Radcliffe himself. They had been tricked, and Crockett noted that there was nothing much to do about it but march on to Camp Wells, between Tuscaloosa and Gadsden. They vowed retribution against the scheming Radcliffe, and for atonement they absconded with "the scoundrell's two big sons . . . and made them serve in the war." At length they came to Ten Islands, on the Coosa River, where Coffee's troops erected a stockade named Fort Strother and began to send out small spy parties to get detailed and confirmed intelligence on the Creek activity and locations. These forays paid off, as it was soon determined that a fairly large contingent of Indians remained encamped at the town of Tallusahatchee only eight miles away. This was it; Jackson's chance to avenge the atrocity of Fort Mims was now at hand.

General John Coffee (he had just recently been given the raise in rank) divided his troops and cleverly marched one line on either side of the town, and in this way used a force of some 900 men to completely encircle a town, and within it, about 180 Creek warriors. They tightened their line. Clearly outnumbered, a good many Creek women began fleeing from houses and shelter and clinging to the soldiers, begging mercy, surrendering. But with Fort Mims still a vivid memory and rallying cry, Coffee's men closed their ranks tight and Captain Eli Hammond, commanding a band of rangers, advanced straight on the town. Crockett remembered that "Indians saw him, and they raised a yell, and came running at him like so many red devils." The outnumbered Indians fired guns and arrows when they could, then quickly retreated into houses and behind outbuildings, waiting. What followed was a scene as gruesome as Fort Mims. Crockett and his contingent chased a group of forty-six Creek warriors into a house, and arriving there, watched as a brave and unyielding Creek squaw drew a bow back with her feet and let fly an arrow that pierced and slew one of their men. It was the first man Crockett ever saw killed by bow and arrow, and the act enraged him and his men. "She was fired on, and had at least twenty balls blown through her. . . . We now shot them like dogs; and then set the house on fire, and burned it up with the forty-six warriors in it." Similar routs took place all around the town, and in a very few minutes the attack was complete, with 186 Creek warriors dead and eighty taken prisoner. Just five of the white troops perished in the raid. Jackson would comment, "We have retaliated for the destruction of Fort Mims."[23]

The next day, November 4, 1813, Crockett and some of his men returned to the Indian town to see what provisions might be salvageable, for the men were by this time exceedingly hungry and without reinforcements or arriving supplies. Crockett witnessed a macabre scene of dead, bloated, and half-charred bodies strewn across the town. "They looked very awful, for the burning had not entirely consumed them, but given them a very terrible appearance, at least what remained of them." Buildings creaked and groaned, half-toppled and smoldering, and they found one large house that had a big store of potatoes underneath, in its cellar, and Crockett noted that "hunger compelled us to eat them, though I had a little rather not, if I could have helped it, for the oil of the Indians we had burned up on the day before had run down on them, and they looked like they had been stewed with fat meat."[24]

The stores of found food proved insufficient, and Crockett returned with these men to Fort Strother, where everyone was near starvation.

They rested and attempted to recuperate for a few days. Crockett noted that food was so scarce they were forced into "eating beef-hides, and continued to eat every scrap we could lay our hands on." Men grew weak, sicker than they had already been, and morale fell dangerously low. Then, on November 7, news came from a runner that Fort Talladega, just thirty miles to the southeast, was under siege by a large band of hostile Creeks. The runner, the chief of a friendly band of Creeks ensconced in the fort, had escaped in a hogskin and himself run the thirty miles to take personal audience with General Jackson.[25] Jackson did not delay, ordering his men to march immediately and not stop through the long night.

At sunrise, Crockett and his cohorts arrived near the fort to find "eleven hundred painted warriors, the very choice of the Creek nation." The hostile Creeks had surrounded the fort, which housed a good number of friendly Creeks, and the hostiles were attempting to coerce the friendlies to join them in a fight against Jackson and his army, bribing them with the lure of guns, money, fine horses, blankets, and a host of other spoils of war, which were exaggerations given the army's actual threadbare condition. The military tactic Jackson would employ was the same that had worked at the bloody massacre of Tallusahatchee: surround and encircle the enemy with two connecting lines of men, then tighten the circle and squeeze them into panic.

Crockett and his men, under the direction of Major Russell, moved in on the fort, but they saw no activity; they heard only the voices of friendly Indians hooting and calling out, attempting to warn the soldiers about an ambush. Enemy scouts had signaled the soldiers' arrival, and thousands of war-ready Creeks lay hunkered down, concealed under the riverbanks of a branch that curved around the fort "in the manner of a half moon." They waited patiently, some almost fully submerged in the icy water, others lurking stealthily quiet in the woods between the stream and the fort. Finally, nervous friendly Indians, noting that the soldiers were not heeding their warnings, ran out from their positions around the fort to the front of the line. The disturbance halted the march, and not wishing to miss the opportunity, the Creeks hidden beneath the stream opened fire. When some of the soldiers began to retreat, Indians poured from the banks in waves, a thousand or more, and Crockett noticed with some trepidation that "they were all painted scarlet, and were just as naked as they were born." The Indians fired as they ran, and "came rushing forth like a cloud of Egyptian locusts, and screaming like all the young devils had been turned loose, and the old devil of all at their head." Some of Russell's men dismounted and ran on foot to the security of the fort, and horses, cavalry soldiers, and Indians swirled in a chaotic mass of gunfire and screams. Crockett's company waited until the Indians ran shrieking within close range, then lowered and let fire, killing many and sending them fleeing toward the other line. The Indians were caught in a downpour of deadly crossfire, and the soldiers killed "upwards of four hundred of them."

In the battle frenzy, the warriors retaliated with guns, bows and arrows, and tomahawks, and a large group managed to create enough sustained pressure to cause a rift in the army's line. Crockett remembers that they were drafted militia whose line parted, and this gap let a considerable number of Indians escape and begin an effective counterattack, forcing a livid General Andrew Jackson to retreat. Jackson later fumed, "If the line had not given way, [we] would have repeated Tallusahatchee."[26] In a separate missive to Governor Blount, Jackson reiterated the gravity of his men's blunder: "Had there been no departure from the original order of battle, not an Indian would have escaped." The error had cost him a quick ending to the war; the breach allowed nearly 700 Creeks to escape and forced Jackson to retreat and regroup back at Fort Strother. In an official report to General Claiborne, Jackson's seething rage is clear: "I was compelled by a double cause—the want of supplies and the want of cooperation from the East Tennessee troops, to return to this place."[27] His situation was most dire: his men were quite literally starving, he'd received no support or provisions, and a large number of his troops, who had been with him since the Natchez expedition clear back in January of 1813, were on expired terms—it was time for them to go home, and mumblings of discord echoed around the camp.

What happened next—a mutiny—has become a matter of controversy, the versions shedding a good deal of light on the character of both David Crockett and Andrew Jackson. In his autobiography, which contains such convincing and accurate firsthand descriptions and observations of the attacks at Tallusahatchee and Talladega that they are considered suitable historical source material, Crockett tells the story of the mutiny and highlights his involvement in it. In Crockett's version, he and a group of volunteers, half-starved and past their enlistment dates, requested of Jackson that they return home for fresh horses and clothing, and in this way they would be prepared and rejuvenated for another campaign. Crockett notes that "our sixty days had long been out, and that was the time we entered for." According to Crockett, Jackson denied the men their wish, but in defiance of the general they saddled up and began to depart. "We got ready and moved on till we came near the bridge, where the general's men were all strong along both sides. . . . But we had our flints ready picked, and our guns ready primed, that if we were fired on we might fight our way through, or all die together."[28]

Crockett relates how they arrived at the bridge and heard the guards cocking their guns, and through fog-thick tension the men marched on past the bridge, Jackson's guns leveled on them: "But, after all, we marched boldly on, and not a gun was fired, nor a life lost." As recounted, it was a defiant, dramatic, and defining act of mutiny, but it simply did not happen that way.

In fact, Crockett and his volunteer cohorts had enlisted for ninety days rather than sixty.[29] It's true that the tattered troops were starving, destitute, and ready for home. On November 17, 1813, Jackson broke his camps and struck toward Fort Deposit, where provisions might be found. About twelve miles from camp they were met by a supply train of "150 beeves and nine wagons of flour,"[30] and the troops halted to devour meat and bread. Jackson, viewing them as sufficiently replenished, then ordered them to march straight back to Fort Strother. But the men were mentally and physically broken, and they could not take the suffering anymore. Some were verbally defiant, barking violent protestations; others merely bowed their heads in silent disdain of their commander. One company, rather than returning toward Fort Strother, turned and continued in the direction of Tennessee.

Jackson immediately mounted a horse and galloped in a long detour ahead of the deserting men. Along the way he met General Coffee and his cavalry (Crockett likely among them). Jackson ordered Coffee to fire on any men who refused orders. He sat tall and angry in the saddle, his eyes blazing with resentment and disgrace; he bellowed that he would shoot to kill any man who did not turn back.

Jackson's fierceness must have been impressive, for the company, after very little deliberation, did an about-face, and as ordered, headed back.[31] But there was even more widespread mutiny afoot at the main encampment, and Jackson returned to find a large brigade readying to leave. His left arm still in a sling from the Benton-Carroll duel injury, Jackson used his good arm to heft up a musket and level it across the neck of his horse. He trotted to the front of the brigade and pointed it at the line of men, raging in near-hysteria that he would kill the first man to move forward. Major Reid and General Coffee eased behind in support.

Disconsolate, but realistic enough to see that Jackson and his supporters were deadly serious, the mutineers turned around and slowly, begrudgingly, returned to their posts. The fiery, unyielding General Andrew Jackson had nearly single-handedly thwarted the mutiny, and Crockett was probably there to witness it.

Of Crockett's entire 211-page autobiography, only the mutiny—and two small subsequent skirmishes which he records, but in which he did not participate—are thought to be intentionally falsified for political purposes. Writing in 1833, perhaps eyeing the presidency himself and certainly considering an audience that was politically educated, Crockett by this time had become nearly rabid in his anti-Jackson rhetoric, and he would have his readers see him as scathingly independent, a man not tethered to the command of another; not a party man. In reconstructing the events, Crockett clearly understood the implications of his historical past and his political future. Later, he would express this independence by pointing out that around his neck you would find no collar with MY DOG printed on it, belonging to Andrew Jackson. The fabrication of the mutiny details suggests yet again that Crockett possessed a keen awareness of how he was perceived—freewheeling, an individual and independent thinker, a man who made his own decisions and stuck by them. His "boasts" also show that he was not beyond what he must have considered a small "white lie," a yarn or tall tale that was very much the domain of the frontier. In his recollection of the mutiny, storyteller Crockett had spun a pretty good one.

In truth, Crockett served out his full enlistment and did not depart until his official expiration on December 24, 1813.[32] But what he had seen in the command of Andrew Jackson must surely have impressed him: a steadfast resolve, an ability to lead men—with violence and fear tactics if necessary, beyond limits they thought they were capable of themselves, "a hard and determined disciplinarian."[33] Crockett would certainly remember the man he'd seen in the fields, a leader whose

> very physical appearance announced his character and personality. His face was long and narrow, his frame gaunt, indeed emaciated. But his manner radiated confidence, enormous energy, and steely determination. It bespoke a spirit that willed mastery over his damaged body. His presence signaled immense authority.[34]

David Crockett had observed this man and been moved by him. He was even, perhaps, envious of Jackson, of his ability to lead, of the respect and deference he commanded, of the way others acted in his presence. It was an envy that would ultimately fester and turn to vehement hatred, a kind of poison that would come to affect and even drive his decisions in Congress, where he would one day oppose Jackson's long-developed position on the Indians. But for the moment, Crockett would take his experiences and war-weakened body back home to Bean's Creek. His first tour of duty was officially up; it was time to head home to Polly and the boys to see how they were keeping.

FIVE

"Mounted Gunman"

CROCKETT WOULD BE HOME for less than a year, just long enough to reacquaint himself with his young wife and two boys. He would hunt as much as he could through the cold rigors of winter, then with the spring thaw make a token effort at getting a few plants in that might realize an early harvest, before the war effort called again. Crockett would later claim that he had a hankering for a "small taste of British fighting," though it is just as likely that the money he had earned on his first enlistment had whetted his mercenary appetite, and the cavalry work had certainly paid better than dirt farming. Plus, it suited his adventurous spirit, his growing notion of what it meant to be a frontiersman. For whatever combination of reasons, and certainly being paid to ride around on horseback and sometimes go hunting was among them, in early autumn—September 28, 1814—Crockett mustered again, this time signing on as one of the Tennessee "Mounted Gunmen."

During his time at home, Crockett busied himself with farm chores, playing with the boys and perhaps showing them the rudiments of tracking and shooting, and no doubt telling them and Polly stories of his adventures. While Crockett was thus engaged, General Andrew Jackson had minor details like an ongoing revolution, and the subjugation of the entire Creek Nation, on his plate. First he endured near disaster at Emuckfaw Creek, where his resting troops were ambushed and nearly defeated. His rear guard collapsed, retreating shamefully until Jackson himself shored up the line under a volley of heavy fire. He barely managed to re-form his columns and organize them into a counterattack that yielded a decisive victory, though he lost some twenty men and more than seventy-five were wounded. After returning to Fort Strother to rest and regroup, Jackson was joined by the 39th Regiment of the U.S. Infantry and additional volunteers sent by Willie Blount of Tennessee. Jackson's force had bulged to almost five thousand.[1] Finally outfitted as needed, General Andrew Jackson would level the blade of his "Sharp Knife"[2] at the Creeks. His plan was deviously simple and yet sinister: he would follow the Coosa River to Horseshoe Bend, where he would annihilate the large encampment of Creeks there and then proceed to the Holy Ground, the confluence of the Tallapoosa and Coosa rivers. Victory here would maim and kill not only physically, but spiritually. The Creeks held the Holy Ground ("Ecunchate") sacred and protected by the Great Spirit, and "no white man could violate it and live."[3] Jackson would take pride in proving their savage religion to be mere superstition.[4]

On March 27, 1813, Jackson spurred his rejuvenated army to Horseshoe Bend (Tohopeka), a deeply wooded curve of the Tallapoosa River, where he found the Red Sticks well prepared for defense. They had situated their fort to use the natural peninsula and bluff for protection. Jackson was grudgingly impressed, noting the clever and efficient use of breastwork constructed of tree trunks, branches, and entire timbers laid upon one another in stacks. The Red Sticks had built the reinforcing wall between five and eight feet high, and left portholes through which to fire, leaving their attackers open and vulnerable in an advance. Jackson later praised their work, noting "it was a place well formed by Nature for defence & rendered more secure by Art."[5]

But the opportunistic and tactical Jackson quickly saw that the situation could be turned to his advantage. He knew he had them significantly outnumbered. And they were so well garrisoned, with only one entry/exit, as to be effectively penned up for slaughter.[6] He quickly surrounded the fort, ordering Coffee's cavalry of 700 men plus almost 1,300 Indians—Cherokees and friendly Creeks—to cross the river and fan out, surrounding the peninsula, hemming the Creeks in. At that, Jackson opened fire and began a bombardment of cannon fire, muskets, and rifles, riddling them for two full hours. The firing did little damage to the fortification, and it became evident that a costly frontal assault might be required. Then, without warning or orders, some of the Cherokees behind the bend hurled themselves into the frigid Tallapoosa and swam more than one hundred yards toward the opposite shore. There they absconded with Red Stick canoes, and, under heavy fire, returned to their men and began ferrying fighters across.[7]

It would prove the move that broke the attack wide open. As literally hundreds of friendly Indians now stormed the rear of the fort, the Red Sticks were forced to shift their attentions from Jackson at the front. Old Hickory seized the opportunity to drive his Tennesseans forward. The 39th Regiment, their bayonets thrust forward and glinting in the sun, were first to reach the breastworks. Taking close-range bullet fire and hearing the haunting drums and war whoops coming from inside, they poured forth. Major L. P. Montgomery clambered to the top of the barricade and waved his men on.[8] As Montgomery frantically waved his hat for his men to follow, a Red Stick musket ball struck him in the head and dropped him in the dirt below. He died instantly.

Right behind Montgomery came a brave and precocious young lieutenant from Tennessee. Sam Houston's adventurous spirit and wanderlust had led him to seek asylum from his uneventful farm life with the Cherokee. His adoptive Cherokee parents had nicknamed him "the Raven," a symbol of good luck. He joined the U.S. Army in 1813 when he learned that they paid cash for enlisting. Now Houston took up the charge when

Montgomery fell, inciting others to follow him up and over the barricade. Just moments later, Houston heard a whir above the screams and gunfire and felt the sharp and searing sting of a Red Stick arrow lodge deep in his right groin.[9] With the arrow protruding from his inner thigh Houston fought on. With the Red Sticks pinched and trapped, the killing became incessant.

Houston enlisted help in extricating the arrow, forcing a fellow soldier to pull it out for him. The barbed arrow withdrew reluctantly, and it tore flesh and veins as it ripped away. Houston limped painfully to find a surgeon to staunch the blood flow. The massacre raged on while Houston lay still, wrapped and recovering, and Jackson himself happened by to commend him and order him to remain there—the day would be won. Then Jackson, calling for more volunteers to follow him and attack a log-roofed structure where more Creeks were hunkered in, departed. Houston, who had promised his family they would one day hear of his famous name, rose in great pain and staggered forward, musket in hand, challenging any in his outfit who were brave enough to follow him. Stumbling down the ravine toward the reinforcing earthwork, Houston was stopped short as two musket balls slammed into his right shoulder and arm.[10] Field doctors tended to him, removing a lodged musket ball from his upper right arm, and dressing his bludgeoned groin with wraps and compresses. Blood issued forth in great spurts, and the doctors assumed he would be dead by morning, so they set him aside to work on others more likely to survive. Houston lay in agony all night, but he willed himself to live, and by morning he was still breathing.[11] He would recover, and his courage in battle, his willpower, and his obstinacy would become traits Jackson would utilize on the plains of Texas.

In the end, Jackson's troops set the breastworks and redoubts ablaze and the killing became point-blank, then hand to hand. The Tallapoosa at Horseshoe Bend came to be called the "River of Blood," and one private crossing the river right after the battle reported that his horse was stained blood red.[12] Perhaps recalling the atrocities of Fort Mims, some of Jackson's soldiers mutilated the dead bodies of the fallen, brandishing their knives and severing long strips of skin to dry, then making bridle reins for their horses. "They started near the heel and cut parallel slits with a knife up the leg all the way to the shoulder blade, then across to the other shoulder and down the other leg."[13] The next day, the Indian fort now a smoldering graveyard, bodies piled high and strewn about the riverbanks, Jackson called for an accurate body count. To achieve this, his soldiers paced among the slain and, taking out a blade, sliced the nose from each fallen Red Stick so as not to double count. The count came to 557 dead, and another 300 or so impaled or shot in the river, setting the total at around 850.[14] Amazingly, only twenty-six Tennessee soldiers lost their lives at Horseshoe Bend, with another 106, the tenacious Sam Houston among them, wounded. Houston would later observe of the carnage at Tohopeka with a sad and metaphoric finality: "The sun was going down, and it set on the ruin of the Creek Nation."[15]

Certainly in the mind of Andrew Jackson, the slaughter at Horseshoe Bend signaled the end of the Creek War and the death knell of the Creek Nation.[16] However, it would prove slightly more difficult than that. As he said he would, "Sharp Knife" marched on toward the Holy Ground, burning and pillaging all towns in a wide swath as he moved south, the Upper Creek country becoming a symbol of the wrath of Old Hickory. But a small and impetuous contingent of remaining Creeks, led by Peter McQueen and other mystics still loyal to Tecumseh and his teachings, had "already fled to Pensacola to seek sanctuary with the Spanish and to continue their war against the Americans."[17] For them, a battle had been lost but the war would be an ongoing struggle they would take with them to their graves if need be. While Jackson returned to Nashville to receive high praise, accolades, and ultimately the rank of major general in the United States Army for his decisive victory at Horseshoe Bend, McQueen, Josiah Francis, and a handful of other prophets ingratiated themselves with the Spanish governor in Florida, and managed to obtain British ammunition and arms to continue their resistance, small bands retreating to the mangrove swamps. These rogues needed to be dealt with, and the vengeful Jackson, acting with no direct orders from his government, called for a sort of "mop-up operation" in the South, along the Gulf. This became the operation—the Florida Campaign of 1814—that would lure David Crockett once more to serve under the now Major General Andrew Jackson.

Crockett hooked up again with Captain Russell, and his company followed on the heels of Jackson's main army march south, through some familiar and foreboding territory.[18] They passed Muscle Shoals, then the dilapidated wreckage of Black Warrior's Town, and then they struck hard southeast to Pensacola. It was a hard march, the last eighty miles on foot (there being no forage for the horses), and Crockett recalled fondly their arrival: "My commander, Major Russel, was a great favourite with Gen'l Jackson, and our arrival was hailed with great applause." Crockett later groused, a bit nostalgically and betraying some regret, that they had missed the real action. "We were a little after the feast; for they had taken the town and the fort before we got there." Crockett would discover, through excited chatter among soldiers who had been there, that Jackson's forces had taken the Spanish-held garrison of some 500 poorly armed, poorly trained, and rather passive soldiers on November 7. The takeover lasted only minutes, after which a white surrender flag appeared, flapping over the rooftops. Next to fall would be forts guarding Pensacola Bay, and Jackson knew these offered the real key to control of the region. He expected a serious skirmish of defense at Fort Barrancas, but the fleeing British and Spanish would not give him the satisfaction. Before Old Hickory could attack the next morning, the British and Spanish boarded ships and blew up the fort themselves, breaching a just-inked treaty.

Crockett remembered that evening of November 8 well, as he and some of the boys took pleasure in seeing the retreating British ships at sail out on the bay, slinking slowly away in defeat. The men procured a bottle and took a few "horns" before eventually returning to camp. Morale was momentarily high. Jackson withdrew his main troops, geared up, and headed west toward Mobile—and toward fame, glory, and military immortality at the Battle of New Orleans in a little over a year.[19]

In the meantime, David Crockett, under the direction of Major Russell and a Major Childs, was sent to the swamps to hunt down Indians who had dispersed under the advance of Jackson's army. His job, as Crockett recollected it in his patented backwoods vernacular, was to "go to the south, and kill up the Indians on the Scamby river."[20] Jackson wanted any hostile elements driven out, and he certainly did not wish them to remain in bands large enough to form and organize defenses again. Crockett, who had already shown his hunting, tracking, and scouting skills, seemed the perfect choice for such detail. The duty was hardly glamorous, and did not even constitute official "battles," but it was deemed necessary and important, so off Crockett waded into the scrubby mangroves.

He went as part of a small special unit composed of some hired-out Indian guides, Major Russell, and sixteen men, including Crockett, who had been promoted to the rank of 3rd Sergeant. Back in Pensacola they had outfitted themselves with what beef they could secure by shooting stray cattle, and had purchased other goods like sugar and coffee, and even some liquor. The terrain they entered appeared foreign to Crockett, a "piney" place pocked with saline lakes and estuaries, briny marshes "where the whole country was covered with water, and looked like the sea." They moved like apparitions through a dank and endless lattice of streams, basins, and tide pools choked by scrub oaks and thorny vines. They waded into the black and brackish water "like so many spaniels . . . sometimes up to our armpits, until we reached the pine hills, which made our distance through the water about a mile and a half."[21] The shivering men built a fire to warm themselves and dry out a little, then moved on, flanked and guarded front and rear by their Indian spies. Six miles up the

Escambia River one of their scouts crashed through the brush in a whirl-wind of panic, saying he had spied a small camp of Creeks ahead and that they ought to go kill them.

As Russell, Crockett and the men deliberated a course of action, their Indian spies readied for battle by ceremonially applying war paint. The scouts came over and told Major Russell that, being an officer and thus a warrior, he should be painted along with them. He consented, and soon he was painted just like the Indians. Russell then informed his spies how the attack would proceed: the white soldiers were to move ahead first, firing on the camp, then falling back to allow the Indians a chance to finish them off and scalp them, as was their custom. They all marched silently for-ward until they came within view of the camp, a small island, where they could see the Creeks working at "beating up what they called chainy briar root" on which they foraged and subsisted. Shots rent the air, followed by piercing war whoops, and Russell's band of men hurried to the scene. They arrived to find their two lead scouts proudly holding the decapitated heads of two Creeks, blood dripping from their severed necks.

As Crockett learned, the scouts had come across two wayward Creeks out searching for their missing horses. Crockett's spies spoke Shawnee, and tricked the Creeks into believing that they were escaping from Gen-eral Jackson. The Creeks believed them, and informed the spies of a large Creek camp on the Conecuh River, an Escambia River tributary. With that, the spies thanked the Creeks and summarily killed them. Crockett arrived to find his spies taking turns smashing the severed heads with their war clubs. Soon all the Indians with them were "counting coup," leveling violent blows on the bloody heads. Then their eyes fell expectantly on Crockett. Apparently it was his turn. "This was done by every one of them; and when they had got done, I took one of the clubs, and walked up as they had done, and struck it on the head also. At this they all gathered around me, and patting me on the shoulder, would call me 'Warrior—Warrior.'" Crockett recalled such reminiscences dispassionately, without irony, pity, or surprise, acknowledging both the brutal facts of war and how easily a soldier found himself caught up in what would today be considered barbaric behavior. At the same time there was self-preservation involved with aligning himself with the "friendly" spies and acting as if he was essentially one of them. He needed them for trustworthy intelligence and reconnaissance, and participating in this way garnered their trust. Crockett's personal communications skills were burgeoning; he was learning how to be an effective liaison.

The band then scalped the disfigured heads and moved along a sparse trail leading to the river. They skulked quietly down the trace, blood still drying on their hands, and came across an equally grotesque scene. A Spaniard, along with what they presumed to be his wife and four young children, lay recently killed and scalped. Crockett used his deft understatement to describe the situation: "I began to feel mighty ticklish along about this time, for I knowed if there was no danger then, there had been; and I felt exactly like there still was." The group pressed noiselessly on, pushing through gnarled thicket, and the trace they followed came to the river, which they took downstream until they were across from the Creek encampment. The spooky place turned out to be entirely abandoned but for "two squaws and ten children."

They were dismally low on provisions, and it was almost dark, the riverbanks and ground inland of them almost impassably thick with cane and vine. Russell determined that the best action would be to scout the camp on the Conecuh, and he selected Crockett to strike out in a canoe that night and search downstream for provisions of any kind. Crockett chose a man named John Guess, and a friendly Creek, and they paddled into the blackness. "It was very dark, and the river was so full that it overflowed the banks and the adjacent low bottoms. This rendered it very difficult to keep the channel, and particularly as the river was very crooked."

In the end the plan to attack the camp on the Conecuh was scrapped by Major Uriah Blue of Virginia, and the scouting parties straggled down the

Escambia to a place called Miller's Landing. Then, after a brief skirmish that included the killing and scalping of a handful of prisoners by the Indian guides, they set out to traverse the panhandle country. Crockett had found little on his night foray, and had then been recalled, so that by now everyone was "in extreme suffering for want of something to eat." They had originally departed with twenty days' ration of flour and only eight days' worth of beef, and had now been out for thirty-four days.[22] They forded the Chattahoochee River, to the country toward the east, needing sustenance in the worst way. Coupled with near starvation, they were also suffering from exhaustion and overexposure to the hostile elements. One evening their spies returned to report they had found a village, and hoping for provisions to pillage, they made a gallant push to reach the place. The delirious men would surely have fantasized about food as they traveled all night. Around sunrise they could see the outline of the town, and they readied for battle, loading guns and snapping bayonets into place. The famished men charged the town, but to their deepest despair, they found not a single human being left to kill, the Indians having departed sometime before their arrival. They poked around, disconsolate, and when they found nothing, not a single pallet of corn or potatoes, they burned the place to the ground, then turned back toward their camp of the previous night, weather-beaten, and, as Crockett put it, "as nearly starved as any set of poor fellows ever were in the world."

With the situation about as grim as it could get, they divided their regiment. Major Childs and his men headed for Baton Rouge, where they would eventually meet up with some of Jackson's forces returning from victory in New Orleans. Major Russell took some of his men, and a few of the fittest horses, in the direction of Fort Decatur, along the Tallapoosa, in hopes of obtaining some food, for death by starvation had become a very real possibility. For fit hunters familiar with the region and its denizens, the country around there should have been rich with game— larger animals like deer and wild hogs roamed the higher, drier ground, and the bogs and marches teemed with smaller fare like turtles and squirrels and other rodents. The brackish waters might provide oysters and fish if one knew where to look, or how to harvest them.[23] But the hunting was difficult and not always productive, especially when conducted by diminished, even emaciated men unfamiliar with this hostile terrain. Days and nights blurred together into a surreal slog as the company struggled on through the marsh. Crockett, clearly the most accomplished and productive of his group, hunted every day now, and "would kill every hawk, bird, and squirrel" he could find. Others followed his lead, and when they would finally cease at night and slump over in exhaustion, the hunters would hurl their kill into a general pile to divvy up at mess.

By now the men were driven insane with hunger, with a few secretly hoarding food. Even raw or barely cooked meat parts like turkey gizzards were worth lying about, fighting for, even killing over. Cooperation, unity, and order unraveled, and Crockett rightly surmised that things had deteriorated to the point that "every fellow must shift for himself," so he took the small company of his mess and decided to strike out from the other troops. Crockett rationalized it this way: "We know'd that nothing more could happen to us if we went than if we staid, for it looked like it was to be starvation any way; we therefore determined to go on the old saying, 'root hog or die.'"[24]

They kept on for three excruciatingly slow days, passing through ghostly remnant towns littered with the bodies of Indians, but still shooting very little game and finding nothing to eat, until at length, as Crockett related, they nearly gave up. "We all began to get ready to give up the ghost, and lie down and die; for we had no prospect of provision, and knew we couldn't go much further without it." Still Crockett kept hunting, and he managed a few small squirrels. He later fired on a hawk, and a group of wild turkeys broke from the thick cane, and a hunting partner of his dropped one. Crockett crept after the scattered flock, following the river bottom, energized with the prospect, at long last, of cooked game.

He calmly lowered his rifle on a turkey sitting alongside the creek, and "blazed away . . . and brought him down."

They ate a large turkey soup that night, their hollow bellies distending. Afterward, some of their messmates related that they had found a bee tree in their absence, so they all took out their tomahawks and hacked into the hives, scooping out handfuls of the honey, gorging themselves to near bursting, growing sick it had been so long since their stomachs had been full. They plopped down to rest, and when Crockett woke he struck out to hunt again, his belly full, hopeful that their luck was changing. He killed a deer that very morning, a fine buck, and flushed a large bear that made him regret he had no dogs to chase after it with, for he "always delighted most in bear hunting." When he returned to camp with his buck, he found that his group had rejoined a division of his "starving army," so he generously gave his deer to the men.

They were fourteen miles from Fort Decatur, where they figured to restock provisions. But when they arrived, they found things were sparse and hard at that fort, too, and after consuming one ration of meat "but not a mouthful of bread," Crockett commandeered a canoe and paddled across the Tallapoosa to Big Warrior's town to see what he could scrounge. Industry compelled him to trade ten bullets and some gunpowder for two hatfuls of corn, a deal which suited him just fine, since he couldn't eat bullets. Crockett recollected that he prized that ration of corn so dearly he "wouldn't have taken fifty silver dollars for it." The next morning they struck out for Hickory Ground, the site of the treaty with the Creeks on August of 1814. Provisions there proved inadequate again, and they kept on, marching nearly fifty miles up the Coosa north to Fort Williams, where they were met with meager rations of parched corn and one ration each of flour and corn. Still, it was food, and they lived on the hope of finally arriving back at Fort Strother, where there were sure to be rations.

By now many of the horses, overworked and underfed, were dying.

Crockett reckoned that as many as thirteen perished in a single day, and they were forced even to abandon good saddles and bridles—an unthinkable waste, but necessary—there simply was no way to carry them.[25] They wandered on day after day, measuring the miles by now familiar landmarks like Fort Talladega. Death and its reminders were all around them, including ghoulish and chilling scenes that only war can conjure: "We went through the old battle ground, and it looked like a great gourd patch; the sculls of the Indians who were killed still lay scattered all about, and many of their frames were still perfect, as the bones had not separated."

Crockett and his mates looked near dead themselves, the few clothes they still possessed rotting off their bodies. The days were bone-numbing cold, the nights a huddled shiver that proved nearly unbearable. At the depth of winter, the creeks froze at their edges, and chill winds tore down from the northern ranges in violent gusts that the men would wince away from. Finally, one frigid morning, the knot of men came upon East Tennessee troops bound for Mobile, and to Crockett's great surprise and happiness his younger brother Joseph was among them. The meeting was a fortunate and timely windfall, for Crockett fueled on fresh provisions and there was even food for his horse, which was about to give out. Crockett spent a rare happy evening with his brother and a number of "the boys" from their own neighborhood, hearing stories and anecdotes from back home near Bean's Creek, which he now began to long for most painfully. The next morning Crockett said farewell to Joseph and the others, then crossed the icy Coosa and at long last arrived at the relative comfort and safety of Fort Strother. He had survived a nightmarish detail that nearly took his life, had participated in killing what few hostile Indians there were to be found, but mainly had been engaged in a protracted struggle for survival in an unfamiliar and inhospitable wilderness. He figured enough was enough, so after recuperating and eating for a few days, he struck out for home and shortly arrived to a joyous homecoming with

Polly and the boys. Crockett reveals a modicum of sensitivity and soft-
ness in his character, as well as a hint of insecurity, when he recalled seeing them after so much hardship and such depravity:

> I found them all well and doing well; and though I was only a rough
> sort of backwoodsman, they seemed mighty glad to see me, however
> little the quality folks might suppose it. For I do reckon we love as
> hard in the backwood country, as any people in the whole of creation.

Crockett had spent only a few happy days at home when he received
unsettling news: he had orders to return to the front, and join an expedition to Alabama, along the Cahaba and Black Warrior rivers, "to see if
there was no Indians there." Having seen what he had, Crockett figured
that there probably weren't too many Indians to be found, and anyway, he
needed to be home for a time. He arranged, in a move that was common,
legal, and in no way considered suspect, to buy off his remaining time of
one month to a young man raring to go. Crockett would later note, with
a hint of "I told you so," that on his return, the young man confirmed
Crockett's suspicions and they did not find any Indians, "any more than if
they had been all the time chopping wood in my clearing." This seemed
to validate Crockett's decision not to go back, and David Crockett's military career was over. He received an honorable discharge from Briga-
dier General John Coffee, and concluded his six-month tour of duty as
4th Sergeant.[26]

It was time to reconnect with his loved ones, to head back into the
fields and try to make a go of farming if he could, to hunt the hollows and
haunts around his cabin and see if he might prosper. He'd proven his
worth as a backwoodsman and knew he could endure most any physical
hardship that might come his way, and he'd seen some of the ways that
politics play out, even on such a stage as a battlefield. He had served under the now famous General Andrew Jackson,[27] a notch on the leather

belt certainly, and undoubtedly fodder for tall tales at taverns around Bean's Creek. But mostly, at almost thirty years of age with practically nothing to show for it, David Crockett was glad to be back home. As it turned out, the joy of his reunion would be as fleeting as a rainbow after a spring squall.

SIX

Trials on the Homefront

H OMECOMINGS WERE INTIMATE and intense times on the dangerous frontier, and the Crocketts' would have been equally close and passionate. A new baby, little Polly (her given name was Margaret), arrived early in the year, but the bliss of her arrival was soon overshadowed by the specter of devastating loss. By summer Crockett's wife, Polly, was gravely ill. Crockett recalled the time with anguish as "the hardest trial which ever falls to the lot of man." Though the exact details of Polly's death are not known, it is conceivable that she died from complications after the birth of her daughter. But myriad killers—including malaria, cholera, and typhoid—plagued the far outposts of civilization and any of these may have been the cause.[1] In any event, Polly apparently suffered for a time before, as Crockett put it with a touch of poetry, "death, the cruel leveler of all distinctions,—to whom the prayers of husbands, and even of helpless infancy, are addressed in vain,—entered my humble cottage, and tore from my children an affectionate good mother, and from me a tender and loving wife."

Prone to almost melancholy lovesickness as an adolescent and a young man, Crockett genuinely adored his Polly, and he never spoke of her at any time with anything other than tenderness and devotion. He took the loss very hard. The event forced Crockett to ponder his own faith (what there was of it) and the divine workings of the world, which he understood are often inexplicable. Crockett described Polly's passing as "the doing of the Almighty, whose ways are always right, though we sometimes think they fall heavily on us." His referral to her "sufferings" suggests she did not perish overnight, or even quickly, but rather hung on and fought for a time.[2] And then, she was gone. Crockett buried Polly in the nearby woods adjacent to the cabin, marking her grave simply with a pile of rough stones, and never spoke or wrote of this trial again. Though it was summer, darkness seemed to fall all around him. Crockett languished in depression, commenting flatly that "it appeared to me, at that moment, that my situation was the worst in the world."

The realities of frontier living, however, did not offer the luxury of moping about feeling sorry for oneself for very long. Crockett was immediately faced with a daunting fact: he was left alone with two young boys and a tiny infant daughter, and he was rather ill-prepared to care for them. The boys, at about eight and six respectively, would have been somewhat accustomed to chores and light farm work, but they were used to having a mother around, and her absence was immediately felt. The situation was bleak, as Crockett needed to try to keep the farm functioning, while hunting for food would keep him away for extended periods. It was an onerous time for the widower.

Under the circumstances, Crockett could easily have buckled, pawning his children off on relatives, but to his credit he sought other alternatives. He loved his boys, and the tiny babe Polly would certainly have reminded him of his wife. Crockett vowed to keep the family together, come what may. "I couldn't bear the thought of scattering my children," he confessed. One solution dawned on him, and he set about convincing his brother and his wife and children to move in and help around the place. They kindly consented, but Crockett admitted that it wasn't ideal. "They took as good care of my children as they could, but yet it wasn't all like the care of a mother. And though their company was to me in every respect like that of a brother and sister, yet it fell far short of being like that of a wife."

Though throughout his narrative he is often philosophical and even poetic, Crockett was primarily a man of action, of deeds over ideas. As a young man he had "set out to hunt" a wife when he determined that he needed one, and now again he looked forward to what he must, of necessity, do. The motto to which he ultimately yoked himself (and which adorns the title page of his narrative) exclaims: "Be always sure you're right, THEN GO AHEAD!" This was not the credo of a man who made hasty or irrational decisions, but rather reflected a man of steadfast optimism. One needed to assess a situation quickly, weigh the alternatives, make a decision, and then act on it—one needed to "go ahead" rather than retreat. There was no time to linger in the past, not when the often bitter realities of the present—hungry young mouths to feed, a farm gone to seed, debts piling up higher than the corn rows—pressed down all around you. So it was that Crockett confronted his current state of affairs and levied his decision: "I came to the conclusion that it wouldn't do, but that I must have another wife."

While Crockett's first courtships were fraught with young love, acceptance, rejection, and all manner of drama, his second round could hardly even be called courting. It was more of a business venture, a contractual arrangement based on mutual needs. Nearby lived a woman recently widowed, whose husband had been slain in the attack at Fort Mims.[3] She had a son and daughter of her own, about the same age as Crockett's children, and one can almost see him rubbing his chin as the notion hit him: "I began to think, that as we were both in the same situation, it might be that we could do something for each other." The woman he was considering was one Elizabeth Patton, an intelligent and resourceful daughter of a prominent North Carolina farmer and planter named Robert Patton who had served in the Revolutionary War. Her good breeding showed in her manners, her managerial skills, and the tidy state of her own small farm, which appeared organized and well-tended compared to Crockett's own grounds, unkempt because of frequent, and extended, absences. She was also rumored to possess some "grit" of her own, a sum amounting to about $800, an eye-opening and fortunate windfall certainly not lost on the perpetually impoverished David Crockett.[4] He therefore began to find reasons for visits, and as she lived nearby, this was quite convenient. He would happen by her "snug little farm" and soon began to formally pay his respects to her. She would certainly have surmised what he was up to—and appears to have enjoyed his blunt entreaties—despite his feigned subtlety: "I was as sly about it as a fox when he is going to rob a hen-roost."

For her part, Elizabeth Patton must have seen that there might be some utility in having Crockett around, even if he hunted and spent as much time out adventuring as rumor held. There was a certain charm to the man, to be sure. At nearly thirty, and having spent the better part of his lifetime outside, Crockett had filled out into a stout, robust man of nearly six feet, with ruddy red cheeks, a swoop of thick cedar-brown hair, and piercing but playful aquamarine eyes. He possessed a beakish nose and a strong chin, set hard and determined.[5] And there were his engaging storytelling and infectious sense of humor, which made him rather irresistible. Crockett modestly recalled that his company "wasn't at all disagreeable to her." Ultimately, it was a match born of hardship and circumstance. "We soon bargained," Crockett said of the union, "and got married, and then went ahead." It was the summer of 1816.

The marriage itself, a low-key event devoid of the traditional rituals like flask-filling attendant to either of their first marriages, was presided over by Pastor Richard Calloway and took place in Elizabeth's parents' home in Franklin County.[6] A smallish knot of family and friends huddled quietly in the living room, where an air of seriousness and dignity prevailed. Crockett and the attendants stood still and expectant, nervously awaiting the arrival through the front doorway of the bride. Without warning, curious grunts and squeals of a pig came from outside, and almost as if herded by devious pranksters, the porker crashed the wedding party, snorting right down the aisle, its hooves skidding and sliding on the hard floor. Children joined the pig's squeals with peals of their own laughter, and adults, previously caught up in the seriousness of the wedding, snickered. Crockett, as he often did, masterfully seized the awkward moment and made it his own. He put on a stern visage, stormed toward the pig and, grabbing it by the scruff of its neck, shepherded the unruly animal out the front door with an emphatic boot. "Old hook," he exclaimed as he clapped his hands clean, "from now on, *I'll* do the grunting around here!"[7]

In the stalwart, steady, and managerial-minded Elizabeth, Crockett had found a reliable business partner, a dependable surrogate mother for his own children, and a companion, if not a soul-mate. Yet they would hardly bask in honeymoon bliss for long. In less than a year Crockett determined, as he often did when he got the itch, that the time was nigh for some exploring of new, more fertile and promising country. His farm on the Rattlesnake Branch was small and in perpetual disrepair, what would today be considered a "tear down." Elizabeth held more acreage, a free and clear title, and combining those two, plus her substantial dowry, had potential. They might get a place big enough, with more tillable ground, to eradicate his debts and begin to see consistent profit. But it would take the right plot of ground, and that quest gave the newlywed David Crockett the perfect excuse to explore new country again. The wanderlust was in him, and perhaps feeling somewhat solvent with the staid Elizabeth taking care of things, he rallied a few of his neighbors for a reconnaissance outing. His traveling companions, named "Robinson, Frazier, and Rich," joined him as they rode toward Alabama, heading through the Jones Valley on overgrown military wagon roads cut during the campaign Crockett had participated in, passing through the very places, like Black Warrior Town, that he had helped to burn to the ground under

John Coffee. The trip, begun in hopeful search of better ground and greener pastures, started ominously and declined.

After only a day of travel, they stopped just across the Tennessee River at the home of one of Crockett's "old acquaintances, who'd settled there after the war." While they rested, Frazier, who Crockett referred to as "a great hunter" (quite a compliment coming from him), headed afield to hunt, but soon returned looking pale and feverish, having suffered a poisonous snake bite. Frazier was left to convalesce while Crockett, Robinson, and Rich rode on through the Jones Valley.

The expedition camped, hobbling their horses along the banks of the Black Warrior River, along a route Crockett would have found eerily familiar, having traveled it to and from Fort Mims. The horses had been tethered carelessly, for in the twilight hours before daybreak Crockett heard the team's bells "going back the way we had come, for they had started to leave us." Crockett waited until daylight so that he could better track the rogue equine, and volunteered to head off alone, on foot, carrying only his heavy rifle. Crockett tracked hard all day, busting through cane and thicket, wading deep swamps and creeks swirling with biting insects, flies, and swarms of mosquitoes. Crockett pushed on and on, following the ever-fainter tinkling of the horses' bells, and confirming at each house he passed that indeed, a small group of horses had recently passed that way. Eventually Crockett couldn't hear the animals anymore and lost their tracks, so he was forced to abandon his pursuit and determined to return to the last house he had passed, where he might rest and sup. The family there took Crockett in, and calculated that Crockett had covered nearly fifty miles on foot that day. When he awoke the next morning Crockett was deeply sore, his legs so fatigued that he feared he would not be able to walk. Still, he felt compelled to rejoin his party and apprise them of the horse dilemma, so he limped away from the safety and comfort of the house and wandered very slowly from early morning to noon, feeling progressively worse, a cold damp sweat overtaking him, his head beginning to throb and pound, his stomach and legs wambling. Finally his long rifle grew so heavy in his arms, and he had grown so feeble, that he could no longer continue, so he decided to "lay down by the side of the trace, and in a perfect wilderness, too," to see if he might improve with some rest.

Later, like a mirage or hallucination, the image of "some Indians" hovered over him; Crockett must have wondered if they were from a dream or a nightmare as they loomed above him. The friendly Creeks offered him some ripe melons, but Crockett felt so sickly he merely shook his head without saying a word. He had spent enough time with Indians to communicate with them, and he quickly learned through their sign language something that he had half-suspected anyway: "They then signed to me, that I would die, and be buried; a thing I was confoundedly afraid of myself." Through more sign language Crockett learned that it was about a mile and a half to the nearest house, and so he got up with their assistance and attempted to walk of his own power. "I got up to go, but when I rose, I reeled like a cow with the blind staggers, or a fellow who had taken too many 'horns.'" One of the Indians proposed to lead Crockett there and carry his gun, an offer he accepted, gratefully throwing a half-dollar into the bargain. By the time they got to the house Crockett was out of his senses with fever. The woman of the house put him in bed and gave him warm teas, but he failed to improve much over the next two days. Though Crockett would not have known it, his condition was malaria, undoubtedly the result of mosquito bites he had received while walking through the bogs and swamps after his horses.

The next day some neighbors from Crockett's home happened by— they were also out scouting new territory. They agreed to alternate horses and give Crockett a ride back up to the Black Warrior River to inform Robinson and Rich of his condition and their situation. Crockett hoped he would get better, but little did he know that his malaria was simply making the transition from the cold and hot stages to the sweating stage.

As they rode, shifting him awkwardly from one horse to another, Crockett's condition worsened; by the time they reached Robinson and Rich he slumped listlessly, no longer able to even sit the horse. Crockett did have the mental capacity to make this understated observation: "I thought now the jig was mighty nigh up with me." He was carried to the nearest house, owned by Jesse Jones; here Robinson and Rich managed to buy horses, and left Crockett for dead.

Crockett quickly fell into cerebral malaria, flopping about in violent fits, sweating, suffering psychosis, and finally settling into a comalike state for nearly two weeks. When he came to, Crockett learned that he had been speechless for five full days, but had revived without the help of a doctor, for none was near. He later joked that at the time, "They had no thought that I would ever speak again,—in Congress or anywhere else." Thinking he was likely to die anyway, the woman took a chance and poured an entire bottle of Bateman's Drops (a frontier medicine containing alcohol and possibly quinine, which would have helped with the malaria)[8] down his throat, and he broke into a deeper sweat all night but then revived, and politely requested a drink of water. From that moment he was on the mend, until finally, after a great deal of effort, he was able to walk on his own. In time a passing wagoner agreed to haul Crockett in the direction of his home, and when they reached the wagoner's destination, he rented Crockett one of his horses so he could continue the twenty miles home.

Elizabeth Crockett had lost one husband to the Creek War, and she would have been prepared for the news that David had met his end during the expedition. Such news was an unfortunate reality on the edge of wilderness. Word had come to her through Robinson and Rich that Crockett had perished. But Elizabeth Patton Crockett was thorough, detail oriented, and she wanted proof—she wanted to know about his personal effects and money, so she hired a man to head out and discover what he could. Somehow this man and Crockett missed each other on the trail, and Crockett arrived home before the man could return with the news. Elizabeth would have been shocked when she opened her door to find the emaciated and ghostly Crockett standing there, no doubt forcing a bemused grin. Crockett remembered the moment clearly: "I was so pale, and so much reduced, that my face looked like it had been half soled with brown paper." After Elizabeth recovered from her astonishment, she informed Crockett that his traveling companions had returned his horse (they'd lucked upon all the horses on the way home) and carried with them the story that not only was he dead, but that they had witnessed Crockett take his final breath and spoken with the men who had performed the burial.[9] Prefiguring Mark Twain's famous line "the reports of my death have been greatly exaggerated," Crockett fashioned his own humorous understatement regarding his reported death when he said flatly, "I know'd that was a whapper of a lie as soon as I heard it!"

Crockett spent the next few months around Bean's Creek, recuperating, doing light work, but still pondering his options, dreaming of better ground. He believed that his own farm was "sickly," unfit to produce crops.[10] Within a year he had determined to leave it for good, and that autumn he set out "to look at the country which had been purchased of the Chickasaw tribe of Indians." Andrew Jackson had secured in writing deals that ceded Chickasaw land in the south-central area of Tennessee, leaving it open to settlement by early 1817.[11] Crockett made it as far as Shoal Creek, some eighty miles from home, when he suffered a reoccurrence of malaria, complete with "ague and fever." Crockett figured it was merely illness from sleeping outside on the soggy ground, but he was incapacitated and remained in that area for some time, hoping to get better. While waiting, he scouted about as he could, and he soon decided that the place was quite suitable—good enough, at any rate, to settle there for a time.

When he felt he could travel comfortably, Crockett went home to inform the family that he had found a nice spot on Shoal Creek and they would be packing up quickly for a move. By now, the Crockett clan included newcomer Robert Patton Crockett, born in 1816, plus his three other children and Elizabeth's other two, a group of eight that would grow even larger soon enough. Over the next four years Elizabeth would be a very busy and hardworking woman, giving birth to the rest of their "second crop," as Crockett liked to call them: Elizabeth Jane in 1818, Rebeckah Elvira (nicknamed "Sissy") in 1819, and finally Matilda in 1821.[12] For the next two decades Elizabeth Patton Crockett would manage a household of nine children, maintain and manage the details of more than one farm, various other holdings, and small businesses involved with leasing land, all while supporting her husband's dreams and schemes and hobbies, which came to include, in addition to his passion for hunting, a run at public office and then politics on a national scale. By any standard imaginable, Elizabeth Crockett was an amazing organizer, a tireless worker, and a fair, flexible, and lenient companion for David Crockett. It's evident that he could not have gotten along without her. He was also conscious (if not a little self-conscious) of the power that her $800 dowry brought to his position, and he understood that with the right financial moves and business decisions, they could perhaps rise from farmer status to "planter" status over time. Crockett may have begun to sense the concept of class stratification, and that with the assistance of Elizabeth and her family, he might begin an upwardly mobile climb.[13]

The Crocketts sold and leased their Franklin County farms (David's twenty acres, Elizabeth's closer to 200) and headed for the picturesque Shoal Creek, sweet grassy pastureland and undulating hills banking gently at the clear, wide stream. They managed to find a perfect spot right near the creek's headwaters, where they built the first of their eventual trio of cabins. Like all of his other homes, these cabins were rough-hewn and utilitarian affairs, the logs semi-peeled and prone to rot, both exteriors and interiors smallish and unadorned. But over the next six years these would suffice. The land looked fertile, the river promising—it could run a gristmill, and they would eventually own and operate a distillery for whiskey making, an iron-ore mine, and a gunpowder factory.[14] It was the closest thing to a real start that David Crockett had seen in his life. And as it would again and again for Crockett, the hope hinged on the land itself, and perhaps even more important, on the idea of the land and what it represented—freedom, the very essence of the American dream.

Their land on Shoal Creek was just a few miles from a small outpost settlement called Lawrenceburg, and an informal community was burgeoning there. Soon after the Crocketts had settled in along the creek side, in October 1817, Lawrence County was officially formed. Crockett would later describe the situation as born of necessity, saying they lived "without any law at all; and so many bad characters began to flock in upon us, that we found it necessary to set up a sort of temporary government of our own." That "government" of sorts would have already been in the works before Crockett's arrival, but things did move quickly once he got there. Crockett's name was added to a list of possible candidates for the position of justice of the peace, and on November 25, the legislature appointed Crockett legal magistrate.[15] Almost by accident, and certainly without trying very hard, David Crockett had run for office and been elected, marking the fledgling stage of what would become a star-crossed career in public life.

That Crockett got selected as magistrate testifies to the solid nature of his character, since he was uneducated in the law, but rather operated from a platform of common sense and decency. Locals in the community would have known about Crockett's recent experiences in the Creek War, noting a rough and unpolished honesty about him, an infectious straightforwardness. Crockett remembered that, while he was magistrate,

My judgments were never appealed from, and if they had been they
would have stuck like wax, as I gave my decisions on the principles of
common justice and honesty between man and man, and relied on natural born sense, and not on law, learning to guide me; for I had never
read a page in a law book in all my life.[16]

That "natural born sense" to which he refers proved to be one of
Crockett's most important character traits—he was a remarkable student
of human nature, possessing savvy, moxie, and street smarts, none of
which can be acquired from books or classrooms.

Crockett presided over everything from domestic squabbles to debt
collection, and he quickly developed a reputation for firm conviction and
fair, common sense. In a very short time he was approached by a Captain
Matthews, a well-heeled local businessman and early settler whom Crockett noted sarcastically "made rather more corn than the rest of us." As it
happened, Matthews informed Crockett that he was running for the office
of colonel, and wondered whether Crockett would run under him for first
major in the same regiment. The fact that Matthews wanted Crockett on
his ticket suggests that Crockett was already esteemed in the region.[17]
Crockett at first politely declined, saying that he was finished with military matters. But Matthews was quite convincing, and Crockett reluctantly agreed, at the same time naturally figuring on Matthews's backing
in the election. Matthews then organized a great frolic and corn husk-
ing that would be part of the electioneering process, inviting the entire
county along. The Crockett family arrived to find that David had been
duped; Matthews's own son was running for the office of major, the same
position that Crockett had been convinced to seek. He had been set up as
a patsy candidate.

Crockett took the challenge in good spirits, then turned around and
took it to another level in the kind of bold and defiant move that would

become his trademark. When Matthews apologetically (and perhaps insincerely) explained that his son feared running against Crockett more than any man in the county, Crockett smiled his devilish grin and told them not to fear. "I told him his son need give himself no uneasiness about that; that I shouldn't run against him for major, but against his daddy for colonel." Matthews, apparently a sporting man with a sense of gamesmanship, took the challenge, shaking Crockett's hand in front of the crowd gathered to hear speeches. Crockett let Matthews finish (a tactic he would often use to his advantage, going last) then "mounted up for a speech, too. I told the people the cause of my opposing him, remarking that as I had the whole family to run against anyway, I was determined to levy on the head of the mess." The voters obviously took to Crockett's straight-shooting style; he came across as a common man, essentially one of them. When the tally came in, Crockett took some pride in noting that Matthews and his son "were both badly beaten." It was a seminal moment in the political career of David Crockett, underscoring a tendency that would surface as one of his mottos: "Never seek, nor decline, office." He was now officially a lieutenant colonel commandant in the 57th Regiment of Militia. He was Colonel David Crockett, a title he would wear proudly for the rest of his life.

That first election also defined Crockett's "electioneering" style, one he would use again and again, partly because it worked but mostly because it genuinely reflected who he was. Reluctantly he would enter the fray, using his humor, wit, and homespun colloquialisms and charm to win the hearts of voters. He affected naïveté, and pointed out that he rarely went looking for public office but rather it periodically came calling on him, and it was his duty as a good citizen to answer the calling.[18] In most cases he was elected for positions for which he had no prior experience, and for which his résumé was spotty at best. But one of his many skills proved to be his great capacity for on-the-job training, and during his one-year tenure as justice of the peace Crockett presided over many cases, from ruling on rightful ownership of butchered hogs to child custody. He issued various licenses, including those of matrimony, "certified bounties for wolves,"[19] and as he remembered, "In this way I got on pretty well, till by care and attention I improved my handwriting in such manner as to be able to prepare my warrants, and keep my record book, without much difficulty." Crockett thrived and learned as much as he thought he needed to in his capacity as magistrate, until he decided to resign on November 1, 1819, ostensibly to focus more on his growing industries.

For the next two years David Crockett remained essentially in one place, unusual for him given his nomadic yearnings. But there was plenty of work to be done, and he spent countless hours working on his concerns such as the gristmill, the distillery, and the gunpowder factory. Elizabeth had generously kicked in her share, but even this fell short of the amount needed to get things up, running, and producing income, forcing the Crocketts to borrow to complete the buildings. David Crockett's growing reputation as a fair and honest man certainly didn't hurt his ability to obtain loans, and by late October 1820 he would write one of his creditors, a John C. McLemore, explaining that he'd be able to pay him back by the following spring. He was already falling behind on his payments on two plots of ground, one just sixty acres, the other a more impressive— and more expensive—320-acre parcel.

> . . . I have been detained longer than expected my powder factory have not been pushed as it ought and I will not be able to meet my contract with you but if you send me a three-hundred acre warrant by the male I will pay you interest for the money until paid. I do not wish to disappoint you—I don't expect I can pay you the hole amount until next spring.[20]

His hope was that by spring his factories would be fully operational and showing profits. Things apparently worked well enough, for by early 1821 he had decided that it was time for him to take a crack at higher office, this time running for the state House of Representatives. In February he left his working industrial entities and set out on a cattle drive that took him down into the lower reaches of North Carolina, then returned to go electioneering, which, as Crockett admitted, was a "bran-fire new business" to him. He looked at it this way: "It now became necessary that I should tell the people something about the government, and an eternal sight of other things that I knowed nothing more about than I did about Latin, and law, and such things as that." Crockett was about to take his woodsy brand of politicking to the people of Hickman and Lawrence counties, using his storytelling and sharp wit to win the people over. He would later muse about this period of his life, "I just now began to take a rise." Things were finally settled and operating at home, with Elizabeth pretty much running the place. It was time to hit the campaign trail to see what he might roust up.

AROUND ABOUT THIS TIME there was arranged what Crockett called "a great squirrel hunt" along the Duck River, where Crockett's kind of people—hunters, farmers, folks making a living off the land—would gather. The squirrel hunt included competition, fun, and politics, as the contest was between Crockett and his backers and those in favor of his opponent. Crockett described the setup:

> They were to hunt for two days: then to meet and count scalps, and have a big barbecue, and what might be called a tip-top country frolic. The dinner, and a general treat, was all to be paid for by the party taken the fewest scalps . . . I killed a great many squirrels, and when we counted scalps, my party was victorious.

At the frolic in Centreville, the candidates were expected to speak on the subject of moving the county seat of Hickman nearer to the center, and a great many townsfolk and folk from all around the county had come for the festivities, as well as to hear what the candidates had to say on the matter. Crockett was asked to go first, and he did a fair bit of legitimate hemming and hawing, partly because in fact he had no real position on the subject, partly to play the role of the reluctant candidate, but mostly because he knew that his opponent was eloquent and "could speak prime," and Crockett used a gambling metaphor to describe his opponent's verbal superiority: "And I know'd, too, that I wa'n't able to shuffle and cut with him." But the opponent's arrogance and overconfidence also piqued Crockett's interest, and he was offended that the man wasn't taking him seriously enough. Here Crockett's insecurity and pride rose high in his cheeks. He remembered the man's attitude: "The truth is, he thought my being a candidate was a mere matter of sport; and didn't think, for a moment, that he was in any danger from an ignorant back-woods bear hunter." That kind of underestimation was always a risky one to take when facing the competitive David Crockett.

Crockett's ire was spurred, his dander up. Still, he had only made one official political speech, and his oratory skills were elementary at best. Facing the expectant crowd, he attempted to speak, but immediately became seized with stage fright: "I choaked up as bad as if my mouth had been jam'd and cram'd chock full of dry mush." The people gawked at him as he struggled. They waited impatiently, and Crockett was at a moment of truth in his political career. He was on the verge of being laughed, then booed, right off the stump. At long last Crockett spoke, explaining his problem and seizing the instant:

At last I told them I was like a feller I had heard of not long before. He was beating on the head of a barrel near the road-side, when a traveler, who was passing along, asked what he was doing that for?

The fellow replied, that there was some cider in that barrel a few days before, and he was trying to see if there was any then, but if there was he couldn't get at it. I told them that there had been a little bit of speech in me a while ago, but I believed I couldn't get it out.[21]

The tactic worked, for as he finished the crowd roared with laughter, and Crockett quickly took the cue to tell a few more amusing anecdotes and tales, and when he had them all in stitches he politely thanked them for their time and stepped down, careful to remark aloud that he was "dry as a powder horn" and that it was a good time for them all to wet their whistles. He led most of the group to the liquor stand, where they all had drinks and Crockett continued with tall tales while his competitor was left speaking practically to himself. Crockett's style and charisma had lured them all over to his side. His behavior and sense of humor that day became the stuff of local legend. He had won their attention and admiration, and he knew he had their votes.

He went on to the town of Vernon, where residents wished the county seat to remain. Crockett quickly comprehended a political reality—he could sway voters simply by agreeing with them. When they pressed him directly on the subject of his opinion, Crockett went coy: "I told them I didn't know whether it would be right or not, so I couldn't promise either way." He had dodged the issue, at least for the moment. The next day a large gathering convened at Vernon, including his opponent as well as those running for Congress and governor, and here Crockett was asked to speak again. Crockett claimed he was nervous again, but his cleverness suggests that his jitters were contrived, all part of his scheme. The major candidates spoke "nearly all day," likely boring and tiring the crowd with politics and posturing. Crockett said that he "listened mighty close to them, and was learning pretty fast about politics." Seeing that the crowd

*Crockett said of this portrait, "I am
happy to acknowledge this to be the only
correct likeness that has been taken of
me." (David Crockett. Engraving by
Chiles and Lehman, Philadelphia,
from an oil portrait by Samuel
Stillman Osgood, 1834.
Tennessee State Library and
Archives, Nashville.)*

was losing interest, Crockett used what he had learned. "When they were all done, I got up and told some laughable story, and quit. I found I was safe in those parts, so I went home, and didn't go back until the election was over."

Crockett had his first major political epiphany: that it is better to be liked, to amuse the voters and tell them what they want to hear, than it is to be knowledgeable but boring. It was a stroke of country brilliance, and it worked. When the votes were tallied, Crockett had more than doubled his competitor's count. Colonel David Crockett had just won in his first bid for the Tennessee state legislature. The rise of Crockett, the man and the legend, had begun.

SEVEN

"The Gentleman from the Cane"

CROCKETT PACKED UP IN THE FALL and left his homestead on the banks of Shoal Creek for bustling Murfreesboro, which was the state capital at the time. His folksy wisdom, sharp and clever wit, and charismatic likability had gotten him elected, and now was his chance to take to the bigger stage of legislature, and also the relatively bigger stage of the Tennessee city. For all his later bravado, Crockett would have felt some intimidation at the transitions he was undergoing personally, professionally, and socially. Along the campaign trail he'd had the opportunity to hobnob with big-shot politicians, and he had participated at functions where his lack of social refinement would have been crudely evident. Though he would later find a way to use that "country bumpkin" image to his advantage politically, overstating his ignorance for his own benefit, at the time it would have bored into him like a tick, a constant reminder of his meager financial and social status.

Crockett relates the story of passing through the town of Pulaski on his way to Murfreesboro, and how he there met and rode with James Knox Polk, who at the time was a twenty-six-year-old lawyer from a prominent family, who had recently been selected as a clerk in the state senate. Polk looked and acted the part of the politician, and he came with real credentials, including a university education and an intimidating command of legal terminology. As they rode along "in a large company," Polk offered to Crockett that in the coming session there might be a "radical change of the judiciary." Crockett claims that he knew no more than his horse the words "judiciary" or "radical change," adding a phrase that would become one of his staples, "If I know'd I wish I may be shot." He simply smiled, agreed, and then got out of there, moving quickly away from Polk for fear that someone might immediately ask him to define the word "judiciary." Crockett seemed intuitively to know that there were times to appear ignorant and times not to.[1] But it was always part of a ruse, and Crockett was a lot smarter than he let on. His feigned ignorance remained a ploy he would use under certain circumstances, and he could turn it on or off at will.

On September 17, 1821, Crockett presided for the first time as an elected official representing Hickman and Lawrence counties at the first session of the Fourteenth General Assembly. The very next day he found himself serving on the Standing Committee of Propositions and Grievances, as it happened his only committee appointment for the session, and a rather mundane one at that.[2] The committee addressed such issues as debt collection, land ownership, and rights of widows and divorced women, some issues Crockett would have been comfortable dealing with from his experience as a magistrate and justice of the peace.[3] Though his first term would be a relatively uninteresting, even quiet one, Crockett did manage to leave a stamp, giving an indication of his passions and beliefs concerning land issues, a passion that would ultimately define his political career. He also surfaced as an outspoken and vehement champion of the underclass, the poor, dispossessed, and disenfranchised, groups with whom he would always align himself. This inflexible political tendency would later hurt him, but at the time he was simply voting his convictions.

Land-reform questions, those which would ultimately become the

Land Bill and his fixation, were of great importance to Crockett, and his initial votes reflected his ardent beliefs. Within the first week, on September 25, he voted "to release landowners in the Western District from paying double tax assessments for delinquent taxes during 1820."[4] His voting and speaking activity over the first term concerned the public lands and land warrants, which at the time was a rather complicated situation. Squatters in Tennessee were sitting on lands which had actually been issued, as far back as the Revolution, as rewards to veterans for services rendered in battle, back when the state was part of North Carolina. So squatters, even those who had lived on plots for years, tilling the soil and building homes, could be kicked off what they believed to be their own lands if a warrant holder showed up waving a piece of legal paper. What made it worse was that many of these people had been migrating farther and farther west, constantly pushed by claimants evicting them from "their" land, until finally this population of people began to inherit the least desirable, least arable plots—rock-filled ground or scrubby, dry hills with no planting potential. Crockett understood these peoples' plight well, for he and his family had been among them, without warrants or money, floating from place to place after each failure.[5]

Quite early in the session Crockett rose nervously and awkwardly to speak, and his discomfort with procedure, as well as his backwoods colloquialisms peppered his speech, marking him not only a fledgling legislator, but an untutored one. James C. Mitchell of East Tennessee stood and referred to Crockett as "the gentleman from the cane," a moniker carrying the same connotation as "hick" or "hillbilly." Some of the assembled chuckled uncomfortably, and Crockett immediately took Mitchell to task, demanding an apology but receiving none. Later, outside the chambers, Crockett strode up to Mitchell and lambasted him, demanding satisfaction in the form of an apology or a fistfight. Mitchell declined, assuring the raging Crockett that he'd meant no insult, but that he'd merely been describing where Crockett was from (the "cane" being what today would be referred to as "the sticks" or "the boonies").

Crockett's own dress at that time reflected his rural origins and his financial constraints. He wore handmade trousers and a rough shirt, a tanned-skin hunting jacket, and perhaps, for evenings out or in the legislative chambers, an unadorned wool coat. By contrast, his counterparts, having greater resources, affected the garb of the landed aristocracy: "pantaloons or knee breeches, waistcoats, cutaway coats, and shirts with fancy cuffs and cotton ruffles at their collars."[6] Crockett's station was obvious, even without Mitchell's public slur. But Crockett's wit and cunning would soon come in handy. Along the roadside Crockett chanced upon a "cambric ruffle," the frill worn at the neck by gentlemen of the day. He squirreled it away and entered the halls, where he put it on undetected. When Mitchell next spoke Crockett waited patiently for his prey to finish, then pounced. Crockett rose to speak, the foppish ruffle garishly evident, a ludicrous ornament contrasting with his functional farm clothes. The pantomime brought the assembly to uproarious tears of laughter, forcing the embarrassed Mitchell to flee the place, and winning Crockett a modicum of respect from his peers. From that time on Crockett acknowledged the nickname "the gentleman from the cane," on his own terms, and he wore it with pride, not only for himself, but for the backwoods folk he had come to represent.[7] Crockett had managed to win the day with his pluck and good humor, and salvage his pride in the process.[8]

Crockett was getting his feet wet, voting against a bill to suppress gambling, offering a speech against allowing magistrates receiving fees for lawsuits, and adapting to the lifestyle of evenings out drinking and playing at the gaming tables, when he received shocking news from home. In an act of nature eerily similar to the "Noah's fresh" which wiped out his father and forced one of his childhood moves, a flash flood had ripped through rain-swollen Shoal Creek, scouring away the streambanks and carrying away much of the Crocketts' industrial complex, including both the powder and gristmills. The buildings had been torn from their very foundations and swept away to oblivion. Crockett would later pun on the situation, playing off the use of "mash" in whiskey-making parlance: "The first news I heard after I got to the Legislature, was that my mills were—not blown up sky high, as you would guess, by my powder establishment,—but swept away all to smash by a large fresh . . . I may say, that the misfortune just made a complete mash of me." At the time, it was certainly no joking matter. The disaster forced Crockett to take an immediate leave of absence. On September 29 he rushed home, expecting the worst and getting exactly what he expected. To compound matters, the distillery would also be lost, rendered useless without the ground corn churned out by the gristmill. It appeared by all measures, having just gotten started and his career on the rise, that the Crocketts were ruined.

Elizabeth Patton Crockett showed her mettle during this devastating time, shoring up her husband when he was as low as he could be. She'd been running things anyway, caring for infant Matilda and the two toddlers, Sissy and Elizabeth Jane, plus six others, getting only token help from the older boys. She had financed much of the complex and managed ably in his absence. Crockett walked the grounds in near depression, his inspection yielding news that was beyond discouraging: he estimated the losses at "upwards of three thousand dollars, more than I was worth in the world." It was a serious moment of truth for Crockett—and his strong and honest wife advised him not to run from their troubles, but to face them head on—the way they always had. She advised that it was best to "Just pay up, as long as you have a bit's worth in the world; and then every body will be satisfied, and we will scuffle for more."[9] Crockett later admitted that her words were salvation for him, exactly what he needed to hear, and he agreed that the only recourse was to clear their debts and start over, embarking on yet another "bran-fire new start." He looked at it this way: "Better to keep a good conscience with an empty purse, than to get a bad opinion of myself, with a full one." They were noble sentiments, and suitable words to live by, and Crockett would carry both—the good conscience and the empty purse—with him to the end of his days.

The Crocketts were forced to sell off property, including the undamaged distillery and equipment, and they were sued by a number of creditors. Those creditors needn't have worried, since when it came to repaying debt, David Crockett bordered on the obsessive. In 1811, leaving his former home in Jefferson County, Crockett had owed a man named John Jacobs a single dollar, not much of a debt, but enough for Crockett to remember. In 1821, herding a group of horses into North Carolina to sell before his next campaign, Crockett happened to pass through Jefferson, and he stopped in at the Jacobs's place. Over a decade had gone by, and still Crockett pressed a shining dollar coin into the palm of a surprised Mrs. Jacobs. She shook her head and tried to refuse. But Crockett stood his ground on this one: "I owed it and you have got to take it," he said.[10]

On October 9 Crockett returned to Murfreesboro, weary and troubled again by the uncertainties back home, burdened by the thought of packing up and moving but confident that the steadfast and stable Elizabeth could handle anything thrown her way. He needed to finish up the first session so that he could return home and help plan another move, perhaps this time to ground west of the Congressional Reservation Line, a significant demarcation separating the state into roughly two halves, with the eastern portion reserved to satisfy the preponderance of the outstanding North Carolina warrants. The western portion remained public lands, "unpreempted,"[11] effectively open for the squatting. Those lands were of special interest to Crockett, now personally (he needed land and it was free) and professionally. Lobbying for their acquisition would influence the majority of his political decisions.

He finished out the session by continuing to represent his constituents with their best interests in mind, announcing himself among his peers as a truthful man of strong convictions. He had made a few friends, including William Carroll, whom he'd first met in Vernon and early in the session voted for in the race for governor. He and Crockett had much in common, having both done battle under Jackson in the Creek War, both men self-made, of humble origins. Carroll was close with Jackson,[12] and that alignment may have influenced Crockett's political leanings at the time; early on Crockett appeared to support the tenets that would become known as "Jacksonian Democracy": a laissez-faire government unfettered by private restrictions, a deep suspicion of special privilege and large business, and a firm belief in the capabilities of ordinary men. Indeed, counting the Mitchell affair, Crockett had made a bit of a stir during his first session.

The assembly adjourned on November 17, and Crockett packed up what little he had and headed for what little home he had left. It was time to set out scouting again. He mustered his eldest son, John Wesley, and a neighbor named Abram Henry, and "cut out for the Obion." The Obion River, a tributary of the Forked Deer, is large and braided, with four branches—North, Middle, South, and the southernmost Rutherford's Fork (near present-day Rutherford, Tennessee).[13] Crockett and the boys headed west more than 150 miles to Rutherford's Fork, and Crockett immediately liked what he saw. The place was wild, unpopulated, and thick with game. "It was complete wilderness," Crockett said, brimming with excitement, "and full of Indians who were hunting. Game was plenty, of almost every kind, which suited me exactly, as I was always fond of hunting." Crockett determined that here was a place he could have some elbow room, a sense of freedom, as the nearest two neighbors were seven and fifteen miles away. The land itself had character, with dense canebrakes— tangled thickets of giant tallgrass—rife with game. The rugged terrain also showed scars of the famous New Madrid earthquakes of 1811–1812, a series of quakes so violent and massive that they were estimated to be the strongest in U.S. history, each far greater in magnitude than the 1906

San Francisco quake. Referred to colloquially as "the shakes," the New Madrid tremors caused the Mississippi River to flow backward for a time, and vibrations were felt from the Rocky Mountains to the Atlantic Coast and from Mexico to Canada.[14] The epicenter of the quakes was at New Madrid, Missouri, in close proximity to Tennessee and Kentucky, and after the first monster quakes, aftershocks would rock the region intermittently for a full seven years in the most dramatic geological upheaval ever witnessed in North America, putting a genuine and continous fear of God into the inhabitants.

Prior to the quakes, Reelfoot Creek flowed through the low-lying area and into the Obion River, but when the terrifying shakes had finally finished rumbling they'd left the eighteen-mile-long Reelfoot Lake in their wake, a huge slurry of water five miles wide and twenty feet deep in places. Violent and persistent storms ravaged the area in the aftermath of the quakes, razing entire forests, rending enormous caverns in the earth, filling the sky with a thick pall of steam, debris, and gas. Crockett referred, almost reverently, to the devastated area as a "harricane," and the thickets, choked by abundant regrowth of native and competing Southern grass and giant cane, some well over head high, provided ample cover and abundant food for ground-dwelling creatures.[15] The result of this upheaval, this tangle of forest and cane, were the game-filled canebrakes Crockett loved to haunt. Here he would sharpen his already considerable skills as a woodsman and a hunter, here where life made sense to him, where he reveled in the simplicity of the hunt, of moving at the pace of wild things.

Crockett became enamored with the landscape and he staked a claim on a spot that looked suitable, then figured that while they were there they might as well hunt.[16] They first rode out to visit a man named Owens who lived across the Obion. The river was near flood stage, fairly bursting and painfully cold, but in they waded anyway "like so many beavers." The going was treacherous, the bottom dropping out from under them at times, Crockett carrying a long pole that he used to feel the river bottom in front of him. Tromping through murky sloughs, Crockett used his tomahawk to fell small trees to fashion into bridges for the deepest sections. More than once John Wesley resorted to swimming, becoming soaked and bitterly cold. Finally they trudged ashore on the far banks, John Wesley shivering and shaking "like he had the worst sort of an ague." They struck for a nearby house, pleased to be greeted by Mr. Owens and some other men, who led the cold and waterlogged travelers inside.

Crockett and his cohorts warmed by the fire, Owens produced a bottle of whiskey. Crockett concluded at that moment "that if a horn wasn't good then, there was no use for its invention." Crockett slugged down half a pint, then passed it on to his boy John Wesley, and they all started to feel better and dry out. Mrs. Owen tended to John Wesley, drying his soaked woolens and plying him with more liquids and some hot food. Crockett accepted an offer to join a run that the men were taking up the Obion, and he and Abram Henry boarded a boat with Mr. Owens and the crew, who had loaded it with "whiskey, flour, sugar, coffee, salt, castings, and other articles suitable for the country." They had struck a deal to deliver these goods upriver at McLemore's Bluff, on the South Fork, for five hundred dollars. Crockett remembered the boat party fondly: "We staid all night with them, and had a high night of it, as I took steam enough to drive out all the cold that was in me, and about three times as much more."

The next day Crockett decided to tag along for the boat trip, and they proceeded upriver until they came to a logjam of downed timber caused by the shakes; the river was too low to be navigable, and they returned to the Owens's place to wait for some higher water. Though it rained, as Crockett put it, "rip-roriously" the following day, the river was still too shallow to accommodate the heavy boat, so Crockett used his charm and gregariousness to convince the boat owner and all the crew to head out to his new claim where they "slap'd up a cabin in no time." Crockett bargained for some provisions, too, putting up in stores "four barrels of meal, one of salt, and about ten gallons of whiskey." The cabin was simple and crude, just a rough-hewn shelter with stone fireplace and straight front porch, but it would do for the moment.[17]

The deal he made for the provisions required that Crockett hire on as boat crew for the trip to McLemore's Bluff, and so after killing a nice deer and bartering for "a large middling of bacon," he left John Wesley and Abram Henry at his new cabin and headed upriver with the boatmen. He figured he'd be gone six or seven days if things went well on the river. They made camp that night below the fallen timbers, and the next morning at first light Crockett headed out hunting along the shores, thinking the men would be unable to get the boat through the jams and debris that day. He crept quietly along in his knee-high leather hunting moccasins, tracking deer and elk and bringing down two bucks before midday, stopping to hang them in trees to keep predators from absconding with them, and marking the spots to retrieve them later. He stalked all day and into the early evening, noting the time by the long slants of shadow through the thick growth, dropping and hanging six deer that day and then bursting through the bramble to the place he figured the boat would be. After hollering and receiving no reply, Crockett fired his rifle, and the shot the boatmen fired back echoed unsettling news; they had made it through the jammed timber and were well ahead, some two miles upriver.

By now it was dark, but Crockett's only choice was to make his way toward the boat, scrabbling over and under nearly impenetrable thicket: "I had to crawl through the fallen timber . . . for the vines and briers had grown all through it, and so thick, that a good fat coon couldn't much more than get along." He moved along this way slowly, the thorns tearing away at his clothes and flesh as he hollered for the boat, and at last they came back for him in a skiff. Crockett was so sliced up from the ordeal that he felt as though he "wanted sewing up all over," and so beaten by fatigue that he could hardly move his jaws to eat his first sustenance in twenty-four hours. In the morning Crockett took a man with him to fetch most of the deer he had hung (leaving a couple to possibly retrieve later), then returned to the boat, and finally, after slow going and some difficult maneuvering, they landed at McLemore's Bluff on the eleventh day.

Their work on the boat completed, Crockett was given a skiff from the captain and his men as a present, and he also took with him a young crew man named Flavius Harris, hiring him on to help get the new farm under way.[18] Crockett and Harris made a speedy return downriver, then, along with John Wesley, began the difficult duties of getting his new homestead ready for the rest of his family to live in. "We turned in and cleared a field, and planted our corn, but it was so late in the spring, we had no time to make rails, and therefore put no fence around our fields." It was by now the spring of 1822, and Crockett needed to get back to Elizabeth and the other children. First, he wanted to hunt some more and put up more dried meat, so after planting what they considered a sufficient amount of corn, Crockett took to the woods and mountains and river, awed by the wildness and remoteness of the place. "In all this time, we saw the face of no white person in that country, except Mr. Owens' family, and a very few passengers, who went out there looking at the country. Indians, though, were still plenty enough." Hunting hard and expertly, he managed to kill ten bears "and a great abundance of deer."

His crop "laid by," loads of dried bear and venison and other provisions put up to store, Crockett reluctantly headed home the 150 miles to Shoal Creek. He knew that things were in disarray there, and he had made some preparations in advance of his scouting departure, including finding temporary housing for Elizabeth and the children, since they lost their homes after the gristmill disaster. During his absence a number of suits had been brought against him, with a couple of judgments granted, and

Crockett's happy homecoming was peppered with despair. Perhaps the worst was arriving to discover that two men, Rueben Trip and Thomas Pryer, had moved in and now occupied his home.[19] Despite knowing that it was likely to happen, the concrete evidence of his own failures must have stung Crockett's considerable pride. Just as Crockett and John Wesley rejoined Elizabeth and as he and Elizabeth began dealing with their legal and situational issues, Crockett received news on April 22, 1822, from newly elected Governor William Carroll that the second session of the legislature would convene on July 22. This would give the Crocketts just enough time to clear their debts, get all their affairs in order, and prepare to leave for Rutherford's Fork when he returned from the second session. Elizabeth would once again take on the significant burdens at home, but to Crockett's great relief, she did so without complaint.

In his second go-round as a legislator, Crockett took to his work with a sense of duty and fairness. His votes were those of a man concerned with social equality and justice, as when he introduced a bill to provide relief for a black man named "Mathias, a free man of color."[20] He opposed bills that would undermine the prevention of fraud in the execution of last wills and testaments, as well as those that would take rights away from widows and their children.[21]

Crockett's other concerns during this time included the Tennessee Vacant Land bill, a foreshadowing of the contentious issue that would eventually consume him. The bill, in brief, asked representatives to authorize the legislature of Tennessee "to dispose of the vacant and unappropriated lands, lying to the North and East of the Congressional Reservation Line, at such price as may be thought prudent by said legislature, for the purpose of education."[22] David Crockett, primarily self-taught, may have already been somewhat dubious of acts structured to raise money for state-funded education, the learned and privileged being two groups he would come to despise and feel threatened by. His voting record during this term illustrates an interesting blend of equanimity and self-interest:

he agreed that vacant lands should be put on sale at the lowest possible prices, prices the poor (which included himself) just might be able to afford. He also voted on August 20 for a bill designed chiefly to promote the construction of ironworks.[23] Given his recent (if failed) dabbling in mills, distilleries, and the gunpowder factory, Crockett appeared to remain intrigued with the potential of such industries and wished to protect them, even garnering governmental support for such entrepreneurship. He managed to get himself placed on a select committee to consider a loan to Montgomery Bell for a "Manufactory and works."[24] Crockett may well have been considering another go at manufacturing once they got relocated.

The short second session adjourned on August 24, and Crockett went home immediately and wasted no time collecting his family and striking out to his new claim on Rutherford's Fork. "I took my family and what little plunder I had," Crockett recalled, "and moved to where I had built my cabin." It would have been a long, slow, cold, and uncomfortable 150-mile trek, burdened as they were with belongings and young children. They arrived in the Obion country in late October 1822. Crockett's hired man, Flavius Harris, had kept things in order, and Crockett and the boys helped to bring in the last of the corn crop they'd planted the previous spring. Once settled in the cabin, Crockett grew excited about the hunting opportunities again. The region he had chosen could not have been any richer in game, any more suited to his favorite pursuit. "I found bear very plenty, and indeed, all sorts of game and wild varmints." He hunted hard and long all autumn and into early winter, filling his larder with venison and fowl, and though still far from financially flush, he would have been somewhat content with the knowledge that he was providing for his family. He had to resort to selling wolf hides for any real income during the difficult early transition to the Obion country.

Just before Christmas 1822, Crockett ran out of the gunpowder he needed for hunting, but also necessary for the tradition of firing "Christmas guns," a common regional celebration. Crockett remembered that a brother-in-law, who lived on the opposite bank of Rutherford's Fork some six miles west, had brought him a keg of powder but Crockett had yet to bring it to his own house. Despite the biting-cold temperatures and recent winter storms, Crockett determined to go after the powder. He later admitted that it was a foolhardy undertaking, with the river over a mile wide in places he'd be forced to ford. The more sensible Elizabeth argued vehemently that he should not attempt such a journey under these circumstances, but Crockett explained that they needed the powder since they were running out of meat. Elizabeth pointed out that they might just as well starve as for David to "freeze to death or get drowned," either of which was likely if he went. Stubborn as always, Crockett dressed in his thickest and warmest "woolen wrappers," and moccasins, tying up a dry set of "clothes and shoes and stockings" and against Elizabeth's entreaties, off he went into the cold, snow swirling around him and collecting in deep drifts. He would later concede that it was a questionable idea, adding that "I didn't before know how much any body could suffer and not die. This, and some of my other experiments with water, learned me something about it."

Crockett plowed through ankle-deep snow until he reached the river, which gave him pause: "It looked like an ocean," he remembered, and was frozen over, glazed with a thin veneer of ice. Undaunted, he waded right in and crossed a long channel, walking in places over downed logs until he came to a large slough, all the while holding his gun and dry clothes above his head and out of the water. Logs he remembered crossing while out hunting were now submerged, and he was forced to wade armpit-deep, then nearly neck-deep. Then he cut saplings to lay down and crawl across sections too deep to wade. He began to lose feeling in his feet and legs, and after crossing a small island in the river he came to another slough, this one spanned by a floating log he figured he could walk over. The log bobbled in the freezing stream and about halfway across Crockett lost his balance and the log rotated, tossing him and completely submerging him. He hurried as much as he could and fought his way to the higher ground, all his limbs now nearly useless as he pulled off his wet clothes right there on the stream bank and struggled frantically into his dry kit. "I got them on," he recalled, "but my flesh had no feeling in it."

He understood the dire nature of his situation, and knew that getting warm was his only way out. He attempted to run to get some blood pumping, but "couldn't raise a trot for some time." He staggered on, zombie-like, unable to step more than one foot forward at a time, and in this way he lurched and limped five miles to his brother-in-law's place, near-dead and dreaming of fire. It was growing dark when he finally knocked feebly on the door, and the family let him in and warmed him slowly back to life in front of the fire and gave him horns of whiskey. The next day dawned bitter cold, snow drifts blowing into cornices along the river, and Crockett agreed to wait out his return. He knew that the river would be freezing over, but doubted its ability to bear his weight. Crockett used the down time to hunt, killing two deer for his in-laws, and the next day chasing after a "big he-bear" until nightfall but failing to bag him. Finally, on the third day, though it remained painfully cold, Crockett decided that he had to get back to his family, who were without food. He "determined to get home to them, or die a-trying."

The river had frozen over more completely, but as he had feared, not solidly enough to hold him, and before long he had broken through the ice up to his waist. He wielded his tomahawk as an icebreaker before him, hacking as he pushed on. Intermittently the ice would bear his weight, and he crawled those frozen distances until he broke through again, completely submerging himself but holding the powder keg dry above the water. He was now partially frostbitten, clearly hypothermic, and bordering on delirious, and he knew he was in trouble:

By this time I was nearly frozen to death, but I saw all along before me where the ice had been fresh broke, and I thought it must be a bear straggling about in the water. I therefore fresh primed my gun, and, cold as I was, determined to make war on him, if we met. But I followed the trail until it lead me home, and I then found out it had been made by my young man that lived with me, who had been sent by my distressed wife to see, if he could, what had become of me, for they all believed I was dead. When I got home I wasn't quite dead, but mighty nigh it; but I had my powder, and that was what I went for.[25]

Though Elizabeth was understandably growing weary of his stubbornness, his near-death experiences, and the constant threat of losing a second husband, she also knew that he had to hunt, both for himself and to keep them in food and furs. Crockett would have measured his own self-worth in part by his hunting prowess, and the very next day he set out for bear, responding to a dream he'd had about a violent battle with one, and viewing it as a sign, adding that "In bear country, I never knowed such a dream to fail."

He went to likely ground "above the hurricane," taking with him three dogs, and heading six miles down Rutherford's Fork and then some four miles over to the main Obion. Sleet drove down in heavy slants across the iron-gray skies, and "the bushes were all bent down, and locked together with ice," making the going cold and difficult. He was soon warmed by the flush of gobbling turkeys, and he brought down two of the largest, and slung them heavily over his shoulders and continued crashing through the cane. Eventually the birds grew too heavy to carry so he stopped to rest, and just then his oldest hound sniffed about a log, then raised his head to the sky and hollered out baying. Then he bolted, and the other dogs followed, with Crockett running hard behind, the turkeys a mass of feathers and wings and necks dangling and swaying. Soon the dogs were well out of sight, and Crockett could only follow the faint sounds of their barking and baying deep into the thickets.

He finally found them barking up a tree, and he laid down his turkeys and readied to fire on the bear, but when he looked up there was nothing there. The dogs bolted, and when he caught them they were barking up an empty tree again, and he grew so frustrated he vowed to pepper the dogs with shot the next time he got close enough, figuring they were baying at the old scent of turkeys. He ran hard to catch them and finally reached a break in the cover, a big open meadow, and up ahead of his dogs he saw "in and about the biggest bear that ever was seen in America." The bear was so big and black and frightening that it resembled an enraged bull, and Crockett understood that he was so large that the dogs had been hesitant to attack him, which explained their curious behavior. Crockett quickly hung the gobblers in a nearby tree, and, flushed full of adrenaline, he "broke like a quarter horse after my bear, for the sight of him had put new springs in me." By the time he managed to get near the dogs and the escaping bear they had entered a deep thicket, and Crockett was slowed to a crawl, as the stuff was too low and tangled to walk through.

Finally, Crockett broke through to see the bear ascending a giant black oak, and he scrambled to within eighty yards of the enraged but frightened creature. Breathing heavily with a mixture of fear and excitement, Crockett primed his rifle, leveled on the great black bear's breast, and fired. "At this he raised one of his paws and snorted loudly." Crockett knew full well that a massive black bear, angered and injured, was an extremely dangerous animal, so he reloaded as fast has he could, aimed once more, and fired. "At the crack of my gun he came tumbling down, and the moment he touched the ground, I heard one of my best dogs cry out." Crockett brandished his tomahawk in one hand, a big butcher-knife in his other, and ran to within a few yards of the bear, which then released his dog and cast his wild eyes on Crockett. Crockett backed off, grabbed his gun again, loaded nervously and quickly, and put a third ball in the bear, this time killing him.

Crockett slumped down and surveyed the bear and could not believe the size of it. He'd need help getting him out of there for sure, so he left the bear and "blazed a trail," cutting saplings as he went to show him the way back. He arrived home and enlisted his brother-in-law and another man to go with him to bring in the bear. Returning to the kill at dark, they built a fire and butchered the animal. Crockett reckoned it was the second largest bear he ever killed, weighing about 600 pounds, and by now, warmed by the fire and the blood lust of this kill still in his throat and mouth, the trek to retrieve his gunpowder seemed justified. He also noted with some humor, using a phrase he might well have coined, that "a dog might sometimes be doing a good business, even when he seemed to be barking up the wrong tree."

Crockett devoted the remainder of that winter to the canebrakes, hunting long hours with his dogs and neighbors and occasionally making the forty-mile trek to Jackson to sell wolf, deer, and bear hides for the few dollars they would bring. And while his family needed any extra money his hunting could generate, his prowess afield transcended monetary value: on the frontier, one's self-worth was measured by one's ability in the hunt, in what a man could bring down with his gun—whether animal or enemy, and in the field, and as a marksman, David Crockett was peerless. Crockett was becoming not just a formidable hunter but a legendary one, and he would later boast of killing 105 bears in less than a year. Many of the pelts he sold, and much of the meat he used, or shared with family and neighbors. Far and wide throughout the South through the frontier grapevine of storytelling his name became synonymous with successful backwoods life. These bear-hunting tales followed the ancient storytelling motif in which the hero confronts a life-threatening adversary and slays it. His own tales of these adventures illustrate a finely tuned skill, the tall tale, the hyperbolic boasting demanded of the hunter and the hero.[26]

He may have been only vaguely aware of it, but David Crockett was in the process of manufacturing the myth and legend that would live long after him.

Crockett's hunts proved so successful that winter that by February, as he put it, he "had on hand a great many skins," and he set out with John Wesley for Jackson, where he sold the hides and did well enough (wolf "scalps" going for three dollars apiece at the time) to purchase provisions, like sugar, coffee, salt, and more lead and powder for hunting, that might take him through to spring. While in town, Crockett ran into a few of his soldier friends from the war, and he decided that rather than return straight away, he'd take a few horns with the boys.

While whooping it up in a local tavern, Crockett became acquainted with three legislative candidates, among them a Dr. William E. Butler, a nephew by marriage to Andrew Jackson. With Butler were Duncan McIver and Major Joseph Lynn, and the three of them would be running against one another in the coming election. Dr. Butler was, among other things, the town commissioner of Jackson; he was quite influential in the area, especially given his connection to General Andrew Jackson. McIver had been among the earliest settlers in the area, and all three men were known politicos, men of high standing and notoriety in the region.[27] During the course of the evening it was suggested, in what Crockett suspected was a joke against him, that he ought to run, too. Crockett pointed out that he lived "forty miles from any white settlement, and had no thought of becoming a candidate at the time,"[28] and the next day he and John Wesley headed home.

Just a week or two later a friend arrived at Crockett's house with a copy of the *Jackson Pioneer*, which contained an article that announced Crockett's candidacy. Crockett immediately assumed, his insecurity flushing his cheeks even redder than they usually were, that he was being made fun of, and he said as much to Elizabeth: "I said to my wife that this was all a burlesque on me, but I was determined to make it cost the man who had put it there at least the value of the printing, and of the fun he wanted at my expense." Riled and testy, Crockett hired an able young farmhand to help Elizabeth, and he set out electioneering, discovering quite quickly that his reputation preceded him. People were talking of Crockett the bear hunter, even referring to him reverently as "the man from the cane."

Butler, McIver, and Lynn were politically savvy, and they understood that they'd have a better chance working together than running against one another, so in March they held a caucus to decide which of the three would be best suited to oppose Crockett, settling on Dr. Butler as the man for the job. That Butler's wife was Andrew Jackson's niece likely played some role in the decision, but Butler was also well educated, articulate, and had the money to sustain a serious campaign. Crockett later admitted that it would be a tough race, and that Butler was a smart and worthy opponent: "The doctor was a clever fellow, and I have often said he was the most talented man I ever run against for any office." Knowing the odds he was facing, Crockett would have to resort to the most creative campaign tactics he could summon, playing off his affability, his growing reputation as a backwoods character, and his uncanny ability to give voters exactly what they wanted to hear. He determined to exploit his authenticity as a man of the people against his opponents' aristocratic background, hoping the people would be able to relate to him more easily than to Butler.

Crockett's first solid opportunity came at a political rally, where Colonel Adam Alexander happened to be campaigning for national Congress. Crockett was in attendance, and he saw that Butler was, too. Crockett relished innocent chicanery, and in the large assembly of people he saw his chance. After Alexander was finished speaking he introduced Crockett to a few folks, explaining that Crockett was running against Butler. People began to mill around, their curiosity piqued to see the bear hunter.

Finally Dr. Butler also recognized Crockett, and he seemed surprised to see him there. "Crockett, damn it, is that you?" he asked quizzically.

A master of comic timing, Crockett took the cue and ran with it. "Be sure it is," he answered, grinning at his now substantial audience and launching into character, laying the backwoods drawl on thick as molasses, "but I don't want it understood that I have come electioneering. I have just crept out of the cane, to see what discoveries I could make among the white folks." By now, people were chuckling, fascinated by Crockett and his antics. Crockett kept right on, explaining to Butler exactly how he would defeat him:

> I told him that when I set out electioneering, I would go prepared to put every man on as good a footing when I left him as I found him on. I would therefore have me a large buckskin hunting-shirt made, with a couple of pockets holding about a peck each; and that in one I would carry a great big twist of tobacco, and in the other my bottle of liquor; for I know'd when I met a man and offered him a dram, he would throw out his quid of tobacco to take one, and after he had taken his horn, I would out with my twist and give him another chaw. And in this way he would not be worse off than when I found him; and I would be sure to leave him in a first-rate good humor.[29]

Dr. Butler had to admit that such a tactic would be very tough to beat. Crockett conceded that in terms of campaign funds, they were certainly not on equal footing, so he would do what he knew how to, using his backwoods skills and ingenuity. With the audience hanging on each new and outrageous sentence, Crockett cited his own industrious children and coon dogs, which he would employ every night until midnight to raise election funds, and that he himself would "go a wolfing, and shoot down a wolf, and skin his head, and his scalp would be good to me for three dollars . . . and in this way I would get along on the big string." The antics had the crowd in stitches, and though the clever Crockett had claimed not to have come electioneering, that's exactly what he had done, selling his infectious personality to the voters.

Crockett employed similar stratagems and more in the official electioneering, taking advantage of the generous and fair Dr. Butler whenever he could. Butler admired Crockett's spunk and appeared to enjoy competing with him; he even sought out his company. Once, hearing that Crockett was in Jackson on the campaign trail, Butler invited him to his home for dinner. Crockett accepted, and when he arrived he could not help but notice the finery, the lovely furnishings, and especially the floor rugs to which Crockett was unaccustomed. The rugs on Butler's floors were so fine that Crockett felt guilty even stepping on them, and he made an exaggerated point not to, hopping over them when he entered to dine with the Butlers. Deviously, Crockett used this episode in later stump speeches, relating the dinner episode to the people: "Fellow citizens, my aristocratic competitor has a fine carpet, and every day he *walks* on finer truck than any gowns your wife or your daughters, in all their lives, ever *wore!*"[30] In this way Crockett undermined his opponent and continued to parade himself as a man of the people.

Opponents often traveled together, coming into towns together and giving speeches one after the other. As this went on for some time, candidates came to know each other's speeches nearly as well as their own. Though Crockett preferred to follow, offering up a comic anecdote and leaving the listener wanting more, once near the end of the campaign he took the opportunity to go first, and with devilish premeditation, he delivered Dr. Butler's own speech almost verbatim. It left the good doctor with literally nothing left to say on that occasion, and Crockett's coup became the talk of the town.[31] David Crockett had found his stride, and expressions that the people understood flowed off his tongue as he entertained them. He promised them that he would "stand up to my lick log, salt or no salt," and he did. When the votes were tallied, Crockett had won by 247 votes. The reluctant candidate, forced to run to save face, was heading to Murfreesboro once again. Though he would employ false modesty in calling this victory luck, he must have sensed his developing expertise in getting himself elected. He was a showman, a born orator with an uncanny sense of comic timing, and he understood intuitively the principle that most fine entertainers come to live by: "Leave 'em wanting more."

Crockett arrived back in Murfreesboro for the Fifteenth General Assembly, which convened on September 15, 1823. By now he would have been fairly comfortable with the town and environs, and with the routines involved in life as a state legislator. He had even gained a degree of respect among his colleagues, for his campaign practices were by now well documented, related at taverns and even in the assembly halls. And although as a campaigner David Crockett assumed the guise of a prankster, as a sophomore legislator he took his role seriously, bearing the added responsibility of representing five new counties—Madison, Carroll, Humphries, Henderson, and Perry. There had been, as yet, no constitutional convention, so his own district was not equally represented, but the fast formation of new counties clearly illustrates the significant migration into the region and the prodigious growth spilling into the West.[32] By the end of the session the district would swell to ten new counties.

Crockett's first week back on the job was frenetic. He immediately found himself on three significant committees, one having to do with specifying new county boundaries, one on military affairs, in which he had at least some experience and interest; and the last having to do with vacant lands, the one to which he would devote most of his attentions.[33] Crockett quickly had the opportunity to assert his growing independence, an independence that would become a kind of contrary trademark and that would eventually be his political unraveling. That independence also signaled his first public and definitive rift with Andrew Jackson, a schism which perhaps began as far back as the Creek War, when Old Hickory quelled the attempted mutiny. Crockett later looked back at the Fifteenth General Assembly with this salient recollection: "At the session in 1823, I had a small trial of my independence, and whether I would forsake principle for party, or for the purpose of following after big men." Principles, voting one's conscience, being true to self and constituents—these were all tenets Crockett cared very much about. Often such idealism—and inability to compromise—hurt him politically.

The test of independence to which Crockett alludes had to do with the election of a United States senator. The term for Senator John Williams had recently expired, and he sought reelection. Around the assembly halls and in the local taverns it was no secret that Williams and Jackson had open enmity dating back to the Creek War. It was also common knowledge that the political machines of Tennessee were priming Jackson to be president. As the senate vote neared, Williams looked like a shoo-in, so much so that in the end Jackson, against his initial interests, agreed to run, fearing that his party's chosen opposition candidate, Pleasant M. Miller, was unlikely to defeat the incumbent. The race was far too close for comfort, with Jackson prevailing by a mere ten votes, and illustrated just how divided the legislators were.[34] Crockett had until this time been openly amenable to Jackson and especially to the idea of his presidential candidacy that would be forthcoming, but he voted for Williams, noting that Williams had been successful and done a good job the last time around, and therefore there was no good reason to discharge him: "I thought the colonel had honestly discharged his duty, and even the mighty name of Jackson couldn't make me vote against him."

It is unclear whether Crockett had other motives for voting against the tide, and against Jackson. It may have been as simple as personality traits, with Crockett beginning to sense that Jackson was moving away from the common man and would be no friend when it came to the western land issues. Crockett was already deeply suspicious of men with money and vast land holdings, and he would certainly have known that while Jackson liked to play on his "self-made" status, they were not on equal footing. By 1798, Jackson owned more than 50,000 acres in central and western Tennessee, much of it worth more than ten times what he had originally paid.[35] Crockett was unapologetic, even downright prideful, about how he voted, though he admitted that the decision was unfavorable politically. He later assessed his first public breach with Jackson in this way: "But voting against the old chief was found a mighty up-hill business to all of them except myself. I never would, nor never did, acknowledge I had voted wrong; and I am more certain now that I was right then ever."

As it turned out, though he was victorious, Jackson later declined the office—he had only intended to run and win, and that was enough to keep Williams out of the position. Jackson had succeeded in ridding himself of Williams as a political thorn in his breeches. Crockett summed up his sentiments on his vote by adding, "I told the people it was the best vote I ever gave; that I had supported the public interest, and cleared my conscience in giving it, instead of gratifying the private ambition of a man." He would be his own boss even if there appeared to be very long and helpful political coattails to ride on. He was having none of it. He did what he believed was right and stuck to his guns, exhibiting an obstinate, unyielding nature that wasn't entirely suited to partisan politics.

David Crockett was in the process of establishing his political tendencies, but also his persona: he would be a man of the people and for the people. He would back any bills or resolutions that were conceived to assist those people with whom he could relate, with whom he felt fraternity, even kinship. Interestingly, James Polk voted with Crockett twice during the session, including on a petition to hear no divorce proceedings—

Crockett was actually in favor of the legislature paying the legal expenses in such cases so that the poor would have fair and affordable access to lawyers. Crockett came out in opposition of using prison labor on state construction projects like roads and improving the navigation of rivers, suspicious as he was of authority and mindful that some of the inmates would have been incarcerated simply for being indigent and unable to pay their bills.[36] In fact, quite early in the session Crockett put forth a bill that would entirely eradicate imprisonment for debt, if that debt could be proved "honest debt." Mindful of the fiscal pains people in the region still felt from the depression of 1819, Crockett aligned with the majority vote to reduce state property taxes, again in an effort to assist the impoverished. In a curious and ironic vote, especially given his own penchant to campaign using the "plug and a dram" technique of luring voters to the liquor stand, and plying them with horns of spirits and twists of tobacco, Crockett voted to prohibit the sale of liquor at elections. Crockett also presaged a later interest in (and deep suspicion of) banking issues, favoring a move toward the state bank of Tennessee and local branches that might provide loans to farmers in need.[37] Crockett had previously spoken outwardly, and scathingly, against the current banking system, and was quoted in the *National Banner* and the *Nashville Whig* in September of 1823 as saying that the "Banking system [was] a species of swindling on a large scale."[38]

The land issue arose again in the form of the North Carolina land warrants, with North Carolina University presenting a large number of warrants of veterans (by now deceased) and requesting authorization to sell them in Western Tennessee as a fundraising technique for the growing university. The North Carolina warrants had the potential to displace untold numbers of squatters; Crockett smelled a rat. He had his own claim on the Obion, and he believed that folks like him deserved the right to buy their land first, before outsiders with dubious warrants. A division within the Jackson supporters had occurred over this issue, with Felix

Crockett's spangled, three-pocket buckskin vest reveals a
man with a sense of style. The glass beadwork is colorful
and attention-getting, just like his character. (Crockett
vest—color transparency. Courtesy of the Daughters
of the Republic of Texas Library, San Antonio.)

Grundy supporting the presentation of North Carolina warrants, and the savvy legislator (and future president) James Polk in opposition. Crockett initially aligned with Polk, but later broke with him, believing that it was a mistake to allow outsiders in the form of North Carolina residents to come in and purchase vacant lands for cash—the poor would once again be priced out.[39] Crockett preferred that the land be sold to those who lived on it, on credit, rather than be bought and used as speculative real estate by outsiders. Crockett's position garnered him a degree of public notoriety when it appeared in the *Whig:*

> Mr. Crockett called up his resolution relative to land warrants . . . He had heard much said here about frauds, &c., committed by North Carolina speculators; but it was time to quit talking about other people, and look to ourselves. This practice was more rascally, and a greater fraud, than any he had yet heard of . . . The speculators then preferring to be great friends to the people in saving their land, had gone up one side of the creek and down the other, like a *coon,* and pretended to grant the poor people great favors in securing them occupant claims—they gave them a credit of a year and promised to take cows, horses, &c., in payment. But when the year came around, the notes were in the hands of others; the people were sued, cows and horses not being sufficient to pay for securing it. He said again, that warrants obtained this way, by the removal of entries for the purpose of speculation, should be as counterfeit as bank notes in the hands of the person who obtained them, and die on their hands.[40]

By the end of the session Crockett had turned over a good number of political cards—most revealing that he would vote his conscience come what may. He'd outwardly broken with Jackson, and with Polk as well, when Polk favored the sale of public land to raise money for universities. Crockett understood too well that universities were the domain of the privileged, so subsidizing land-grant institutions was of no interest to him. By now his name and position on such matters were getting out into the regional papers, developing his reputation as a representative of the poor and downtrodden. It was a role Crockett played well.

EIGHT

"Neck or Nothing"

CROCKETT'S MODEST SUCCESSES in the last session whetted his appetite for politics enough to convince him that a run at Congress was a reasonable next step. He had now begun to feel a modicum of comfort moving in the elite circles of Murfreesboro, playing on his persona to win voters and using his contrary nature to stir things up in state politics and get himself noticed. Elizabeth would have been very happy to have him home, as his hunting skills were responsible for their food. The pressure to provide was increased by the lease of an additional tract of land on the Obion, and coupled with the hunting were the need to continue tilling, planting, and harvesting viable crops for vegetable sustenance, which Crockett oversaw in a rather distracted way, leaving much of the toil to his boys and few hired hands. He would always prove a very reluctant farmer, much preferring the chase, whether for wild animals or public office.

Crockett later postured that he was coerced into his first congressional race, again against his wishes and better judgment, but that others urged him into the fray. Colonel Adam Alexander was then representing the western district, which now numbered eleven counties, and though he possessed significant power and influence, and was a wealthy planter and extremely well-connected, he had blundered in his previous term by voting in favor of high tariffs, leaving his constituents bemused at best, and leaving himself potentially vulnerable to defeat.[1] Crockett remembered that Alexander's "vote on the tariff law of 1824 gave a mighty heap of dissatisfaction to his people. They therefore began to talk pretty strong of running me for Congress against him." Crockett went on to say that his initial feeling was to decline, citing lack of preparation and knowledge as ostensible reasons, though a spotty or nonexistent résumé had never stopped him before. "I told the people that . . . it was a step above my knowledge, and I know'd nothing about Congress matters."

He might have been slightly disingenuous here, for in 1824, some months before he officially offered himself for the candidacy, and perhaps while still serving in the state legislature, Crockett sent out a circular to the district that included the following appeal:

> I am not one of those who have had the opportunities and benefits of wealth and education in my youth. I am thus far the maker of my own fortunes . . . If in the discharge of my duties as your representative, I have failed to exhibit the polished eloquence of men of superior education, I can yet flatter myself that I have notwithstanding, been enabled to procure the passage of some laws and regulations beneficial to the interests of my constituents.[2]

Clearly Crockett plays on the emotions here, underscoring his humble origins, while at the same time jabbing barbs at the moneyed and educated. Throughout his political career he would face opponents with more money, connections, power, and influence, always assuming the role of the reluctant underdog. His ill-fated first attempt at Congress was no exception, and Crockett said that finally, at continued pressure from friends, "I was obliged to agree to run." It was a mistake, for he wasn't ready yet, and the result would offer schooling in the dirty machinations of national politics, games and power plays about which Crockett was untutored.[3]

First of all, Crockett didn't have the financial means to run a successful campaign, which would require printing costs, travel expenses, and worst of all, more time away from farm and fields and hunting grounds. He felt that he was well liked in his local area, but the congressional district covered an impressive eighteen counties, and Crockett would need to venture far and wide to make himself known. It was simply beyond his current means.

His opponent, Adam Alexander, did not share Crockett's indigence or lack of influence. He was close with Jackson, and with two other significant "Jackson supporters," Felix Grundy and Judge John Overton. Crockett had already alienated Grundy in the previous legislative session when he voted in favor of Williams over Jackson for senate, and Crockett would quickly come to understand that such decisions came with consequences. In politics, allegiances mattered, and people tended to hold grudges.

A number of factors conspired to doom Crockett in that first attempt at Congress, though he would later blame it all on the price of cotton. It's true that cotton prices ran miraculously high in 1825, up to $25 per hundredweight, nearly five times the average price, and it's true that Alexander was quick to jump on this fact, taking credit for it in the two main papers, with which he had connections and influence while Crockett did not.[4] To complicate matters, John Overton began to have some fun at Crockett's expense, partly in retaliation for Crockett's vocal opposition two years earlier to moneyed planters and speculators, of which Overton was both. Writing under the nom de plume of "Aristides," he took Crockett to task for attempting to change court days and to add an East

Tennessee brigade to the militia of the Western District.[5] Overton made
a convincing case against Crockett with sustained newspaper postings, an
onslaught that lasted over three months and kept Crockett constantly on
the defensive. In the end, with the peoples' purses bursting from the high
cotton prices, and Alexander promising that there would be equally high
prices for everything else they manufactured and sold, Crockett's entreaties fell on deaf ears. "I might as well have sung *salms* over a dead
horse, as to try to make the people believe otherwise; for they knowed
their cotton had raised, sure enough, and if the colonel hadn't done it,
they didn't know what had."

He was unable to persuade the voters differently, and this, combined
with his general political naïveté, cost him dearly. Though years later in
his autobiography Crockett would remember incorrectly that he lost by
"exactly *two* votes," the real tally difference that August was not two, but
267. Given his lack of preparation, Crockett's showing was better than he
let on; he had received 2,599 votes of the 5,465 total cast.[6] But he was not
accustomed to losing, and the fact that he later fudged the poll figures suggests that he took defeat hard. In a move that would become a pattern,
Crockett chose to pacify his hurt pride by heading back out into the canebrakes to hunt, out into open country where he conjured schemes for
making easy profits to get ahead, always dreaming of ways to make his
fortune.

One such enterprise involved some speculation of his own, for no
sooner had Crockett returned home from his defeat than he made a trip of
some twenty-five miles to Obion Lake, where he hired a small crew and
put them to work building two large flatboats, which he intended to pile
high with cut barrel staves and float to market in New Orleans. The plan
seemed sound, if a bit ambitious for the self-described landlubber Crockett, and he felt confident enough to leave the construction of the craft to
his men while he got down to the more serious and enjoyable business: "I

worked on with my hands till the bears got fat, and then I turned out to hunting, to lay in a supply of meat." It would be his most productive winter hunt ever, and he ended up supplying not only his family, but many other friends and relatives, with an abundance of meat, sustaining, and even augmenting, his backwoods legend. Crockett by this time had acquired an impressive pack of "eight large dogs, and as fierce as painters [panthers]; so that a bear stood no chance at all to get away from them." Crockett took his dogs and hunted for a few weeks with a good friend, and when he'd filled the friend's larders he spent some time helping his boys with the flatboats and the collection and cutting of barrel staves, but the work grew tedious and his mind wandered. "At length I couldn't stand it any longer without a hunt," he admitted. The hunt coursed through his veins, so he took one of his younger sons (either Robert Patton, nine, or William, sixteen), with or without Elizabeth's complete blessing, and headed out for a long hunt. The hunt proved notable because during this winter, in an oft-told story, he killed a massive bear with nothing but a knife.

One day early in the winter hunt, Crockett came across a downtrodden fellow who he described as "the very picture of hard times." The man bent over a rough field, hacking away with a heavy implement and trying to clear the ground of roots, stumps, and boulders in a process called "grubbing." Crockett stopped to chat with him, and commiserating when the other informed him that it wasn't even his field; he was grubbing for another man, the owner, to get money to buy meat for his family. Crockett struck a deal with the man: if he would go with Crockett and his son and help pack and salt the slain bears, Crockett would provide the man with more meat than he could earn in a month of this backbreaking grubbing. The man retired to his rustic cabin, conferred with his wife, then reappeared with her blessing, and off they went. They killed "four very large fat bears that day," and in the course of only a week added seventeen more. Crockett relates that he quite happily gave the man "over a thousand weight of fine fat bear-meat," pleasing both the man and his wife, and when he saw him again the next fall, he learned that the meat had lasted him out the entire year.

Crockett and his son later hooked up with a neighbor named Mc-Daniel, who also needed a good supply of meat. They struck out to likely ground between Obion Lake and Reelfoot Lake, the brambly "harricane" country some of Crockett's most coveted and productive, the strewn and tangled timber providing perfect cover for the animals. They followed ridges dense with cane, peering inside the hollows of black oaks in search of hiding bears, using Crockett's wily techniques of finding treed bears by noting the differentiation of scratch marks on a tree bark. On the third day Crockett and McDaniel left the young boy in camp and headed deep into the cane, but found the going slow "on account of the cracks in the earth occasioned by the quakes." The deep troughs and fissures forced them to go around in places, and soon they met a bear coming straight at them, and Crockett sent his dogs off and they howled in pursuit. Crockett remembered this bear well, noting that "I had seen the tracks of the bear they were after, and I knowed he was a screamer." Crockett kept hotly after the bear, the foliage so tight in places that he was reduced to traveling his hands and knees: "The vines and briars was so thick that I would sometimes have to crawl like a varment to get through at all."

In time he managed to scramble through, and he found that his dogs had treed the bear in an old dead stump, and shaking with fatigue Crockett just managed to shoulder his rifle and bring the bear down. With McDaniel's help they butchered and salted the bear, "fleecing off the fat" as they skinned the animal and packed the prepared meat on horses. They rode when they could, but mostly they walked, and they reached the camp around sunset. Crockett called out and his son answered, and as they moved in the direction of camp, the dogs opened up again, baying into the sunset. Never one to forgo a fresh chase, Crockett handed his reins to McDaniel and trotted off after his hounds into the darkening skies.

The night fell fast under the canopy of cane and Crockett stumbled along, bashing his shins on fallen logs and falling into clefts in the earth left by the quakes. He forded a wide cold creek, then broke from the stream bank to scale a severe incline, clawing his way up the hillside. When he made the summit, he located his dogs and found they had treed the bear in the fork of a tall poplar. It was so dark that all he could see was the outline of a large lump in the fork of the tree, and aiming by guess-work, he fired. He missed, but the bear obliged by venturing out onto a limb where Crockett could see him better and he reloaded fast and fired again. He didn't see the bear drop so he began a third reloading. Suddenly there was the bear, down on the ground with the dogs all about him in a snarl of teeth and claws. Crockett was too close for comfort, so he pulled out his big butcher knife as protection and waited while the roaring roll and tumble of flesh and fur went on and on, his one white dog showing as an occasional flash amid the brown and black of the bear and other dogs, the whirl of animals coming at times within a rifle length of Crockett.

Finally the dogs forced the bear into a large crevasse in the earth and Crockett could tell "the biting end of him by the hollering of my dogs." He pushed his rifle into the crack, felt around, and when he thought he had it pressed against the bear's body he fired, but he only wounded its leg, and the bear, injured and enraged, broke from the hollow and went another round with the dogs before they drove him back into the crevasse again. After spearing the bear with a long cut pole, Crockett determined to risk crawling in after him, hoping the bear would remain still long enough for him to "find the right place to give him a dig with my butcher." He sent the dogs in first to keep the angry bear's head occupied, and he snuck around behind, placing his hand bravely on the bear's great rump, feeling for the shoulder. "I made a lounge with my knife, and fortunately stuck him right through the heart; at which he just sank down."

Crockett quickly got out of the crack, and when his dogs backed out too, bloody and panting, he knew the bear was finished. It had been a tremendous fight, and now Crockett had the difficult task of getting the massive animal out of the hollow, which he managed with great effort, dragging the bear a few feet at a time until he had him up on the ground and could butcher him. Exhausted, Crockett slumped on the ground to sleep, but his fire was too feeble to warm him, and he was wet through from sweat and the river he'd crossed. Soon he was shivering and shaking, his teeth chattering, his core body temperature plunging dangerously low. He tried to find dry wood to burn but it was all green or wet, and he knew he was in trouble. He began leaping and hollering in the air, hurling himself "into all sorts of motions," but hypothermia began to set in: "for my blood was now getting cold, and the chills coming all over me." At last he was so spent that he could barely stand, and he understood that he absolutely must get warmer or else he would perish:

> So I went to a tree about two feet through, and not a limb on it for thirty feet, and I would climb up it to the limbs, and then lock my arms together around it, and slide down to the bottom again. This would make the insides of my legs and arms feel mighty warm and good. I continued this till daylight in the morning, and how often I clomb up my tree and slid down I don't know, but I reckon at least a hundred times.[7]

His ingenuity having kept him alive, Crockett hung his bear and headed back to camp, where his boy and McDaniel were very happy to see him. They ate breakfast, and Crockett told them about the tough night he'd been through. Then he led them back to retrieve the big bear. McDaniel wanted to see the crack where Crockett had slain the bear with only his knife, and after he looked it over he came out shaking his head and exclaimed that he'd never have gone in there with a wounded bear, not "for all the bears in the woods." McDaniel would certainly have told that story at taverns, and to visitors, time and time again.

They concluded this hunting trip by bagging a few more bears, then salting and loading all the meat on their five pack horses and heading home. McDaniel went home with meat enough for the year, and that fall and winter Crockett counted fifty-eight bears that he and his hunting partners had brought in. In spring, the bears out of hibernation, he went out again, and in just a month he bagged forty-seven more, boasting a historic count of 105 bears in less than seven months, a number that would be considered illegal and "game hoggery" by modern standards but was perfectly acceptable and plausible at the time. Though Crockett, like many hunters and in keeping with the tall-tale tradition, sometimes lapses into hyperbole, his legendary abilities as a hunter are confirmed by a host of his contemporaries.[8]

Sated emotionally with his best hunt ever, Crockett returned to his barrel-stave project in mid-January 1826. In his absence his hired hands had been productive, piling the two flatboats with some 30,000 staves, which Crockett figured would turn a healthy profit in New Orleans. The flatboats were large and unwieldy rectangular craft, fashioned of roughhewn wood and finished with a central cabin where those off duty could sleep or eat out of the weather. They were basic, utilitarian boats often made for single trips, as they could be easily dismantled at the end of a run, their lumber sold along with whatever cargo they carried.[9] Men navigated the sluggish boats as well as they could, standing on top of the cabin, in the bow, and along the sides and rowing with long, sweeping strokes. Crockett had no nautical experience, but the lure of profit drove him even into the unknown, mysterious element of dangerous waters, and when the boats were completely loaded and tied down and some provisions stored, he and his crew boarded and pushed off into the Obion. Everything seemed to float smoothly until they converged with the great, churning Mississippi, at which point Crockett discovered that "all my hands were bad scared, and in fact I believe I was scared a little the worst of any; for I had never been down the river, and I soon discovered that my pilot was as ignorant of the business as myself."

The river was bigger than any of them had imagined, the deep water dark and eerily powerful. Soon the boats yawed and spun uncontrollably, and Crockett lashed them together, hoping to steady them. This made the boats "next akin to impossible to do anything with, or guide them right in the river." The awkward tandem drifted sideways in the river, and Crockett discovered to his dismay that they could not even intentionally land the boats, or even run them aground, though he tried to do so more than once. They were at the absolute mercy of the river.

Just before nightfall, some Ohio river boats passed and recommended, against Crockett's wishes and instincts, that they float on through the night. All night long they made futile attempts to land, as people along the shore communities would run out with lanterns swinging, shouting directions that the inept boatmen were unable to follow. Eventually they came to a tight turn in the river called the Devil's Elbow, which Crockett allowed was perfectly named: "If any place in the wide of creation has its own proper name, I thought it was this. Here we had about the hardest work that I ever was engaged in, in my life, to keep out of danger; and even then we were in it all the while."

Finally Crockett threw his hands up in futility and quit trying to land, resigned to just float along, come what may. He went below into one of the cabins and rested, thinking and reminiscing. "I was sitting by the fire, thinking on what a hobble we had got into; and how much better bear-hunting was on hard land, than floating along on the water, when a fellow had to go ahead whether he was exactly willing to or not."

Crockett's boat rode behind, and about that time he heard men scurrying on the deck above, their voices crying out hysterically as they heaved and pulled, and then the boat slammed violently into the head of a "sawyer," a bobbing sunken tree that impaled the boat. The current instantly sucked the first boat down, and feeling his own boat swamping, Crockett scrambled for the hatchway but water poured through in a thick cold current "as large as the hole would let it, and as strong as the weight of the river could force it." The boat flipped over sideways, "steeper than a housetop," and the main hatch offered no escape.

Crockett remembered another small hole in the side, which was now above him, and he clawed for that. It was too small to crawl through but he thrust his arms and face out and hollered for his life. Water had filled the cabin and now crept up almost to his head when some of the deckhands heard him screaming and leapt to grab his arms.

I told them I was sinking, and to pull my arms off, or force me through, for now I know'd well enough it was neck or nothing, come out or sink. By a violent effort they jerked me through; but I was in a pretty pickle when I got through. My shirt was torn off, and I was literally skin'd like a rabbit.

As it turned out, Crockett was well pleased to get out any way he could, because the moment they pulled him out, the craft went entirely under. They all managed to jump to a foundered mass of logs. It was the last he would see of his boats or his staves. He and his crew remained on the logjam through the night, shivering in what little clothing they had on. All else, including Crockett's would-be fortune, had been lost. They were marooned at a place called "Paddy's Hen and Chickens," just above, and within sight of, the bustling city of Memphis. Crockett later remembered that deep in that night, shaking with cold and now penniless and destitute, he did not feel sorry for himself: no anguish, despair, or self-pity. Rather, a curious kind of calm, a surreal contentedness, washed over him as he sat stranded on the island: "I felt happier and better off than I ever had in my life before, for I had just made such a marvelous escape, that I forgot almost every thing else in that, and so I felt prime."

Early the next morning a passing boat recognized their distress and sent a skiff for them, where they found the men tired, wet, cold, and hungry, the cantankerous and revitalized David Crockett sitting buck naked on his shredded shirt. News of the men had traveled downstream, and their sinking stave boats were spotted plummeting headlong down the river, and when the rescue skiff arrived at the docks in Memphis, curious onlookers were on hand to see what all the hubbub was about. Among the throng was a man named Marcus B. Winchester, a prominent Memphis businessman who owned department stores and would later become postmaster of Memphis during the Jackson administration. Winchester kindly took the distressed travelers to one of his stores, where he clothed the men, and then he offered to host them in his home, where his wife gave them much needed food and drink.[10]

Warmed, fed, clothed, and happy to be alive, Crockett and his men hit the town, partying all night long, sharing horn after horn and telling tales of their travels and near-death adventures, Crockett the most vociferous and animated of the group, and certainly the best storyteller. Small crowds gathered at each tavern they visited, and Crockett held forth, cheers and laughter going round with each unbelievable tale. Marcus Winchester took keen note of the attention Crockett received, impressed with the way people gravitated toward him and responded to him.

Winchester was so taken with Crockett that the next day he took him and his crew again to his store and outfitted them with shoes, hats, and enough clothes for their return upriver, and he even decided to give Crockett some money, urging him to run again for Congress and promising to back him if he did so. Crockett sent most of his men home, and took just one comrade downstream by steamer to Natchez, to see if by some miracle they might recover their rogue flatboat, which had actually been spotted some fifty miles downstream. Crockett noted that "an attempt had been made to land her, but without success, as she was as hardheaded as ever." She would remain so, and though Crockett made a strong effort, the boat was never recovered.[11]

As was often the case with Crockett, once disaster was averted, he emerged stronger and more vital than before. In this case, he had become something of the darling of Memphis, with stories circulating about the larger-than-life bear hunter who washed up naked and bleeding on the shore. Major Winchester observed this growing notoriety and reiterated that he would back Crockett in the upcoming congressional election of 1827, providing him with campaign money as needed to make a second run against Alexander. So, though he had lost his entire entrepreneurial enterprise, he finally returned to his Elizabeth and his family in good old Gibson County, sometime in the early part of the summer of 1827, with quite a story to tell. Instead of having his tail between his legs, he arrived spry and sassy, flush with some hard grit in his pocket and a new benefactor down in Memphis, a thriving and politically influential river town in the huge Ninth Congressional District.[12]

Elizabeth and the young Crocketts would have been happy to see the truant patriarch, but the reunion was tempered with the news that he needed to get right out on the campaign trail for the upcoming elections, to be held in August. If Crockett knew that it would be a difficult task to unseat an incumbent as strong and savvy as Alexander, he did not let that challenge dampen his spirits or his conviction, and in fact he appears to have been bolstered by a new positive attitude after surviving yet another close call, this time at the providence of the mighty Mississippi River. Not only did Winchester agree to provide campaign support and a loan to Crockett, he also made frequent business trips down in Crockett's region, and the two would meet and socialize. Winchester promised to talk Crockett up to his influential friends, a fact about which Crockett felt no compunction; it was simply the way politics worked.

> My friend also had a good deal of business about over the district at the different courts; and if he now and then slip'd in a good word for me, it is nobody's business. We frequently met at different places, and, as he thought I needed, he would occasionally hand me a little more cash; so I was able to buy a little of 'the creature,' to put my friends in a good humour, as well as the other gentlemen, for they all treat in that country; not to get elected, of course—for that would be against the law; but just, as I before said, to make themselves and their friends feel their keeping a little.[13]

Crockett benefited from other social factors as well. The price of cotton, which he used as an excuse in his loss to Alexander two years before, was now back down to earth at $6 per hundredweight, so Crockett cleverly keyed on this fact, plus the very real situation of occupant dispossession in the Western District as a result of extensions to the North Carolina warrants. Crockett harnessed his campaign simply: he would run "against the tariff and for a congressional solution to the land problem."[14] To help things even more, two other candidates entered the skirmish: John Cooke and General William Arnold, and their presence could potentially take some of the vote away from Adam Alexander, especially the addition of Arnold from Jackson, who took his open animosity against the incumbent to the forum of public debate, undermining some of Alexander's credibility.[15]

Crockett had three recent campaign races under his belt, and he had learned from each one, so that he came to the summer of 1827 as a seasoned campaigner with a firm command of his public persona. His strategy this time around was simple: he would give the voters what they wanted to hear, and he would most importantly give them what they wanted to see—a real-life backwoodsman who was a mouthpiece for them, who shared their dreams and aspirations but also their frustrations and concerns, a thigh-slappingly funny storyteller who lived "out amongst 'em."

His first challenge was to deal with the loud-mouthed and long-winded John Cooke, who launched an aggressive personal attack on David Crockett's character traveling all about the district and publicly reviling Crockett as an adulterer and a drunk, and generally trying to undermine him as indecent.[16] Crockett responded by fighting fire with fire (in much the same way politicians use mud-slinging commercials today), casting equal and worse aspersions against Cooke, most of them utter fabrications, but who cared? He was having a good time trading lies with Cooke, stooping to his level and then crawling even lower. Cooke decided to ensnare Crockett in his egregious lies by attending a political rally with his own witnesses in support, and, after one of Crockett's lengthy tirades, coming forward and exposing him publicly as a liar. Thus caught in the act and exposed by his witnesses, Cooke reasoned, the disgraced Crockett would wither away and perhaps even withdraw from the race.

The plan backfired in Cooke's face like a ten-pound cannon. At the event, Crockett rose to speak with unusual bluster, laying on outrageous falsehoods even thicker than usual. Now an expert at timing, Crockett let the air grow still and pretended to be finished, feigning a move to take his seat but then pausing, clearing his throat, and stepping up again. He wished to add one last comment. At length he informed the gathering that his opponent was among them, and planned to expose him as a liar; he'd even brought his own witnesses with him for the purpose of doing so. Crockett grinned his patented wildcat smile and pointed out that the witnesses were entirely unnecessary—they could all be witnesses, for he was quite happy to admit that he'd been telling lies. What choice did he have?

His opponent had started the fight by slurring him with slander and out-right lies, and so, to keep things fair and even, he had responded with lies. In fact, truth be told, they were both liars![17]

An informer had obviously tipped Crockett off, and the result was devastating for Cooke, who never even had an opportunity to respond, so uproarious was the laughter from the crowd. Crockett was the hero of the day, and Cooke could only burn with indignation as the crowd rallied around their man, David Crockett. Cooke soon withdrew his name from the running, claiming that he was morally superior and could not in good conscience serve a constituency that would cheer an acknowledged liar. Cooke felt the embarrassment for a long time, and could see that he was outgunned, for "two years later he rejected an opportunity to face Crock-ett in a rematch."[18] Using his trademark humor, and embracing his role as a trickster, Crockett had single-handedly dispatched one of his opponents by simply being funny and, ultimately, truthful.

In the meantime, Alexander and Arnold locked horns, and in doing so, made a fatal error: they completely overlooked Crockett as a serious threat. Alexander remembered his decisive victory of two years earlier and seemed little threatened or concerned by Crockett this time around, instead focusing his attentions on Arnold, who by necessity responded in kind. Crockett put it this way: "My two competitors seemed some little afraid of the influence of each other, but not to think me in their way at all. They, therefore, were generally working against each other, while I was going ahead for myself, and mixing among the people in the best way I could."

His mixing proved to be just right, and around the region Crockett was now entrenching himself as the peoples' candidate. He was a self-made man, and he began to comprehend what being popular felt like. His talk was so straight and genuine that people simply couldn't help but like him. He had developed a style, complete with a country accent, manner-isms, and scathingly funny comic timing, and most remarkable of all, it was really him. He made certain to season his short speeches with regional jargon, understanding the efficacy of homilies like "A short horse is soon curried," knowing that the common folk would appreciate the slang. He may have been exaggerating some, but he wasn't faking it. What Crockett gave them in the congressional race of 1827 was pure and authentic Crockett.

For years after the election Crockett liked to tell the story of how all three candidates convened once at a stump meeting in the eastern counties, and how, as usual, Arnold and Alexander had completely ignored Crockett, treating him as if he did not even exist. On this occasion Crockett went first, and spoke very briefly and simply, knowing from experience that the other two would be remembered for their long, protracted, and boring speeches, and he for his good humor and cunning wit. Crockett listened attentively as they railed away at each other, first Alexander, then Arnold:

> The general took much pains to reply to Alexander, but didn't so much as let on that there was any such candidate as myself at all. He had been speaking for a considerable time, when a large flock of guinea-fowls came very near to where he was, and set up the most unmerciful chattering that ever was heard, for they are a noisy little brute any way. They so confused the general, that he made a stop, and requested that they might be driven away. I let him finish his speech, and then walking up to him, said aloud, 'Well, colonel, you are the first man I ever saw that understood the language of fowls.' I told him that he had not had the politeness to name me in his speech, and that when my little friends, the guinea-fowls, had come up and began to holler 'Crockett, Crockett, Crockett,' he had been ungenerous enough to stop, and drive them all away. This raised a universal shout among the people for me, and the general seemed pretty bad plagued.[19]

David Crockett's eccentricities were getting him noticed, and crowds of people came just to get a peek at him, and if they were lucky, to hear some of his well-wrought anecdotes. At the same time, Crockett had learned just enough in the legislature to understand that political allegiances mattered, though he never learned that lesson well enough to make it stick—when it came down to a vote, his conscience and his principles always triumphed over any political alliances. Still, despite his vote against Jackson in 1825 and his suspicion of him as privileged rather than one of his own kind, Crockett was outwardly and honestly a backer of Jackson at that time: "I can say, on my conscience, that I was, without disguise, the friend and supporter of General Jackson, upon his principles as he laid them down, and, as 'I understood them.'" Of course, the provision between Crockett's quotation marks became important later on, foreshadowing a moment when Crockett would make the case that even Jackson himself no longer ascribed to his own principles, but for the moment, Crockett supported Jackson's upcoming run for the presidency in 1828.

By election time in the late summer of 1827, Crockett had done all he could in an attempt to unseat an incumbent, one who had beaten him the last time around. His face and voice and outlandish storytelling had been spread all around the district; Marcus Winchester's endorsement, introductions to influential circles, and fiscal backing had ensured that. The rest was pure Crockett. When the polling numbers came in, even Crockett had to be a bit surprised. Before the election, he had admitted that he was a long shot, as unseating an incumbent like Alexander was difficult in the best of circumstances, and in Arnold he faced a very clever major general in the militia, and a lawyer as well, which Crockett viewed as nearly insurmountable: "I had war work, as well as law trick, to stand up under. Taking both together, they make a pretty considerable of a load for any one man to carry." But the resilient Crockett managed to shoulder that load, and more, for the final count shocked everyone and sent tremors rumbling all the way past Memphis to Washington City. The turnout had

The last portrait of Congressman Crockett, dressed as a
gentleman, as he would have appeared during his days
in Washington. (David Crockett. Portrait by Asher
Brown Durand, engraving on paper, copy after Anthony
Lewis de Rose, print circa 1835. Smithsonian National
Portrait Gallery, Washington, DC.)

been excellent, and 2,417 had voted for the barrister Arnold. Alexander received an impressive 3,647, nearly a thousand more than the number that got him elected in 1825. But it was the quirky and enigmatic David Crockett who carried the day, his remarkable 5,868 votes representing a solid whipping laid on his opponents.[20] His election signaled a new era in American politics, one that gave hope to the common fellow. A man like Crockett spoke his piece and then went ahead—no posturing, no empty or blanket campaign promises, no obfuscation and misdirection by belaboring complicated and dull issues. Here was an original straight shooter, a rustic and woodsy neighbor you'd be comfortable with trading yarns at the local tavern, and one in whom a new generation of voters could see themselves.

The bear hunter from the cane had wrestled and yarned his way into the tricky arena of national politics, and he was heading to Washington City. David Crockett was ready for the challenge, and if it turned out that he wasn't quite qualified for the job, he was a quick study and he would learn as he went. In truth, he really had no idea precisely what he had gotten himself into. What remained even less clear was whether Washington City was ready for Congressman David Crockett of Tennessee.

NINE

Political Reality

IT WAS TIME FOR A VICTORY LAP. Crockett, in good spirits but fatigued by the rigors of campaigning, decided to take Elizabeth on a well-earned vacation to North Carolina, where she could visit her relatives and he could revel a bit in his new station as U.S. congressman, accepting backslaps and horns of whiskey as they came his way. In the first week of October, Crockett, John Wesley—now a fit and hearty twenty-year-old—and Elizabeth set out for North Carolina. In about the third week of September they paused in Nashville, where Crockett paid a visit to Henry Clay's son-in-law, James Erwin, hoping to receive an introduction to the young man's influential father-in-law, the secretary of state. Crockett believed, or at the very least hoped, that the powerful Clay shared some of his own ideas on western land issues, and Crockett would have been champing at the bit to meet someone with his vision, especially to make a potential allegiance of that magnitude.[1]

They later stopped to visit with friend James Blackburn, and passed a pleasant time reliving old stories and swapping tales of the recent election. Just a day after departing Blackburn's, Crockett fell violently ill, overtaken by what he later described as "billes feaver" (bilious fever), a presumed liver infection that was actually a recurrence of his old nemesis, malaria. It hit Crockett hard, and though he managed to ride the distance to Swannanoa, North Carolina, he arrived an emaciated figure. Doctors bled him, as was then believed the proper treatment, and he required nearly a month of bed rest before he was up and moving about on his own again.[2]

When he was finally sufficiently recovered Crockett rose to find himself embroiled in a duel between his good friend Sam Carson and a man named Dr. Robert Vance. Carson, who would later be named the first secretary of state of Texas, had defeated Vance in a congressional race in 1825, and in 1827 the two squared off in a hotly contested rematch that included negative campaigning, verbal jousting, and a flurry of personal attacks and insults that each man took seriously. Vance publicly questioned Carson's manhood, calling him a coward, and Carson (who had just won the election) responded with a challenge to a duel, to be held in Saluda, North Carolina, dueling being illegal in Tennessee.[3] On November 6, 1827, Crockett followed his friend Sam Carson to the field of honor, where he watched the two men step off their paces, turn, and fire. Crockett hardly waited for the gun smoke to clear before he mounted his horse and, still weak from his bout with malarial fever, galloped off to report the news. According to an account from Carson's daughter, "David Crockett was the first man who brought the news to Pleasant Gardens. He rode his horse almost to death, beat his hat to pieces and came dashing up yelling 'The Victory is Ours.'"[4] Dr. Robert Vance died the following day.

With his first session as a congressman looming on the horizon, Crockett said good-bye to Elizabeth and entrusted John Wesley to chaperone her back home to Tennessee. His own illness had taken up so much time that he would be unable to backtrack to the west and make it to Washington City by the start of the session on December 3rd. Elizabeth and John Wesley departed with three young slaves her father had given her, and Crockett, weakened once more, remained some time to allow doctors to again treat him with blood-letting. A tough man accustomed to bearing significant pain and discomfort, Crockett rode toward Washington City, accompanied by Sam Carson, Lewis Williams, and probably Nathaniel Claiborne.[5]

The journey should have been exciting and adventurous, Crockett happy to be traveling with a good companion in Carson and an experienced statesman in Williams, but a relapse in his condition made the trip across the mountains excruciating for the frontiersman. By the time he finally arrived in Washington Crockett was nearly dead, and along the way he feared the worst: "I have thought twice that I was never to see my family anymore," he admitted later in a letter to Blackburn. The illustrious bear hunter had lost a good deal of body weight. He experienced "the worst health since I arrived here that I ever did in my life," and he went on to report "I am much reduced in flesh and have lost all my Red Rosy Cheeks that I have carried so many years."[6] Still, Crockett managed to suffer through the arduous journey, and just before the opening of the session he took a room at Mrs. Ball's boarding house on Pennsylvania Avenue, along with a handful of fellow representatives that included Nathaniel Claiborne, Thomas Chilton of Kentucky, and William Clark of Pennsylvania,[7] as well as Gabriel Moore of Alabama, and Joseph Lecompte of Kentucky.[8]

Some of the men Crockett caroused with and shared lodgings with would go on to achieve greatness, and the upstart congressman felt humbled and perhaps even a little intimidated by the stature of those around him. Yet he was never one to cower before anyone or anything, and quite soon he managed to convince himself that he belonged. "I think I am getting along very well with the great men of the nation," he told Blackburn in confidence, "much better than I expected." What he likely did not expect was the difficulty of the political waters he would soon be forced to navigate. Quite soon he would be paddling upstream against a heady current.

STILL PALE AND FEEBLE, Crockett nonetheless went straight to work, enthusiastic and optimistic that he would be able to make a difference and effect change working alongside those "great men" to whom he had alluded. Just three days into his first session, Crockett began hammering away on his pet project, the Tennessee Vacant Land Bill. The freshman congressman was still wet behind the ears, and naïve enough, to make the following unrealistic claim: "I have Started the Subject of our vacant land on the third day after we went into Session I have no doubt of the passage of the Bill this Session I have given it an erly Start."[9] He had grown accustomed to seeing administrative and political processes move with relative celerity at the state level, but he would soon realize that such speed on issues and bills simply wasn't possible at the national level, and the slow-grinding pace would eventually wear on him. He would complain to friends and constituents about the sluggish movement in Congress, betraying an impatience in his character. "Thare is no chance of hurrying business . . ." he griped, "thare is such a desposition here to Show Eloquence that this will be a long session and do no good."[10]

Crockett quickly, if unhappily, came to understand at least one political reality—change, if it came at all, would take a great deal more time than he'd bargained for. Patience and compromise were two necessities for political success at the highest levels, and Crockett would never possess either. He needed to be going somewhere, moving forward, and no doubt he daydreamed of riding the outlands at sunrise, the call of birds in the air, the sound of his baying hounds echoing through the cane, as the endless murmur of speeches droned on through the stuffy halls.

At least the nightlife was entertaining. A series of hotels and boarding houses strung along tree-lined Pennsylvania Avenue accommodated most politicians, and a vigorous social scene abounded when the gavel fell at day's end. Once Crockett felt well enough, he ventured out, tugged into a whirlpool of taverns and bars, of backroom gaming, gossip, drinking, and dinner parties. In this milieu Crockett flourished, his gift of gab and magnetic personality and humor perfectly suited to the social scene. Certainly he would have felt a tad self-conscious at his lack of presentable clothes, his redundant outfits compared to the many suits worn by some of his more well-heeled contemporaries, but he compensated by being himself, by plying friends with whiskey and sidling up for an amusing yarn or two.[11]

While he was having a fine time of it, his eccentricities and rustic manners did not go unnoticed by his peers, some of whom would become his political opponents, even enemies. His uncultured grammar and general lack of refinement became fodder for the papers, and one particular account detailed how, at a gala dinner hosted by President John Quincy Adams to welcome incoming congressmen, Crockett drank from the finger bowls and accused a waiter of trying to steal his food. He was still publicly aligned with Jackson, and the accounts were published by anti-Jacksonians in hopes of casting Jackson's supporters in an unfavorable light, characterizing them as unruly, barbarous, and generally ill-suited for the gentility of public life.[12] Crockett initially ignored the slurs, since his personality was at the same time making him some friends, and he was becoming something of a curiosity, frequently invited to parties, dinners, and social functions for his affability.

The first few months in office also helped Crockett comprehend the divisive nature of partisan politics and the political climate he'd entered. John Quincy Adams had been chosen by the House of Representatives in 1824 when, after Jackson had taken the majority of the popular vote, he'd failed to be confirmed by the Electoral College. At the time, Crockett and many others figured some collusion must have been arranged against Jackson, and he carried that suspicion with him to Washington City, noting that Henry Clay was immediately made secretary of state.[13] By 1828 the political camps, formerly called "Republicans," were now split into two centralized groups, the Democratic Republicans and the National Republicans. Jacksonians, in a holdover from the notions of Jeffersonian Democracy, courted and even embraced the notion of the "common man," while Adams and Clay came across as elitists, and even "evinced a strong distaste for, if not actual fear of, the rule of the masses, which they often equated with the mob."[14]

Crockett paid attention to the camps, noting how allegiances and alignments ebbed and flowed, and was pulled for the moment to follow Jackson and his principles, the man who had won New Orleans, defeated the British, and opened the West to expansion by subduing the Indians. The presidential election of 1828 was on everyone's mind, and Crockett could see the potential benefits of remaining outwardly a Jackson supporter, especially if it might later assist him in pushing through his vacant land bill. Nearly all of Crockett's fellow Tennessee delegates backed Jackson, and that group included James Polk. Crockett could see that "Old Hickory is rising,"[15] and he had no doubt that "Jackson will in a short time begin to receive the reward of his merit."[16]

Thus Crockett spent his time between the laborious day sessions and the evening revelry attempting to make sense of where and how he might fit into the scheme of things, all the while trying to remember the desires and needs of his constituents back home in Tennessee. But after a full two months in office he had nothing tangible to offer them, and the painfully slow wheels of bureaucracy drove him to agitation. His introduced land bill still lay on the table, gathering dust, and Crockett noted with great frustration that his colleagues yammered on endlessly about nothing: "Their tongues keep working, whether they've got any grist to grind or not."[17] It was painful to bear, and Crockett began to leave early if speeches blathered on and on and seemed mere partisan posturing unrelated to issues. He missed roll calls here and there as well, citing his ill health, which was a fact, but the malaise he suffered from most was a general ennui at the slow proceedings.

One significant acquaintance Crockett made during his first term was with a fellow freshman representative from Kentucky, Thomas Chilton. Chilton enjoyed Crockett's style and affability. They often voted similarly, and in fact they teamed up on an odd little bill that would provide a pension for the war widow of a man named Major General Brown. On April 2, 1828, Crockett and Chilton argued vehemently against the proposed bill, contending that providing public funds to individuals would be a "special privilege" they weren't entitled to. Though he voted against the bill, the generous Crockett empathized with the plight of the poor woman and went so far as to offer his own money to aid her, and only Chilton rallied in support. As it turned out, their money wasn't required; the bill passed and Mrs. Brown was awarded her much-needed pension.[18] Crockett and Chilton struck up a friendship, and Chilton began polishing some of Crockett's writing, assisting with his speeches and other correspondence such as circulars and letters to his constituency. The relationship would develop over time, and Chilton became a ghostwriter for Crockett, ultimately co-authoring his autobiography. Chilton stayed at Mrs. Ball's boarding house whenever he was in Washington City, and the two men spent a great deal of time together.[19]

The union also marked the development of a kind of split personality in Crockett, a conscious construction of the dual nature of his persona. He understood that it was the bear hunter from the canebrakes who managed to get elected, but Crockett felt the tug of the gentry, the need to be accepted by his peers, and, ironically he wanted to be like the very people he despised and criticized. Chilton's assistance in the formal writing refined Crockett's voice, grammar, punctuation, and spelling, smoothing out his rough edges, at least superficially.

It isn't difficult to understand why Crockett would have felt compelled to appear slightly more refined, given the company he was keeping. Among these was Duff Green, an eclectic renaissance man (variously a surveyor of public lands, a lawyer, and an editor and publisher) who had purchased the *United States Telegraph* in 1825, was politically well-connected and powerful, and was increasingly chummy with John C. Calhoun of South Carolina (Calhoun's son would eventually marry Green's daughter).[20] Green had recently been appointed public printer, a position awarded by the House, replacing Joseph Gales, who returned to his post as publisher the Washington *National Intelligencer*. Joseph Gales and his partner William Winston Seaton were brothers-in-law and enemies of the Jacksonians, and on Crockett's arrival in Washington, still spewing party rhetoric, he had called them "treasury pap Sucking" editors. Crockett wrote this lovely epithet to a friend before he had ever met the men, and he would later get to know both Gales and Seaton well; Seaton referred kindly to Crockett as an "odd but warm-hearted old pioneer."[21]

Seaton, like Chilton, tightened and edited Crockett's speeches for publication in *Gales and Seaton's Register of Debates in Congress*. The Clerk of the House at this time was the recently reelected Matthew St. Clair Clarke of Pennsylvania, with whom Crockett also struck up an acquaintance. And finally there was James Polk, an aggressive Presbyterian delegate and a remarkably quick learner with an uncanny knack for the legislative process and the intricacies of political posturing.[22] Crockett had no way of knowing, of course, that his contemporary and fellow delegate would rise to greatness, eventually to be elected governor of Tennessee, Speaker of the House, and ultimately President of the United States, and earning the nickname "Young Hickory." For now, he was simply someone to squabble with over the land bill.

And squabble they would. Initially, the views of the two men were somewhat in concert concerning public lands, and in fact Crockett was a member of a select committee, chaired by Polk, formed to deal with the state of Tennessee's request to cede lands in the Western District to the state, which would inject any profits from their sale into "common schools" rather than colleges or universities. Crockett stood behind this notion, especially regarding common schools over universities; he contended that the children of West Tennessee farmers and squatters would be unlikely ever to tromp their muddy work boots inside a university.[23] Crockett believed that should the vacant lands ultimately be offered up and sold, it would be at prices the poor squatters might be able to afford.

He soon came to understand that the state had other intentions, as did other members of Congress.

On April 24, after Polk debated the issue within the committee and had done some independent research as to the relative worth of the vacant Tennessee lands, he rose to speak for the bill when the House finally agreed to open up discussion on it. Polk's position was concise and simple: the state of Tennessee had been shorted significant public lands—the so-called "set aside" lands left over from the 444,000 acres provided for when it seceded from North Carolina in 1806. The infamous North Carolina warrants claimed all but 22,000 acres, and the bulk of what was claimed was the best available ground. It wasn't fair, Polk argued.[24] Crockett offered an enthusiastic second, adding that much of the remaining ground was low-lying, prone to flooding, and so thickly timbered as to render it devoid of worth. "The low ground or bottoms, contiguous to the streams in this western division, are frequently from one to two miles in with; but an important reason why they neither are, nor can be, valuable, is . . . that they are usually inundated. This I know to be fact personally, having often rowed a canoe from hill to hill."[25] Some heated discussion ensued, Polk essentially deferring to Crockett and allowing him the limelight on the issue. Crockett concluded emphatically and with a touch of emotion: "The rich require but little legislation. We should, at least occasionally, legislate for the poor."[26] His appeal was that the bill would finally allow these poor farmers to own their own property, the squatters being a class of people that Crockett felt should be compensated for their courage. Crockett considered squatters "the pioneering advance guard of the American nation . . . that in return for their services they were entitled to the plot of land which they had improved, and on which they made their homes."[27]

However eloquent his entreaties, they fell on the deaf ears of the Adamsites, who on May 1 managed to get the bill tabled until the second session, which would not begin until the following December. They feared making special provisions for Tennessee, and wondered if it might create a domino effect, with other states falling in behind. Crockett was indignant, insulted, and frustrated with the pace of the process. On May 10 he tried a different tactic, requesting that the Committee on Public Lands ponder donating 160 acres to each and every settler in the Western District, including improvements made upon the land. It was a bold, if last-ditch, attempt, but again Crockett was skirted, as the session adjourned without addressing his suggestion.[28]

The emotional malaise of Crockett's failure to get movement in Congress was compounded by his physical maladies, which had returned during the session on at least three occasions. Neither he nor the doctors who attended him could have known that the illness they diagnosed as "pluricy" (pleurisy) was actually malarial relapse, coupled with probable pneumonia, and to counter it they "took two quarts of blood" from him, diminishing his condition even more. He felt so ill and weak that he remained in Washington City after the close of the session, trying to recover for the journey home.

When he finally did make it home, he was met with the wrath of a wife now worn threadbare by taking care of literally everything—from the mundane domestic duties to the more complex and tedious bookwork and business affairs—without a stitch of help from her husband. To make matters worse, though he was fairly well compensated in his job at around $8 per day, he arrived back in Gibson County nearly penniless, having paid a $250 debt to Marcus Winchester. Debt would never be a stranger to Crockett, and he immediately had to borrow more money when he sold his Gibson County place to finance a newer, bigger spread to the north, in Weakley County, and hired men to fabricate a new gristmill, this one run by horse-power.[29] Crockett spent the remainder of the summer and fall on these projects and others necessary to move his family into the new place and get it and the 225 acres up and running. There remained little time for hunting, and he idled at the new farmstead, Elizabeth all the while tongue-lashing him for his drinking and poor business acumen, which she attributed to his lack of religious conviction. Crockett must have slunk around the place like a scolded dog with his tail between his legs, promising her he would try to improve himself, because by the time the second session came around on December 1, 1828, Crockett was a man with new convictions. Actually, he was a week late, arriving December 8, the beginning of the second week.[30] His tardiness remained unexplained, though he certainly could have been detained visiting relatives and stopping to see friends in Nashville along the way. At any rate, Crockett intimated in a letter to George Patton that he was going to mend some of his ways, including swearing off spirits stronger than cider, and even making allusions, however vague, to religious conviction. He would need all the strength he could muster against the hostilities he was about to receive from his opponents in Washington.

Things grew complicated as soon as the session started. On November 25, 1828, the Nashville-based *National Banner and Nashville Whig* ran the story about Crockett's coarse behavior at the Executive Mansion while he dined with President Adams and four other dignitaries, citing his uncouth claim that the waiter was trying to steal his food and that he had drunk the water from all the finger bowls. Nurturing a backwoods reputation was one thing, but these blatant lies were another matter entirely. Crockett was outraged, and he immediately enlisted two prominent Republicans, James Clark and Gulian Verplank, to write statements of retraction in the papers attesting to the falsity of these accounts and assuring that Crockett had behaved with perfect and gentlemanly propriety. "I would not make this appeal," he assured them, but "I have enemies who would take much pleasure in magnifying the plain rusticity of my manners into unparalleled grossness and indelicacy."[31] The two men, close allies of Clay and ardent Whig Republicans in opposition to Jackson, agreed to pen the letters, which they did, the retractions appearing in the *National Banner* after January 9 and 23, 1829.[32]

Crockett may have saved some face among his colleagues, but the damage was already done, and many of his constituents, aware of his colorful behavior and antics, found the accounts of his decorum plausible, if slightly embellished. Readers of the newspapers understood partisan apparatus in place, and were quite accustomed to lampooning, but certain images, despite their relative truth or falsity, were hard to shake, and these stuck. Already the papers had run exaggerated stories of the new representative from Tennessee who claimed he could "wade the Mississippi, carry a steamboat on his back, and whip his weight in wild-cats."[33]

Crockett was in the midst of being penalized and lampooned for the very boasts that he had employed to such salutary effect in the stump speeches that got him elected. The *Nashville Republican* of January 27, 1829, published right on the heels of the retractions by Clark and Verplank, claimed that "Col. Crockett, a member of Congress from this state, arrived at Washington City on the 8th day of Dec. and took his seat. It was reported before his arrival there, that he was wading the Ohio towing a disabled steamboat and two keels." The jargon and vernacular that he had honed, the conscious construction of his aura, were already posing problems for him in Washington. He would need to attend to his image, that was for certain, to rein in the flatboat drawl and show a more gentlemanly countenance. Or at the very least, temper it in specific contexts.

Crockett's behavior during the second session heralded a changed man, one even more fiery and independent than before, with new personal convictions perhaps foisted upon him by a spouse losing her patience. The messiness in the papers had peeved him, and made him a trifle paranoid, too, for it wasn't precisely clear who could have orchestrated the mudslinging and manipulated the press. The obvious culprits were the National Republicans, on the surface his opposition, but two of their party had agreed to write retraction letters. It seemed unlikely that the insults and lies would have been spearheaded by the Clay-Adams contingent, who were perhaps considering wooing the gullible Crockett over to their side when the time was right. Whoever it was, Crockett would need to be looking over his shoulder more often in the coming sessions.

In early January, Crockett presented a formal amendment to Polk's land bill, stubbornly including a resolution that the government would provide 160 acres to anyone who settled on vacant Western District land, and produced improvements, on or before April 1, 1829. Polk and others warned Crockett that it went too far and would never pass. Crockett, reveling in his contradictory, even obstinate nature, went ahead, generating a circular (with the help, as was becoming custom, of Gales and Seaton) to his constituents and delivering a rousing if uncharacteristically formal speech on the merits of his proposed amendment. He referred to his people in ennobling language, calling them "hardy sons of the soil, men who entered the country when it lay in a state of native wilderness; men who had broken the cane, and opened in the wilderness a home for their wives and children."[34]

Impassioned as his speech and circular were, his delegation opposed him, suggesting a compromise, but Crockett would not budge. Polk began to become suspicious of Crockett, wondering if he might not have another agenda altogether, one that pandered to the Republicans. There was little overt evidence of this, though Polk had observed Crockett in public fraternizing with enemy factions of prominent Whigs. Crockett, driven by a combination of hubris and political naïveté, was marooning himself. His amendment took immediate criticism, and while the experienced and erudite Polk attempted to soften the measure by including a provision that the lands be ceded to the state, Crockett balked at this last feature.[35]

Delegates Pryor Lea and John Blair of East Tennessee came out nettled, taking firm positions against Crockett, and subsequently each member in turn spoke out against Crockett's amendment. Crockett's bullheadedness turned pathetic when he offered to trade votes with members of his delegations straight across: anything they wanted him to vote for in exchange for a yes vote on his version of the land bill. Polk viewed this action as deceitful, commenting of Crockett, "He associated himself with our political enemies, and declared . . . he would vote for any measure any member wished him to vote for, provided he would vote for his foolish amendment against the original bill."[36]

Crockett appeared desperate. For nine days heated argument raged, and then it waned. The slim chance of being passed that the bill had had in its original incarnation, was now gone. Polk placed the blame for the bill's failure squarely on the shoulders of Crockett, whom he suspected of being coddled by Adamsites and "opporated [operated] on by our political enemies." The vitriolic Polk, convinced that Crockett has betrayed his own party, went on to attack vigorously:

> The cause of its defeat is to be attributed in great degree to the course taken by our man *Crocket* . . . You may suppose that such a man under no circumstances could do us much harm . . . but in this instance many of the *Adams men* . . . seized upon the opportunity to use Crockett, and to operate upon him through his measure, for their own political purposes . . . Rely upon it he can be and has been operated upon by our enemies. We can't trust him an inch.[37]

Polk added a personal attack on Crockett's inability to speak in "measured language," citing this as a reason that he could not understand the remarks he made "against his own state."[38] On January 14 the bill was tabled in a vote of 103 to 65. It was a defeat from which Crockett derived misguided pleasure, thinking its failure might pave the way for him to introduce in a future session his own, reconstructed version.[39] Crockett was deceiving himself, however, and things would get worse before they got better. Polk had fair reason to believe rumors circulating about Crockett's inclination to vote Gales and Seaton in the upcoming election for House printer over Democrat Duff Green.[40]

Crockett was getting a real taste of business-as-usual in Washington. His own party affiliations, or those tenuous links he had managed to establish, were unraveling around him. His constituents, swayed by published materials that showed Crockett being lured from the Democrats, now had cause to doubt his intentions, and whether he had their best interests in mind. Pryor Lea followed Polk's lead and continued to attack Crockett, intimating that he'd deserted his delegation and was sleeping with the enemy. The argument got ugly, the papers spanning the region running particularly effusive and lively exchanges between the two men. Crockett took particular offense to some of Lea's charges, finally calling him "a poltroon, a scoundrel, and a puppy," and challenging Lea to a duel or a fight when they next crossed paths.[41] The public tête-à-tête unraveled into something of a circus, with no verifiable winner in the verbal skirmish. But an already frustrating and unproductive session had drawn to a close, with Crockett doubtful of his abilities to persuade his delegates and insecure about his own effectiveness.

But above all Crockett's optimism always shone through, despite the circumstances, and he was heartened by his improving health. Though he received devastating news from home that his niece, Rebecca Ann Burgin, had been killed in a tragic accident at Crockett's mill (her head crushed by oxen), he maintained his pledge to Elizabeth to swear off hard alcohol, and was quite obviously moved enough by the event to reconsider his own behavior:

> I have altered my cours in life a great deal sence I reached this place
> and have not tasted one drop of Arden Spirits sence I arrived here nor
> never expect to while I live nothing stonger than cider I trust that god

will give me fortitude in my undertaking I have never made a preten-
tion to religion in my life before I have run a long race tho I trust that
I was called in good time for my wickedness by my dear wife who I
am—certain will be no little astonished when she gets information of
my determination.

Crockett added in the same letter to George Patton, in reference to his
niece, his heartfelt and honest condolences, relating how much he cared
for the young girl: "I thought almost as much of her as one of my own I
hope she is this day in eternal happiness where I am endeavoring to make
my way."[42] Crockett's references to religion, and to his pride in staying on
the straight and narrow, suggest that Elizabeth gave him some ultimatums
before he left for the session. He would mend his ways as he could, cur-
tailing his consumption so as to remain in control, even if he never quit altogether. And the language in his letter to Patton reveals that, for all his
bravado, Crockett had a sensitive, vulnerable streak.

Crockett loitered in Washington City long enough to see one positive
political outcome, the inauguration on March 4 of Old Hickory as the
seventh president of the United States. Large crowds lined the streets, and
many packed the White House to get a chance to shake hands with the
great military leader about to lead a nation. Crockett would have been
among the throng, but for him the victory was likely bittersweet, since he
was now at the very least feeling uncertain about his role in party politics,
and probably suspicious about whether he belonged to any party at all. He
might have raised his eyebrows at part of Jackson's inaugural address,
when the new leader declared "I shall keep steadily in view the limitations
as well as extent of executive power."[43] In Jackson he saw a powerful
statesman, a man of his kind in theory but in fact above his rank and station, with his elegant and sprawling Hermitage, his libraries and guest
quarters, his separate cooking rooms. Crockett could only dream of such
dwellings, still wondering whether he could catapult himself to planter

status, while questioning whether or not that was his real goal. He would have time to think about it on the road. And so David Crockett rode for home, the confusing and contradictory halls of Congress behind him as he clomped along for yet another temporary reunion with his family in the new Weakley County home where they had settled, at least for a time.

TEN

Crockett's Declaration
of Independence

DESPITE FEELING PHYSICALLY BETTER than he had in recent memory, Crockett arrived home psychologically battered. Learning to be thick-skinned was one thing, but not knowing friends from enemies was quite another, and by now Crockett had begun to look over his shoulder. To complicate matters, he faced a short campaign season ahead, and probable ire from Elizabeth at home, having incurred another significant debt, this one for $700, in order to square up his bills at the boarding house and finance his journey back to Tennessee.[1] Crockett had developed a pattern of borrowing and spending more than he had, then spending months or years to work off the debt. As a lad he had witnessed the same cycle in his father, and try as he might, he could not seem to shake it. That burden of debt load prefigured the American Way for the twentieth-century American middle class, but all Crockett knew at the time was that he must remain solvent if he could, and that meant some brief "howdies" at home, then off to circulate in his district and see what kind of damage had been sustained by the papers and his inability to push the land bill through.

Crockett spent less than two weeks at home attending matters of the farm, and likely having words with Elizabeth about his perpetual absence, before striking out on a three-week sojourn through his own and adjacent districts that was part campaigning and part damage control. In addition to the embarrassing accounts relating his alleged behavior at the presidential dinner, a March 7 lampoon in the *Jackson Gazette* derided his campaign techniques as unethical, citing his drunkenness and penchant to buy votes with booze, despite his having sworn off the stuff in the last session. The cartoon ran an image of Crockett exclaiming that he could always find willing constituents "who will sell both body and soul for good liquor. Let alone their votes."[2]

But Crockett was renewed physically, perhaps the result of his temperate lifestyle, and he hit the hoistings hard, making important political visits along the trail. It appeared that his old nemesis Adam Alexander would also run for Congress again, and this fact pleased rather than worried Crockett. Confident that he could thrash Alexander once again, he went so far as to boast that he would outstrip him by 5,000 votes.[3] He moved through the districts, acting as the independent he had become, relying on his tried and trusted antics. In Memphis he made a stump speech from the deck of a flatboat very much like the one that had marooned him there, naked, back in 1826, an episode that had been elevated into lore around the city.[4] To adoring crowds he retold the barrel-stave disaster, exaggerating the details for effect, and once he knew he had the audience under his thumb he made the broad boast that he could "jump higher into the bay, make a bigger splash, and wet himself less than any other man in the crowd."[5] To his great surprise a monolith of a man took the bet, and Crockett begged off, paying up to the great delight of everyone, and the politics quickly turned to partying, more storytelling, and tavern camaraderie.

But while Crockett was busy winning votes in the only way he knew how, his tactics fueled the fire of the opposition and allowed them to continue their onslaught of slurs. Though it was still unclear to Crockett what the sources of the accusations were, the press and its readership devoured them. Broadsheets, newspaper articles, and rumors circulated citing

Crockett's gaming, debauchery, even adultery.[6] Crockett fended off some claims, ignoring most, while narrowing his eyes to discover their source. Alexander himself was certainly in the mix as his only real opponent, but Crockett had to wonder if larger forces were at work, perhaps those inside the Jackson camp, or allies of Polk.

In Nashville Crockett visited with his friend and colleague Sam Houston, who was in the throes of personal and professional upheaval: he had just resigned his gubernatorial post and separated from his wife, Eliza Allen. The entire state of Tennessee was in shock over the news, and during their meeting Crockett asked Houston what his plans were now. Houston remembered fondly his years living among the Cherokee, and he considered the Indians his brothers. He painfully recalled how, in his role as an Indian agent and infantry lieutenant, he had helped drive his own family of the Cherokee nation, the Hiwassee, into exile in the Arkansas Territory. Houston told Crockett that he intended to go once again to be among his people, this time in Arkansas.[7] Although neither would have known it at the time, the independent and maverick ideals of the two men would meet again some years later, becoming immortalized—in quite different ways—on the rugged Texas plains.

Crockett's skills as an orator and campaigner, coupled with his familiarity with the people and region, made him a formidable opponent in 1829. But his fierce, even obstinate independence remained ill suited to party politics. Crockett took everything personally, and he often had difficulty seeing the larger scheme of things, the apparatuses of politics beyond the hand-to-hand combat of a stump campaign. As a result, he failed to understand that the feisty independence which made him popular as a candidate also ostracized him and made him potentially dangerous in the eyes of the Jacksonian Democrats as well as the Whigs, the anti-Jackson group formed within the Democrats. The upshot was that Crockett was in the process of becoming a man without a party. At the time, "Jackson forces were trying their best to make Crockett an object lesson—the first in American politics—of the price to be paid for the sin of breaking ranks."[8] They viewed such independence as treason. The problem was, the naïve good ol' boy never saw it coming. He was too busy hamming it up on the stump trying to get reelected.

His efforts that spring and summer paid off, and by close of the election in August, Crockett had indeed routed Alexander. Though he failed to equal his brash prediction of crushing him by more than 5,000 votes, he did manage the significant margin of 6,773 to Alexander's 3,641, receiving 64 percent of the vote.[9] Despite all the mudslinging, Crockett had emerged victorious once again, confirming his belief, if not in politics proper, in himself and his ability to convince people that he was right, that he was a man with their best interests at heart. He had also learned to refine his image somewhat—at least in part to keep the hawkeyed Elizabeth appeased—and also as a role for the benefit of his constituents—playing on his newfound religious conviction, his at least temporary sobriety, and his balance of earthy backwoodsman and sophisticated gentleman. That was a difficult balance, for he knew that he needed to speak the language of the folk so as not to appear as though he was succumbing to the lure of the city. At the same time, he understood that he must possess some of the refinements of gentlemanly culture, lest he appear the boor depicted by some of his foes.[10] It would be a duality he would attempt to perfect during his entire run at politics, a kind of "image schizophrenia" that would eventually tear away at him. But for the moment, he considered himself the darling of Western Tennessee, and to a large extent he was. In fact, his name and aura were beginning to attract attention beyond the small sphere of his home state. His persona was taking on a life of its own. And at the same time, he seemed to represent the sharecropper's yearnings for independence, their humble desire for opportunity, that hopeful if tenuous vision shared by thousands of settlers migrating west and trying to make a go of it on the land.[11]

So it was that David Crockett returned to Washington City when the

Twenty-First Congress convened on December 7, 1829, and immediately took up his obsession, the land bill. In a bold move, Crockett set out to extricate the issue from the Committee on Public Lands, headed by Polk, and position it instead within a special or select committee, which he himself would chair. He received a bit of impetus from the Henry Clay faction, and perhaps to his surprise, his motion was granted over Polk's vehement protestations. Crockett's desire was confirmed in a vote of 92 to 65, "approving his amendment and rejecting Polk's."[12] The tide appeared to be shifting Crockett's direction, if only temporarily, and it looked to him like he might finally get some action on his coveted bill. He now had a stronghold on the committee, and he believed naïvely that things boded well. For weeks Crockett's committee wrangled over the wording of the bill, and at last Crockett felt like the iron must be hot enough to strike, so on December 31 he moved that the House reconsider the Tennessee Land Bill, but to his continued chagrin his motion was denied.[13]

After weeks of further debate, much of it vitriolic, Crockett proposed a revised version of the bill in early January, but it failed once again. An optimist to the very end, Crockett must have begun to sense some futility, as well as understand that something larger than the merits of the bill were at stake and being debated here. It had become personal, and Crockett was being singled out and alienated for his break with Jackson.[14] Against his nature and his political tendencies, Crockett and his committee finally came forth with a revised bill, one that made some concessions. The bill's central tenet was to cede to Tennessee 444,000 acres in the Western District, equivalent to the sum of the 640 acres in each of the state's townships set aside for "common schools."[15] The state would be able to sell the land and apply the profits toward education, but it would also give squatters the option of buying, at twelve and a half cents per acre, up to 200 acres that they either intended to improve or had already improved.

Crockett could only shake his head, outwardly hopeful at the compromise he had made. He later admitted that "this is the best that I could do for my constituents."[16] Delegates of North Carolina balked at the bill's terms, claiming that their warrants were being overlooked, and on May 3 it was defeated 90 to 69. Livid, Crockett quickly moved for the bill, in further revised form, to be reconsidered, though by now he appeared to be begging. He was floundering, with only Cave Johnson remaining an ally among his own Tennessee delegation, and his motion was tabled until the following autumn session. It was a bitter defeat for Crockett, and a confusing one, especially when things had looked so promising just weeks before. Even a man as politically obstinate as David Crockett must have suspected collusion. He was proud enough to interpret the failure of his bill as due not to his own shortcomings, but to more widespread and venal operations that were beyond his abilities to counter.

WITH HIS MEASURE TABLED until the following session, the fall/winter of 1830–1831, Crockett's frustration led him into a pattern of monkey-wrenching that alienated him even further from his peers. He vehemently opposed the Military Academy at West Point, his feelings toward officers and privilege developed back in the Creek War when his own reconnaissance was ignored, but that of an officer's was listened to attentively and then acted upon by his commander. Crockett believed that West Point was an institution reserved for the sons of the nobility and the wealthy, and that only graduates of the academy were granted commissions as officers, so that it became a self-perpetuating mechanism where once again the poor were shortchanged.[17] Crockett went so far as to propose the abolishment of the entire academy, adding in a qualification that sounded insulting, that "gentlemen were not up to the task of commanding soldiers" because they were frail and "too delicate, and could not rough it in the army because they were too differently raised."[18] His motion struck his typical contrary chord, and it was summarily tabled and eventually died a quiet death.

Having lived his entire life in far-flung outposts many miles from civic centers or even modest-sized towns, Crockett knew the importance of viable roadways and navigable rivers and canal systems to encourage transportation and commerce. From his brief time in the East, Crockett could see the benefits brought by "internal improvements" such as good roads, workable harbors, and an organized infrastructure. Especially in his region, navigable rivers were paramount for transportation and for the sale and trade of personal goods.

Additionally, Crockett had long believed that the pioneers, who were the nation's brave and underappreciated scouts, forging a life out of a dangerous wilderness, deserved at least some of the benefits enjoyed by inhabitants of the more established and developed East, since pioneers were the ones literally grubbing the way for western expansion. Crockett favored a bill for a national road extending from the famous port city of New Orleans all the way to Buffalo. But in a regionally motivated provision, Crockett went so far as to propose, for the good of the people in his area, that the road section originating in Washington should end in Memphis. He suspected that once again, the people of his district were being bypassed. "I cannot consent to 'go the whole hog,'" he said, "but I will go as far as Memphis."[19] He also reasonably argued that winter frosts and drifts rendered roads impassable, whereas rivers tended to be navigable year round. And he posed an interesting observation rife with foreshadowing, asking anyone to explain to him the usefulness

of a road which will run parallel with the Mississippi for five or six hundred miles. Will any man say that the road would be preferred to the river? And if the road should so terminate [that is, at Memphis], it would be on the direct route from this city to the province of Texas, which I hope will one day belong to the United States, and that at no great distance of time.[20]

His amendment failed, and when the original bill surfaced again for a vote, Crockett grudgingly voted for the entire route, since it was once again the best he could do for his constituents. Crockett's side lost badly, and the grim pattern of his ineffectuality persisted.

And something else was afoot. In April, Jackson had vetoed the Kentucky Maysville Road Bill, taking a firm position against internal improvements, and, unquestionably, in a political maneuver to spite Henry Clay, whose own position on such improvements mirrored Crockett's for the most part.[21] Jackson himself, in a move that catered to Southern and Eastern Jacksonians, argued that local projects ought not be funded with federal monies. During the early part of Jackson's first term, one of his primary concerns was paying down the national debt, and he viewed internal improvements as unnecessary expenditures counter to his aims. That was his official, public position. But behind the scenes, his veto was intended to undermine the Clay-Adams allegiance; at the same time, the move illustrated to Crockett that Jackson was a political opportunist, an equivocator, a leader who would flip-flop on an earlier position (prior to his election Jackson had supported improvements as long as they were for defense)[22] if it was personally and politically advantageous, even at the expense of the good of the nation. At least that's how Crockett perceived the situation. And though up until this point Crockett had remained a supporter of Jackson's administration and its central goals and platforms, now a serious rift began to form, one which would ultimately define Crockett as a rogue individualist and leave him politically isolated, a lone flag flapping helplessly in the wind.

The impending debates over the controversial Indian Removal Bill would hammer a wedge into that rift, splitting it violently into splintered cordwood.

. . .

ANDREW JACKSON HAD MADE NO SECRET about his position on Indians. His desire to subjugate them dated back to before his military victories in the Creek War, a position he voiced during the Jefferson administration when he resoundingly declared that if the Cherokee could not be civilized, "we shall be obliged to drive them, with the beasts of the forests into [the] Stony [Rocky] mountains."[23] Now, having waited long enough and finally in a position of enough power to realize his desires, Jackson seized his opportunity for action. On February 22, 1830, Senator Hugh Lawson White of Tennessee, a man whom Jackson had earlier considered for secretary of war and who currently chaired the Senate Committee on Indian Affairs, put forth a bill that would come to be known as Jackson's Indian Removal Act, and which set off a nationwide controversy.[24]

Between late February and mid-May rancorous debate raged through the House. Many members, Crockett included, opposed the unbridled authorization of a $500,000 to carry out the relocation of remaining peaceful tribes to lands west of the Mississippi. In the first place, the sum was drastically insufficient to perpetrate such a scheme; relocation would ultimately require millions of dollars. Furthermore, the money would be allocated devoid of congressional accountability.[25] Opponents of the bill also contended that Jackson himself was meddling dangerously close in the due processes of legislature, intruding in the proceedings "without the slightest consultation with either House of Congress, without any opportunity for counsel or concern, discussion or deliberation, on the part of the coordinate branches of the Government, to dispatch the whole subject in a tone and style of decisive construction of our obligations and of Indian rights."[26] Indian rights—now that was a novel concept. Senator Theodore Frelinghuysen spearheaded the opposition, objecting not only to Old Hickory's heavy-handed intrusions, but also on basic principles: the government had broken a string of treaties with these people, yet continued to marginalize them, herding them south and west while devouring their land by forcing them to sign it over. Senator Frelinghuysen rightly noted the hypocrisy of calling them "brothers" while simultaneously stealing their sacred homelands.[27]

Jackson's cleverly worded position on the issue had couched the "removal" in a positive, hopeful way, one bent not on destroying these remaining, generally peaceful tribes of Choctaw, Creek, and Cherokee, but rather designed to save them and their culture from complete assimilation. He noted the fate that had befallen the Eastern tribes, including the Mohegans, the Delawares, the Narragansetts, and warned that extinction awaited the Southern tribes if they were not voluntarily removed to

> an ample area west of the Mississippi, outside the limits of any state or territory now formed, to be guaranteed to the Indian tribes, each tribe having distinct control over the portion of land assigned to it. There they can be Indians, not cultural white men; there they can enjoy their own governments subject to no interference from the United States except when necessary to preserve peace on the frontier and between the several existing tribes; there they can learn the 'arts of civilization' so that the race will be perpetuated and serve as a reminder of the 'humanity and justice of this Government.'[28]

Crockett and many others could see through the wording to the reality for the tribes in question. And Crockett himself had been shepherded from place to place long enough to understand what such forced migration felt like. It was true that his grandparents had been slain by the Creeks, and it was true that he had fought against the Indians in the Creek War, sent on special missions to "kill up Indians," but David Crockett possessed a basic, central morality that told him this bill was unfair and unethical. He empathized with the Indians because in many ways he was exactly like them. At his core, all he really wanted was a modest piece of ground he could call his own, some likely and productive cane where he could hunt when he wanted, and the freedom to move about unencumbered by undue governmental regulation and jurisdiction. Additionally, Indians had saved his life more than once, picking him up and carrying him to the safety of an Alabama farmhouse as he lay dying from malarial fever, and aiding him and his starving men as they staggered through Florida. No, Crockett believed that this was an unjust measure—bad politics and bad for the country—and it would not stand. The Indian Removal Bill would be Crockett's public break with Jackson.

When the bill finally came to a vote in late May, it passed by the excruciatingly slight margin of 102 to 97, falling along strict party lines and creating plenty of tension vis-à-vis alliances and coalitions, especially with the specter of election ramifications looming in the next cycle. Crockett antagonist Pryor Lea referred to the debate and vote on the bill as "one of the severest struggles that I have ever witnessed in Congress."[29] Crockett himself, as he would to the very end of his days, stuck to his principles:

> I opposed it from the purest motives in the world. Several of my colleagues got around me, and told me how well they loved me, and that I was ruining my self. They said it was a favorite measure of the president, and I ought to go for it. I told them I believed it was a wicked, unjust measure, and that I should go against it, let the cost to myself be what it might. That I was willing to go with General Jackson in everything that I believed was right; but, further than this, I wouldn't go for him, or any man in the whole creation; I would sooner be honestly and politically d-nd, than hypocritically immortalized.[30]

It was a bold and noble act. With the verbal stroke of a "nay," Crockett had conspicuously cast the only Tennessee vote against the Indian Removal Bill, effectively hanging himself politically. After the contentious passage, Jackson wasted no time, signing the monumental bill on May 28, 1830. It was a deeply dividing event in the history of the United States, one that made legal the efficient and expeditious expulsion of entire Southern Indian peoples from their ancestral homelands.[31] The victory for Jackson propelled into motion a series of events that would culminate in the tragic Trail of Tears.

Crockett would later reflect on the proceedings, steadfast in his belief that he had done right: "I voted against the Indian bill, and my conscience yet tells me that I gave a good and honest vote, and one that I believe will not make me ashamed in the day of judgment."[32]

Perhaps not, but before long he would have plenty of people, including his confused and angered constituents, to answer to. He had publicly snubbed the will of the executive leader Andrew Jackson, and the decision would go neither unnoticed nor unpunished.

Within the next month Crockett would attempt to assuage the fallout from his singular dissention within his state, penning a speech in which he attempted to simultaneously clarify his position and placate the voters. He acknowledged openly that it was an unpopular position to take, and that it would be difficult for him to find a person within 500 miles who agreed with his decision, yet he stuck by his vote to the end. In the speech, published in the *Jackson Gazette* on June 19, less than a month after the vote, he implored his electors to understand that "If he should be the only member of that House who voted against the bill, and the only man in the United States who disapproved it, he would still vote against it; and it would be a matter of rejoicing to him till the day he died, that he had given the vote."[33] He eloquently added that he could not bear to see "the poor remnants of a once powerful people" driven from their land and homes against their desires. He honestly told the people that "If he did not represent the constituents as they wished, the error would be in his head and not his heart."[34] The editors of the *Gazette*, while willing to publish Crockett's speech, vehemently disagreed with him, and printed a note saying they "regretted" his stance. The headstrong Crockett never regretted his stance, unpopular as it was.

Ironically, while Crockett drifted into turbulent political waters, his general popularity blossomed. His name, his peculiar sayings and idiom, and stories about his character, even about meetings with him, were circulating from Washington City outward across the growing nation. While his brash and unwavering independence ostracized him from the powerful Jackson forces, it was becoming his notable trademark, establishing him as an "eccentric" and "original character."[35] He was becoming more than a curiosity—he was on the verge of achieving celebrity at home and even abroad. Alexis de Tocqueville, a young French civil servant and aristocrat visiting America in 1831, wrote about Crockett in his work *Journey to America*. Tocqueville learned of Crockett from others, and became fascinated by his unlikely ascension from the canebrakes to one of the greatest political bodies in the world. He marveled that a common man could rise to the distinguished halls of power in America. But more important, his assessment of Crockett's character contributed to Crockett's growing celebrity.[36] Crockett was the living, breathing embodiment of a *type*, a Western character writ large, one that audiences and individuals yearned to glimpse more of.[37] He relished the interest, even if later, feigning modesty, he claimed that he could not understand it.

Strained relations with Elizabeth made recesses awkward, and Crockett spent as little time as he could at home, instead focusing on nurturing what positive associations he still had in Washington and around his region—such as his Adams-Clay connections, and others on the routes to and from the capitol and his home. By late summer, Crockett's break with the Jacksonians was widely known. The Jacksonians themselves noticed his movements and the fact that he spent more and more time with known anti-Jackson types, including "Henry McClung, a friend of Houston's

*This portrait highlights Crockett's high cheekbones, which he
described as "Red Rosy Cheeks that I have carried so many
years." (David Crockett. Watercolor drawing by
James Hamilton Shegogue, 1831. Smithsonian
National Portrait Gallery, Washington, DC.
Gift of Algernon Sidney Holderness.)*

and himself an outspoken Adams-Clay man."[38] Crockett also fostered
camaraderie with Matthew St. Claire Clark, whom he'd met during his
first term and who was rumored to be an Adams-Clay crony. Crockett's

defection would have consequences, as he would come to understand in a few short months.

Crockett finally returned to Washington in December a week late for the Twenty-First Congress, immediately scrambling to salvage something of the land bill if he could, understanding intuitively that failure to push it through would seriously threaten his chances at reelection. On three occasions he tried to get the bill reconsidered, failing each time, though the vote was painfully close. Frustrated, Crockett was suspicious of the apparatus that was keeping the land bill tabled, and he now took it personally. He openly argued with other members of his delegation and made thinly veiled references to Jackson's dictatorial tendencies. On January 31, he created a brouhaha over the formation of a committee to review a petition of three Cherokee Indians claiming 640 acres of land apiece. Crockett believed the petition should be dealt with by the Committee of Claims rather than by Polk's Committee on Public Lands. Crockett argued reasonably and compassionately that though the Indians had brought suit to reclaim land confiscated from them, they were too indigent to obtain proper legal assistance in the matter, and effective counsel from the state of Tennessee had been denied them.[39] His points were well taken, and after vigorous discussion the petition did find its way to the Committee of Claims, a token victory for Crockett but one that would have been noticed by Jackson and his forces, who had earlier repealed part of the 1789 Judiciary Act keeping the court from ruling on the issue.[40] Crockett was once again at direct and defiant odds with Jackson on questions involving Indians, and he felt that Jackson's interference outstripped the bounds of his office's duties and power.

Crockett fumed for the remainder of the session, losing a fight to gain appropriation for improved navigation on the Mississippi and Ohio rivers, another internal improvement issue, and now his choleric temper took hold of him. He could no longer contain his feelings about Jackson the man, whom he increasingly believed to be a hypocrite, an autocrat, and a powermonger. He lashed out at Jackson personally, accusing him of betraying the very principles he had espoused in getting elected. "When he quitted those principles, I quit him. I am yet a Jackson man in principles," Crockett railed, "but not in name. I shall insist upon it that I am still a Jackson man, but General Jackson is not; he has become a Van Buren man."[41] Crockett's venomous barbs were aimed at Martin Van Buren as well, whom he believed had manipulated Jackson. Crockett referred to Van Buren as the Fox, alluding to what he considered a sneaky, oily character (another nickname for him was the Magician) who would do anything for personal advancement. "The *fox* is about," he had warned in a letter published in the *Gazette*, "let the *roost* be guarded."[42] Though Crockett's attacks were public and personal, he at least couched them with an eye toward the upcoming congressional elections, hoping his complaints would show him in a positive light, making the case that it was Jackson, not he, who had changed:

> He has altered his opinion—I have never changed mine. I have not left the principles which led me to support General Jackson: he has left them and *me;* and I will not surrender my independence to follow his *new opinions,* taught by interested and selfish advisers, and which may again be remolded under the influence of passion and cunning.[43]

Those were fighting words, and Jackson interpreted them as such. Meantime, Jackson had bigger problems than one disgruntled congressman. Jackson's administration continued to grapple with fallout over the so-called "Eaton Affair," which had begun at the outset of Jackson's first term the moment he selected his cabinet and appointed his reliable and dutiful understudy John Eaton as secretary of war. Eaton's wife had died, but he had entered into a relationship with a woman named Margaret

O'Neale Timberlake, herself recently widowed by her young, tall, and handsome Navy purser rumored to have taken his own life as a result of her infidelity.[44] As gossip swirled around the social functions of Washington, Jackson forcefully suggested that Eaton marry Margaret Timberlake as the honorable course of action. Eaton consented, but by now other wives within the administration had snubbed her, and many viewed this wedding as conspicuously hasty. The whole affair created internal administrative tension that Jackson hardly needed. Additionally, there were rumblings within his own cabinet on another matter, as it was becoming evident that Vice President John C. Calhoun was now actively eyeing the presidency for 1832, Jackson having intimated that he sought a single term, and no more.[45]

Perhaps knowing that Jackson and his core people had public relations problems to contend with, in late February Crockett generated a circular explaining his recent break with the president, as well has his failure to hammer the land bill legislation through. Ghostwriter friend Thomas Chilton certainly had a hand in the prose, which employs a clever combination of indignation and self-exoneration:

> Why I have not entered into some arrangement with my colleagues to secure the land to them [his constituents]? I can only reply that I thought that I had done so. After it was ascertained that my first proposition would fail, I prepared a substitute for it, which I understood as being satisfactory—and which I again repeat I believe would have passed without difficulty, if they had not prevented me from getting the subject before the house. Heaven knows that I have done all that a mortal could do, to save the people, and the failure was not my fault, but the fault of others.[46]

By this time he appeared to be reaching, however, and the squatters were primarily interested in results, not excuses. Despite Crockett's emotional appeals, he was losing his stronghold, even in his own district, and he was clearly on the defensive.

Crockett closed his circular with patriotic language aimed at the heart, hoping for loyalty:

> You know that I am a poor man; and that I am a plain man. I have served you long enough in peace, to enable you to judge whether I am honest or not—I never deceived you—I never will deceive you. I have fought with you and for you in war, and you know whether I love my country, and ought to be trusted . . . I hope that you will not forsake me to gratify those who are my enemies and yours.[47]

There was no question that the circular was a campaign speech, and sincere as it may have been, many saw through the rhetoric. He was blaming others for his shortcomings, and even if his constituents believed him to be honest and trustworthy, they could also see that he was ineffectual. The Jacksonians rallied, putting forth William Fitzgerald from Crockett's own Weakley County as their man to oppose him. They would do what they could to unseat the incumbent, and in April, Jackson himself entered the fray, taking time from his own extremely busy schedule to write his friend Samuel Hays: "I trust, for the honor of the state, your Congressional District will not disgrace themselves longer by sending that profligate man Crockett back to Congress.[48] Jackson, who typically did his best to ignore Crockett and, as a matter of course, used envoys or henchmen to do his bidding, apparently found Crockett a nettling inconvenience and wanted him out of office. That he would personally confront the matter suggests he took Crockett seriously and reckoned that he must be dealt with. It set up an ugly and bitter campaign.

Crockett was on his heels from the start, broke, in debt yet again, and behind in his electioneering, having lingered for weeks in Washington to pose for a portrait he may have been intending to use as a campaign prop. He borrowed money from William Seaton, a Whig supporter, and having finally attended to some remaining personal matters, he took the completed portrait and started home, heading overland by coach through Virginia via Maryland, eventually boarding a steamship for the final leg down the Ohio River.[49] Paradoxically, while he might have had cause for depression during the journey, knowing full well that he was in for an uphill battle for reelection, something beyond Crockett's power was taking hold of the American consciousness. Earlier in the previous session, people began to speak of him in metaphoric terms; a man hearing him speak at the House referred to him as "the Lion of Washington," and added that he was practically hypnotized by his charisma and magnetism. "I was fascinated with him," he said.[50] Visitors to the city, knowing that he lodged at Mrs. Ball's Boarding House, would try to get a peek at this object of "universal notoriety" if they could. A newspaper article in 1831 exclaimed that he was one of the "Lions of the West,"[51] alluding to a fierce, fearless, and independent nature that led Crockett to roar his principles across the aisles. But he would need all the press he could get if he hoped to retain his seat.

Along his journey Crockett lost his new portrait, a bad omen. He arrived home fraught with fiscal worry, having been sued in April, for outstanding debts, by John Shaw, and in late May he was forced to sell twenty-five acres at his Weakley County residence to his brother-in-law George Patton. He made only $100 in the transaction, so he included Adeline, a slave girl, for another $300.[52] It wasn't much, but canvassing required ready cash. Then, as if to bolster his own waning confidence in himself, he wrote down for the first time the maxim that would come to define his brand of "can-do" attitude, scribbling across the bills of sale for the property and the slave, "Be allways sure you are right then Go, ahead."[53] It was as if he was convincing himself that continuing the campaign against such odds was the right thing to do.

Certainly Elizabeth would not have thought so; she had grown accustomed to fiscal irresponsibility and disaster in nearly every one of his schemes, and their relationship by now was growing distant and frayed. That he had risen in stature from regional curiosity to folk hero would have impressed her but little; Elizabeth would have seen him only as an absentee husband and father, and a financial hurricane. It did not help that the *Jackson Gazette* now supported Fitzgerald and began to print anti-Crockett propaganda and smears, including the recurring accusations of public indecency, gambling debts, and violent bouts of drinking. Though he had previously assured Elizabeth of his continuing sobriety, she surely must have suspected that at least some of the claims were true, much as she wanted to believe him. How could he always be so broke, always struggling to catch up, borrowing money from one man to pay off his debt to another?

Crockett had committed, however, and despite being a lone eagle now, essentially a party pariah, he went ahead with the campaign, fending off a running series, called *The Book of Chronicles, West of the Tennessee and East of the Mississippi Rivers* and printed in the *Southern Statesman,* that depicted his meteoric rise and cataclysmic descent. The scathing satire turned out to be the handiwork of a barrister from West Tennessee named Adam Huntsman and nicknamed "Black Hawk."[54] Using pseudoreligious jargon and tone, the hyperbolic parodies depicted Crockett as the would-be savior of the river-country dwellers, but who had failed—so that, instead, the river people should elect Fitzgerald. Crockett hadn't the time or the energy to parry all the attacks, but Huntsman would be a nemesis for the next few years, and Crockett would eventually have to contend with him. Crockett generated a few responses for publication in the *Southern Statesman,* taking the opportunity to coin the nickname "Little Fitz" as a slam on Fitzerald, whom he accused of being base, unprincipled, and prone to gambling.[55] The insults flew back and forth, and were made particularly awkward since the men ended up touring around the district virtually together on the stumping circuit, and had plenty of face-to-face interaction. Prior to one rally in Paris, Tennessee, Crockett issued a verbal warning that if the diminutive Fitzgerald continued to make spurious charges against him, he would be forced to bludgeon him.

An expectant crowd watched and listened as Fitzgerald rose to speak, first placing a white handkerchief on the hardwood table before him. Against modest restraint by his own backers, who did not like the odds or the roughness of the place that better suited Crockett, Fitzgerald stood anyway, and promised he would verify the charges he had made against his opponent. Crockett shot up and exclaimed that he had come to "whip the little lawyer" who would continue to make such claims.[56] Eventually, as everyone in the crowd anticipated, Fitzgerald did come to the points of controversy, and Crockett flew toward Fitzgerald in a rage, storming the stand. He hardly expected what followed:

> When he was within three or four feet of it, Fitzgerald suddenly removed a pistol from his handkerchief, and, covering Colonel Crockett's breast, warned him that a step further and he would fire. The move was so unexpected, the appearance of the speaker so cool and deliberate, that Crockett hesitated a second, turned around, and resumed his seat.[57]

Crockett's backing down showed excellent common sense, but it wasn't the behavior expected of a man with a reputation for killing bears barehanded. Embarrassed and on the defensive, Crockett resorted to lengthy and redundant anti-Jackson harangues, most lacking his patented humor and sounding mean-spirited, not his hallmarks. He continued his petty name-calling, referring to Fitzgerald as "a little court lawyer with verry little standing" and "a perfect lick spittle."[58] Through the campaign Crockett remained true to his tenets of individuality, independence, and sticking to one's principles no matter how unpopular they seemed. It was not enough, however, and in the end Crockett was out-campaigned by a man with backing much stronger, more influential, well financed, and more organized than his. With the infrastructure of the Jackson forces behind him, William Fitzgerald eked out a victory over Crockett in a devilishly close election, with a margin of only 586 votes out of 16,482 votes cast.

THOUGH HE SHOULD HAVE SEEN IT COMING, Crockett had not expected to lose (he never did), and he officially contested the results of the election at the next Congress, citing fraud in vote counting at Madison County, but the House Committee on Elections refused him, and the vote stood.[59] The sour Crockett had shown himself to be a poor loser, and he bowed out of Congress for the time being with anything but grace. He looked to be unraveling, his regional popularity in question (at least politically), his marital relations disintegrating, his financial situation perilous. Perhaps Black Hawk's prediction in the *Book of Chronicles* had been correct, perhaps David Crockett's shooting star was on the wane, crashing headlong back to earth after its brief flight to fame, to flicker until it was extinguished.

ELEVEN

"Nimrod Wildfire" and "The Lion of the West"

D AVID CROCKETT HATED TO LOSE, and now it seemed that he was losing everything around him: his family, his spouse, his farm, his constituents. He had been ousted from office by a combination of his own
failings and a political mechanism beyond his scope of comprehension,
and he was left to pick up the pieces and try to move ahead. It would take
some doing. Ironically, what Crockett failed to grasp completely was that
while he struggled to maintain his political career and more important, his
tenuous sense of self, something outside his direct influence was happen-
ing to his image, and to the desires of the American psyche. And he would
be the beneficiary of that new hunger.[1]

A few years prior, in 1829, playwright William Moncrieff had introduced a play called *Monsieur Mallet; or, My Daughter's Letter*. The play
featured a notable character named Jeremiah Kentuck, played by popular
actor James Hackett. The character was "a bragging, self-confident, ver-
satile and vigorous frontiersman . . . Congressman, attorney-at-law, dealer
in log-wood, orator, and 'half-horse, half-alligator, with a touch of the
steamboat, and a small taste of the snapping turtle.'"[2] The parallels to
Colonel David Crockett were impossible to miss, and the play enjoyed
some success. Hackett relished the role, but he wanted a play that cast him

as the lead specifically, so he enlisted friend and playwright James Kirke Paulding to write a play for him. Paulding, familiar with the characteristics of Jeremiah Kentuck, sought a real-life model on which to base his play, and his muse was obvious: Colonel David Crockett. Paulding wrote his friend, the painter and writer John Wesley Jarvis, asking him to pen a few "sketches, short stories, and incidents, of Kentucky or Tennessee manners, and especially some of their peculiar phrases and comparisons." But what he really wanted were replications, real or imagined, of the man himself. "If you can add, or *invent*," Paulding prodded Jarvis, "a few ludicrous Scenes of Col. Crockett at Washington, you will be sure of my everlasting gratitude."[3]

Paulding and Hackett intended to draw their caricature, in the role of Nimrod Wildfire, directly from Crockett, borrowing from his antics and episodes in Washington, which would have been rich material. The play, which was hotly anticipated, given leaks regarding the subject matter and a widespread desire to see Crockett portrayed in this way, would be called *The Lion of the West; or, A Trip to Washington*. In the play, which has the distinction of being "the first American comedy to place a crude backwoodsman in a lead role,"[4] allusions to Crockett were beyond obvious. Nimrod (the word means "hunter") Wildfire roared around the stage clad in hunting buckskins and a hat fashioned from wildcat skin: "My name is Nimrod Wildfire—half horse, half alligator and a touch of the airthquake—that's got the prettiest sister, fastest horse, and ugliest dog in the District, and can out-run, outjump, throw down, drag out, and whip any man in all Kaintuck."[5] Crockett was just egomaniacal enough to relish the connections when it finally opened, despite the fact that the farce was viewed as either mocking him, or as a "Jacksonian political piece" intended to deride Crockett and further alienate him from the Jackson administration.[6]

Evidently, Paulding felt that Crockett was prominent enough to warrant his blessing—or at the very least, he wished not to offend him, and on December 15, 1830, he wrote a note to Crockett, passed via an emissary, Georgia Congressman Richard Henry Wilde, assuring Crockett rather deceitfully that he had not drawn the character for comic purposes, and had no intention of making a mockery of him.[7] Crockett naïvely bought the rouse, and sent a reply to Paulding on December 22, 1830, humbly accepting his assurances that the play had no direct references "to my peculiarities."[8] By the time the play opened in New York in November of 1831, nearly everyone knew that the overt parallels were intentional, and Crockett ended up relishing the publicity he gained from the play's highly successful run. In fact, Hackett went on to portray Nimrod Wildfire for years, eventually taking the play across the Atlantic to London. At the moment, though, the desire for such theater simply confirmed a ravenous American appetite for characterizations of eccentric originals who had risen against unlikely odds to power and position, and who had come to represent the personality and temperament of a nation. Such people showed what was possible for common men, illustrating the achievements of "natural gentlemen."[9]

Once again, just when he appeared lowest, David Crockett was buttressed by public acclaim, bucked up when it looked as though he ought to quit. The acclamation shored up his confidence when he was out of work and deeply indebted, and it gave him the notion to consider running for office again. He began eyeballing the 1833 election, writing to his financial backers in Washington to notify them of his plans and appealing to their generosity in letting his outstanding debt ride and agreeing to additional funding during his hiatus.[10] At the beginning of the new year he would write imploringly to the cashier of the Second Bank, hoping to orchestrate further bank withdrawals and suggesting that he would pay his already outstanding notes when he could.[11]

With some fiscal salving in place, and sights lowered on the next election, he attempted something he'd missed for the last few years—quiet and predominantly settled home life. But there wasn't much for him to return to. Fed up with his dreams and delusions, Elizabeth had packed up and sought refuge with her more stable and solvent Patton relatives in Gibson County, taking the children with her. In Washington, Crockett had the fraternity of fellow congressmen and the social fabric of legislative life, and it would have been depressing for him to live alone on the farm, in a skeletal version of his former family life. In late August of 1831, Crockett wrote to a friend named Doctor Jones, informing him of his dire financial situation and asking for a six-year lease on twenty acres adjacent to his place on the Obion, and when Jones agreed, at decent terms and offering an option to purchase, Crockett set in to his old routine, clearing and grubbing the tough top ground, and planning a viable farm that would include a few cabins, a smokehouse, corncribs, stables, a well, and even a modest fruit orchard.[12] Optimistic to a fault, he determined to make the place flourish; perhaps if he made good on his plans, Elizabeth would even agree to move back in with him.

Whenever he could, David Crockett turned to hunting again. After being cooped up in the constrictive confines of a boarding-house room, he longed to lace up his knee-high moccasins, to pull on his buckskins and head out into the open air, cool breezes pouring down the valleys and draws, his feet padding soundlessly through dew-damp grasses as he struck for the pine forests and grapevine thickets. It would have been a difficult time for him, the loss of his people's confidence lodged in his crop. He would have plenty of time to think about his indigent condition and what he planned to do about it. Crockett always believed optimistically that the answer to his problems lay in the land itself: that possession of it, at nearly any cost, was his path to freedom, his way out from under the ominous thundercloud of debt. If he could just get enough acreage, free and clear, he would be able to build security for himself and his family, but he also knew that time was running out. He certainly must have hoped that by the time his dreams were realized, there would be a family and friends left to share it with him.

When not out hunting or working around the new farmstead, Crockett traveled extensively through his own district, connecting with old friends and such political allies as remained after his last showing in Congress. He passed through Kentucky, and made it as far back East as Washington and Philadelphia, maintaining casual contact with potential backers, courting powerful figures like Daniel Webster.[13] Other than that, Crockett lay low, relatively quiet for a man of his notoriety. The brief caesura of 1832 to 1833 would be the quiet calm building on the national horizon before the impending arrival of the torrential David Crockett storm.

Crockett's timing, as usual, was fortunate. When the electioneering season rolled around in 1833, he surfaced refreshed but famished, like a bear rousing from hibernation. Shaking off his slumber, Crockett would have been pleased to note that his alter ego Nimrod Wildfire had indeed caught fire, expanding Crockett's own reputation. *The Lion of the West* proved a blockbuster, drawing strong reviews and huge crowds wherever it went; even where it didn't play, excerpts of the text were printed and reprinted in hundreds of newspapers all across the nation, including prominent papers like the New Orleans *Picayune* and the St. Louis *Reveille*.[14] The general public began to associate Crockett with passages from the play, including variations on the boasts "I can whip my weight in wildcats and leap the Mississippi." By April of 1833 the play had swept the nation and even leapt the mighty Atlantic, playing at the famous Covent Garden in London.

At the same time, Crockett adopted the phrase "Be always sure you're right—THEN GO AHEAD," which he had scribbled innocuously on two bills of sale back in 1831, as his own motto, and the aphorism stuck. He would use it as his own credo, and it defined his attitude of right and forward thinking.[15] As he had known all along, from the moment he lost the election to William Fitzgerald in 1831, he would "go ahead" and run again. Now that he had officially announced, and Fitzgerald would be his opponent once again, everyone else in the land knew it, too. And this time the tables were turned—it was Crockett's chance to unseat an incumbent.

The electioneering during the 1833 campaign immediately took on a courteous and convivial tone, a complete reversal from the previous combat. Apparently, Fitzgerald himself, and his colleague Adam Huntsman—author of the previously damaging *Book of Chronicles*—had agreed in principle to a verbal ceasefire with Crockett, each camp accepting the terms of the treaty and promising none of the dirty sabotage and mudslinging that had typified the 1831 contest.[16] For the most part the parties would stick to the truce. And if he was going to take the moral high road, to better combat the considerable opponent he knew he had in Fitzgerald, Crockett would need something to find some political nugget or vulnerability within the Jackson administration. A couple of issues and circumstances immediately presented themselves.

First, in 1832 Jackson had been elected for a second term, amid some controversy and administrative unrest. John C. Calhoun, who had served as vice president for four years under John Quincy Adams, rode his position right into the first term of Jackson's presidency, "in an unprecedented and never repeated event."[17] The ambitious Calhoun, himself coveting the presidency, had erroneously assumed that the gaunt and aged Old Hickory was a one-term president, and it rankled him when Jackson stuck around, and tensions strained their relationship further as Jackson began to rely on the shrewd counsel of Martin Van Buren. The division with Calhoun bore into Jackson deeply, for he was a military man who insisted on loyalty and viewed dissent as treason. Late in his life, reflecting on his presidency, Jackson made the offhand but ominous comment that his one main regret "was not having ordered the execution of John C. Calhoun for treason."[18] When the smoke had finally cleared and Jackson's new cabinet materialized, Calhoun was out and the slick Van Buren was in. Crockett would want to exploit the turmoil within the administration to see if he might undermine the man he now viewed as a nemesis.

This process found legs in the controversy over the Second Bank of the United States, which Crockett supported in principle, partly because the bank offered loans to cash-poor squatters who subsisted on credit to keep their meager parcels of land running, and partly just so that he might oppose Jackson, a known antagonist of the Bank. Jackson viewed the bank, which by now was headed by Nicholas Biddle of Philadelphia, as a monolithic "monster" and vowed to kill it, and stop the bleeding of the national debt in the process.[19] Jackson believed in hard currency over debt, thinking the latter contributed to economic downturns, even depressions. Crockett viewed Jackson's position on the bank as greedy and nepotistic, and he made that case clearly and passionately in stump speeches, intimating that Jackson's intention to remove the deposits was illegal.

By Crockett's own admission the campaign of 1833 was "a warm one, and the battle well-fought."[20] Though Crockett still used some scathing language (he referred to Fitzgerald as "That Little Lawyer" and Jackson's "puppy"), he played fair, sticking to the issues for the most part, and he benefited from the fact that Fitzgerald had not succeeded in pushing through any vacant-land legislation.

Simultaneously a fortuitous series of publishing events, one of them quite likely orchestrated by Crockett himself,[21] conspired to rally support for Crockett, at the very least providing momentum for his surging notoriety. January 1833 heralded the release of a new book, *Life and Adventures of Colonel David Crockett of West Tennessee*. The anonymously authored book flew off the shelves, selling out its initial print run immediately, and appearing later that year in New York and London with the revised title: *Sketches and Eccentricities of Colonel David Crockett of West Tennessee*.[22] Though Crockett would later use the publishing of *Life* rather disingenuously as his rationale for publishing his own *Narrative*, he very likely knew that the book was being written, having contributed anecdotes and factual information, and sanctioned its development and publication, knowing it stood to contribute to his reputation. In the preface to his *Narrative*, Crockett made the following clever claim:

> A publication has been made to the world, which has done me much injustice; and the catchpenny errors which it contains, have been already too long sanctioned by my silence. I don't know the author of the book—and indeed I don't want to know him; for he has taken such a liberty with my name, and made such an effort to hold me up to public ridicule, he cannot calculate on anything but my displeasure.[23]

Crockett's tongue could not have been more firmly in his cheek. It was all part of an elaborate spoof, for Crockett most certainly knew the author of the book in question, and had likely provided him, verbally, with much of the subject matter.[24] He had met Matthew St. Claire Clarke back in 1828, during the early years of Clarke's lengthy post as clerk of the House of Representatives. Clarke was a close friend of Nicholas Biddle, president of the Second Bank of the United States, and a Whig sympathizer. Clarke was also something of a raconteur, a literary mind, and a writer.[25] Crockett liked trading stories with Clarke, and he sent personal letters to the man as early as spring of 1829, during his first term in Congress.[26] The book itself was riddled with clichés, offering little new about Crockett the man but contributing greatly to Crockett the myth. Plenty of readers made the reasonable assumption that Crockett had written the book. Though Crockett publicly scoffed at the content and pretended to be affronted by the clownish caricature it made of him, he secretly could not have been happier with the timing and the attention the work received.

Almost as if on cue, a New Englander named Seba Smith (who incidentally shared Crockett's politics, first sanctioning and later splitting with Jackson) created a character by the name of Major Jack Downing, a down-home and likable country bumpkin who unwittingly stumbled into public life. The Portland, Maine, *Daily Courier* ran the letters of Major Downing, and the Yankee audiences ate the stuff up, loving the homespun vernacular and more than willing to chuckle at the unsophisticated and unrefined mind and manners of the character.[27] The good-humored Crockett went along with the ruse, even responding to a letter from Major Jack addressing him personally and requesting that they meet in Washington to observe the political climate. An excerpt from the 1833 diary of John Quincy Adams reveals that Crockett remained playful and true to the artifice. Adams wrote that on leaving the Capitol building he

> Met in the Avenue . . . David Crockett of Tennessee. I did not recognize him till he came up and accosted me and named himself. I congratulated him upon his return here, and he said, yes, it had cost him two years to convince the people of his district that he was the fittest man to represent them; that he had just been to Mr. Gales and requested him to announce his arrival and inform the public that he had taken for lodgings two rooms on the first floor of a boarding-house, where he expected to pass the winter and have for a fellow-lodger Major Jack Downing, the only person in whom he had any confidence for information of what the Government was doing.[28]

Crockett must have had difficulty keeping a straight face as he related this conceit to Adams. The Downing letters became widely popular, reprinted in newspapers across the eastern seaboard, filtering across the entire country, and people immediately linked Major Jack Downing with Colonel David Crockett. The country was ready for frontier heroes, real or imagined, and Crockett filled the role as best he could, confirming in human form the desired ideals of freedom, commoner-gentleman, and values like courage and independence.[29]

The opportunistic Crockett took the attention and ran with it, and his campaign opponent Fitzgerald, though a strong incumbent, could do little to counter the onslaught of printed matter keeping Crockett's name and image in the news. Commoners flocked to the polls to confirm and appreciate someone in their own mold, this bumpkin of a gentleman, this enigma named David Crockett. Crockett squeaked past in an extremely close vote, winning by a mere 173 votes out of nearly 8,000 cast, the interest in David Crockett verging on feverish. He was poised to become a cult figure, a folk hero, and bona fide celebrity, the first person in American history famous for being famous, a media-manufactured "personality" with the potential to make a living from his celebrity.[30] It was clear that Crockett had earned his celebrity status, and even had a hand in its construction. What wasn't clear was how the notoriety would affect him, or what he intended to do with his fame. One way or another, it was time to cash in on his persona.

Crockett arrived back in Washington in November 1833 newly confident. Two years before he'd slunk home sheepishly, spiritually broken and bitter with the loss, and only a few months earlier he'd been financially strapped, paying for a crude wooden shanty on a hardscrabble tract of leased ground. His enthusiasm showed in his early arrival, well before the December 2 opening of the session. He had plenty of reason to celebrate. For Crockett, victory always salved a variety of wounds, and defeating William Fitzgerald this time around, even if by a small margin, was a kind of affirmation. But something more significant had happened just months after his successful election: members of Mississippi had come forward and requested that they be authorized to put forth his name as a potential candidate for the presidential election of 1836.[31] Could they possibly be serious? Crockett possessed enough vainglory to think so, and in his own *Narrative* he alluded to it, connecting himself and the presidency several times. But at this point he would have taken the suggestion as an enormous compliment and also seen the political rationale behind the Whig courtship. After all, what were their other options?

Everyone knew that Van Buren would be offered up at the end of Jackson's second term. He represented the moneyed, propertied class of people that Crockett outwardly criticized yet paradoxically wished to be accepted by and become a part of. His known vitriol toward both Jackson and Van Buren made him an obvious choice, and it would be impossible to find someone with greater media cachet, even if his political effectiveness was dubious. If his image and popularity could be sustained, and even expanded, over the next few years, who knew what might happen? As Crockett had proved more than once by his very presence in Washington, nothing was impossible.

At the session's commencement, happily ensconced at his familiar lodgings in Mrs. Ball's Boarding House, Crockett took up some old scores and readdressed one that had raged during his absence, the issue and ongoing argument over the Second Bank. Crockett's position, and his vehement opposition to Jackson, had been faithfully trumpeted by Henry Clay, John Calhoun, and Daniel Webster, who had railed mightily against Jackson by calling him a despot, nicknaming him "King Andrew," and aligning him with dictators like Napoleon.[32] He would let that ride for a time, concentrating his attentions instead on his old obsession: land. On December 17, he introduced a pair of motions, one proposing a select committee of seven members to investigate the most prudent and equitable method for disposal and distribution of lands west and south of the Congressional Reservation Line, and the second insuring that all files, papers, and correspondence of the House related to the Tennessee Land Bill be referred to this committee.[33]

Crockett's subsequent optimism regarding the bill reveals a confidence gleaned from his recent time in the limelight, and shows that his memory for frustration, bitterness, and defeat was short. In a letter to a Tennessee constituent, Crockett rode on false hopes when he scribbled enthusiastically: "My land Bill is among the first Bills reported to the house and I have but little doubt of its passage during the present Session."[34] His con-

The congressman looking stately and reserved, which contrasts his actual ranting and raving behavior on the House floor. (David Crockett. Portrait by Chester Harding. Oil on canvas, 1834. Smithsonian National Portrait Gallery, Washington, DC. Future bequest of Ms. Katharine Bradford.)

tinued naïveté is a bit surprising given his experience with congressional debates, the sloth of their movement, and his own history with the land issue. Still, Crockett was riding high, though his mind was elsewhere.

Feeling good about himself was one thing, but being financially flush was quite another, and Crockett, as he always would, retained some outstanding debt that niggled at his pride. Nicholas Biddle had been good enough to cancel one hefty outstanding note, and though Crockett was humbled and grateful, that only began to staunch the bleeding.[35] It dawned on Crockett that the series of recent literary and media events magnifying his public image and some nudging and prodding by friends and associates, as well as constituents, during the previous election cycle all conspired to an obvious conclusion: it was time to write his own story, a narrative of his life, at once to set the record straight as well as to immortalize himself in print, and if all went as planned, financial and political success was in the offing. But Crockett knew that the scope of the project was too daunting to take on alone, doubting privately whether his own literary skills were up to the task.

He turned to Thomas Chilton, fellow boarder for years at Mrs. Ball's, his friend, confidant, and sometime ghost writer. Crockett trusted Chilton: they had come into the house together as freshmen back in 1827, and they had worked together productively before. Chilton had been trained in the law, so he could negotiate any contract with a potential book publisher. Crockett certainly took notice of the frenzied sales of both Clarke's *Life,* and later the wildly successful *Sketches and Eccentricities.* Frankly, he was tired of seeing others profit from his name, image, adventures, and near-death escapades—he might as well taste the pie he had helped bake.

The way his image had degenerated into caricature also needled Crockett, even if he had benefited from the mirage. A narrative of his life and adventures, written in his stylized vernacular and from his unique point of view, would clarify who he was, separating the flesh-and-blood Crockett from the mythical one threatening to overwhelm him. This was his chance to decide, once and for all, how he would be perceived. "I want the world to understand my true history," he would write, "and how I worked along to rise from a cane-brake to my present station in life."[36] He would be puppet and puppeteer, his choice of words and the selection of his anecdotes cleverly manipulating the strings of the marionette that was his public image. Here was his opportunity to finally construct the David

Crockett he wished to be, the authentic and legendary folk figure-cum-congressman, the *true* "Gentleman from the Cane." Here was his chance to portray himself "in human shape, and with the *countenance, appearance,* and *common feelings* of a human being."[37] But most important of all, Crockett now understood that his fame was reaching its zenith, that the public craved him in many versions and permutations, and he desperately wished to capitalize on his popularity. One can imagine him grinning widely and with the dipped brow of feigned humility as he claims in his preface:

> I know that, obscure as I am, my name is making a considerable deal of fuss in the world. I can't tell why it is, nor in what it is to end. Go where I will, everybody seems anxious to get a peep at me . . . There must therefore be something in me, or about me, that attracts attention, which is even mysterious to myself. I can't understand it, and I therefore put all the facts down, leaving the reader free to take his choice of them.[38]

He was certainly right about everyone wanting to get a "peep" at him. Just as he was in the preliminary stages of the writing, Thomas Chilton having mailed off a flurry of prospecting letters including one to the publishers Carey and Hart of Philadelphia, James Kirke Paulding's blockbuster play, *The Lion of the West,* arrived in Washington, in its own way heralding the *arrival* of David Crockett. When Crockett himself went to see the benefit performance, in a much talked-about and written-about sequence, artifice and life converged. Nearly drowned by the cheers of a knowledgeable audience, Crockett was escorted like a dignitary to a special reserved seat in the front row, center, where he waited, hoots and hollers of recognition coming from all around him. At last the curtain slowly rose, and star actor James Hackett sprang onto the stage, bedecked in the leather leggings and wildcat skin hat of Nimrod Wildfire. He stepped to the edge of the stage and bowed deliberately and graciously to Crockett, who smiled, paused, then rose and returned the gesture. The enthralled audience, bowled over by the poignancy of the moment, erupted in a frenzy of cheers and applause.[39] It was a powerful convergence of fact and fiction, where the mythical legend and the real man met, the past, present, and future of David Crockett all morphing into one. Crockett must have been intoxicated by the applause, and one had to wonder whether his addiction for that very praise would consume him the way "Arden spirits" had before.

By day Crockett attended to the mundane matters of congress, growing distracted and occasionally missing sessions; he devoted the evenings to his book. He and Chilton had agreed to a collaborative effort that would retain Crockett's "style" and "substance," with Crockett scribbling down the tales of his boyhood, the anecdotes, and the recollections of his life up to the present, and Chilton using his editorial eye to "clarify the matter."[40] Probably at Chilton's likely insistence, Crockett made sure to elucidate that his collaborator was entitled to "one equl half of the sixty two and a half percent of the entire profites of the work."[41] He valued Chilton's editing skills and his strong eye for structure and grammar, but he wished to retain the flavor and nuance of his own personality. Where useful and pertinent, Chilton retained Crockett's idiosyncratic language. In the preface, Crockett humbly explained the plain style, wondering what might be criticized by "honourable men." "Is it on my spelling?" he reflected. "That's not my trade. Is it on my grammar?—I hadn't time to learn it, and make no pretensions to it. Is it on the order and arrangement of my book?—I never wrote one before, and never read very many, and, of course, know mighty little about that."[42]

Even in explaining the shortcomings of the book, Crockett was endearing himself to the audience. How could they not be enamored with his honesty, his candor, his utter lack of pretension? He came across as he wanted to, the "plain, blunt Western man, relying on honesty and the woods, and not on learning and the law, for a living."[43] It was an ingenious rhetorical device, and it worked better than Crockett, Chilton, or the publishers could ever have imagined.

Crockett wrote furiously, knocking out a good portion of the manuscript by the end of January, and, finding he was quite comfortable with the task, he managed to finish well ahead of his initial deadline. But the long nights burning the proverbial midnight oil took their toll, and he fell weak and feverish once more with a touch of malarial croup. Feebly handing over his handwritten manuscript to Chilton for polishing, editing, and revising, Crockett must have been quite relieved, pleased with his efforts as a first-time writer, but with no idea of what, if anything, he had accomplished.

As providence would have it, the incomparable David Crockett had written something of a masterpiece.

TWELVE

A Bestseller and
a Book Tour

A Narrative of the Life *of David Crockett of the State of Ten-nessee, Written by Himself,* hit the booksellers' racks in early March of 1834 and flew off the shelves faster than fowl spooked from a canebrake. Publishers Carey & Hart had anticipated the frenzy, having done some promotion the minute they realized they had a winner on their hands. They must have been thrilled when they saw the readable, authentic volume—tidied up by Chilton but retaining Crockett's quaint spelling and grammar, which he had ultimately specified remain unaltered. It was a gem of a book, and they quickly made Crockett an offer by the end of January, which he accepted on February 3.[1] Mere hours after receiving his acceptance in the mail on February 7, the publishers distributed a broadside heralding the following:

> It may interest the friends of this genuine Son of the West to learn, that he has lately completed, with his own hand, a narrative of his life and adventures, and that the work will be shortly published by Messrs. Carey & Hart, of Philadelphia. The work bears this excellent and characteristic motto by the author:

I leave this rule for others, when I'm dead:
Be always sure you're right—THEN GO AHEAD!

The broadside included the very reasonable terms for what was destined to become a collector's item: twelve copies and upwards, sixty-five cents.[2] Crockett helped his own cause as well, writing a promotional preface that he leaked to the press just prior to the book's release.[3] Sensing interest in the narrative to be at near-hurricane levels, Carey and Hart produced the book with remarkable speed, taking it from edited manuscript to published work in less than a month. The public responded, shelling out happily for multiple copies and the first print run sold out in a matter of weeks. Carey & Hart went back to press and offered them up again. The phenomenon continued, and within a few short months the book was in its sixth printing, an undisputed bestseller.

Everyone, from statesmen to commoners, bought the book, some out of sheer curiosity, spurred by Crockett's name and interested in his outrageous stories and tall tales. But what they all got when they opened the 211-page narrative was an American classic, an autobiography on the order of favorite son Benjamin Franklin's. Certainly there were similarities between the two texts, and as Franklin's *Autobiography* was among the very few books Crockett owned or had ever read, he borrowed structural elements from that book.[4] But the content, and the result, was pure Crockett, with just the slightest peppering of Chilton for political effect. *Narrative* is complex in its simplicity, revealing the playful, sincere, moral and even vulnerable voice of a real man, a man of his times. At once a morality tale, a political treatise, an adventure story, and a manifesto for the common man, the *Narrative* was the first truly "Western" autobiography,[5] and "*the* great classic of the southern frontier."[6] The book prefigures by some fifty years the literary genre of "realism,"[7] with nothing remotely like it, or nearly as good, appearing until 1884 with the publication of Mark Twain's *The Adventures of Huckleberry Finn*. Crockett's *Narrative* is real, vital, touching, and shrewdly humorous. It is the work of a master storyteller and truly gifted humorist.

For its apparent minimalism and straightforwardness, the *Narrative* is also remarkably multifaceted, at once deliciously revealing and frustratingly obfuscating about the man David Crockett. Crockett claimed, in a letter to his son John Wesley penned during his work on it, that "I am ingaged in writing a history of my life . . . I expect it will . . . fully meet all expectations."[8] That the book met expectations is grand understatement, for it managed to far exceed them, giving a host of reading audiences precisely what they desired. City folks and the gentility from established centers like New York, Washington, and Philadelphia reveled in the stylized language and the original frontier humor, and the frontier folk themselves could see their own stories in the book's narrator: a common man of humble origins and scant formal education who had risen to national prominence through his own wits, hard work, tenacity, and common sense. The book reflected their humility, decency, sense of adventure, and their role as pioneers of westward expansion. It ascertained, once and for all, that the democratic experiment of America was working and came to represent the national identity.[9]

The humor of the narrative prefigured and no doubt influenced the work of Mark Twain, and set a very high standard for future American humorists, precisely because it appealed to a wide range of readers.

The question of whether Crockett accurately conveyed the history of his life presents a host of vexing considerations. His recollections are uneven and evidently fabricated in a few places, and there is no doubt, given the timing of its release, that the book was politically motivated. As such, it's a performance of sorts, playing on the desire for tall tales his readership would have expected from him, and giving him an opportunity to justify his very public break with Andrew Jackson. He cleverly avoids much discussion of his time in Congress, likely because it was ineffectual, but also since he seemed to genuinely prefer tales of his boyhood adventures and days afield to what he considered the painfully slow churning of the country's political wheels.

It's true that he fudged his involvement in the Creek War mutiny, probably as a way to set forth an early and justifiable animosity toward Jackson; it's also true that he wrote of some battles in which he never took part, aware that a respected war record reflected well during political campaigns. And while he failed to include such fundamentals as the names of his own wives, siblings, and offspring,[10] he managed to infuse the text with pertinent political satire, so that the book can be read as a thinly veiled campaign circular. But those are minor transgressions given the breadth of what he managed to achieve in writing his *Narrative:* a peerless American voice that stood to represent the desire of a nation. It was, and remains, a remarkable literary achievement.

Crockett hoped that it could right his listing financial ship. During the writing process he corresponded with John Wesley and mentioned that he was considering a tour in the east at recess to help promote the book, convinced that his presence would "make thousands of people buy the book."[11] The nagging fact of his indebtedness still ate away at him, becoming an element of shame so profound that he could barely face the people he owed, and if things went well, the book might just be his ticket to solvency. "I intend never to go home until I can pay all my debts," he told John Wesley, "and I think I have a good prospect at present and I will do the best I Can."[12] At the same time, perhaps fired by the apparent ease with which writing came to him and the potential for profits, he conspired to help produce the first two *Almanacs,* which were essentially reprinted excerpts from his autobiography and contained bear hunting yarns and other amusing anecdotes, and these he mass-marketed, producing on the order of 20,000 to 30,000 copies, many of which he hoped to sell himself along his book tour route.[13]

But before he could depart on his book tour, he had to face the tedium of his role as congressman, while preoccupied by the hullabaloo of the book release. The truth was that what little patience he ever possessed for the ennui of congressional proceedings was now completely gone, replaced by the very real excitement of the potentially lucrative book tour, and a feeling of importance, perhaps even superiority, at the attention his book won him. His behavior on the House floor, which had grown progressively more "eccentric" and idiosyncratic over the years, now bordered on erratic and even unstable. Fueled by the controversy over Jackson's removal of the bank deposits between sessions, Crockett launched into scornful rants, becoming disorderly, breaching the decorum the congressional halls demanded.

His verbal assaults grew hackneyed, for he and others had used many of them before, describing Jackson in hyperbolic epithets like "King Andrew," and even aligning him with dictators and despots, remarking in a letter to friend William Yeatman:

He [Jackson] has tools and slaves enough in Congress to sustain him in anything that he may wish to effect. I thank God I am not one of them. I do consider him a greater tyrant than Cromwell, Caesar or Bonaparte. I hope his day of glory is near at end! If it were not for the Senate God only knows what would become of the country.[14]

Crockett's public seething managed to get attention, and had the effect of keeping his name in the papers, cementing his reputation in politics as one of Jackson's most vehement critics. Seeing that any movement on his lame land bill appeared remote, Crockett achieved the nearly inconsequential victory of procuring postal service for diminutive Troy, Tennessee, through Obion County.[15] Other than that, he effectively ignored the business of Congress and, as a result, the desires of his constituency, focusing instead on himself and the business of solidifying his name and image in the popular consciousness.

He was so impatient, so intoxicated with stardom that he did not even wait until the end of session to begin the process. He would leave smack in the middle of the session, despite some earlier criticism about his tendency toward absenteeism. But before he left, there was some socializing to do, and Crockett hooked up with his old pal Sam Houston, who was in Washington after his self-imposed exile among the Cherokee. The two were seen at parties, dinners, and in the company of a woman named Octavia Walton, whom Houston was apparently courting and whose guest book each signed while they visited and shared drinks.[16] Houston was in town on official business, having recently come from Texas, which he likely told Crockett was ripe for the picking. He may have reiterated what he had recently told James Prentiss: "I do think within one year it [Texas] will be a Sovereign State and acting in all things such. Within three years I think it will be separated from the Mexican Confederacy, and will remain so forever."[17] Houston understood firsthand already what Crockett would later see—that Texas offered the newest frontier of the West, where opportunistic men, in the right place at the right time, might make their fortunes.

As they reminisced about old times and pondered the future, Houston must have described to Crockett the wild and undeveloped hunting grounds and the seemingly endless expanses of land for the taking. Houston was utterly intoxicated with Texas, his unbridled enthusiasm evident in a note to his cousin some months before: "Texas is the finest portion of the Globe that has ever blessed my vision."[18] The prospects in Texas would have piqued Crockett's interest considerably. They parted ways, perhaps with plans to meet again in Texas.

Plagued as he had been over the years by relapses of malaria, Crockett could sometimes use his health as a fairly legitimate excuse for his tendency to be a congressional truant, and when he was later criticized for packing up and going on a "Towar Through the Eastern States," he would play the health card once again. But he fooled no one. There were other factors at work as he departed Washington on April 25, 1834, later ensconcing himself in Baltimore's Barnum's Hotel and preparing for a lovely meal with Whig cronies to discuss his upcoming tour. He had already intimated to John Wesley that he intended to advance book sales through public appearances, and on April 10 he wrote a letter to Carey and Hart requesting 500 copies of the book that he could take along and peddle on his own.[19] His Whig friends and political supporters had arranged an elaborate speaking tour and public appearance itinerary for him, and the shrewd, innovative, and media-savvy David Crockett figured to hawk as many books along the way as he possibly could, creating what was the first ever official "book tour."[20]

It was at once a stroke of marketing genius and political suicide.

GETTING OUT OF WASHINGTON would have been a great relief to Crockett, and the trip was one of the most delightful and electrifying he ever made, as he was paraded, wined, dined, and fêted through the most vital cities along the eastern seaboard, including Baltimore, Philadelphia, New York, and Boston. It was a highly structured and tightly monitored publicity tour orchestrated by the Whigs, who were trotting Crockett out to see how he played, the better to determine whether the obstinate and headstrong frontiersman-cum-congressman and a noted loose cannon might prove malleable enough to make presidential material two years hence. Massive crowds turned out at every stop along the way, all hoping to get a glimpse of the American original, all hoping to hear him utter some outlandish anecdote. For the most part, he did not disappoint, though he was also expected by the Whigs to come out in defiance of Jackson and Van Buren, pacifying partisan crowds with practiced rhetoric, including the old contention that "I am still a Jackson man, but General Jackson is not."

In Baltimore, he gave a speech in the affluent community of Mt. Ver-

President Andrew Jackson, Crockett's archnemesis. Of
their political rift Crockett would claim, "I am still a
Jackson man, but General Jackson is not." (Andrew
Jackson. Portrait by Albert Newsam, copy after William
James Hubard. Lithograph, print 1830. Smithsonian
National Portrait Gallery, Washington, DC.)

non Place beneath a statue of George Washington.[21] He then boarded the
steamship *Carroll-of-Carrolton,* which bore him across the Chesapeake,
then went by train to Delaware City, and "re-embarked there for a trip up

the Delaware River, and arrived in Philadelphia that evening, April 26."[22] The tour was well conceived, with adoring, cheering throngs greeting him at every stop along the way.

In Philadelphia, Crockett made a brief speech and was then paraded to a hotel directly across the street from the United States Bank, certainly no mere coincidence. In the next few days he was whisked about the city, touring the civic waterworks, the asylum, the Navy Yard, the stockyard, the mint, and the exchange, where as requested he launched into his patented anti-Jackson oratory.[23] Prominent young Whigs of Philadelphia presented the beaming Crockett with a watch, chain, and seal bearing his now-famous motto, "Go Ahead," and offered him the present of a new rifle, to be delivered upon completion to his personal expert specifications. It was the perfect gift for a man whose reputation had been made in part by his skills with the long rifle, in target and sport as well as in the pursuit of wild game.

On April 29, Crockett left Philadelphia for New York, sailing (for the first time) up the Delaware on the *New Philadelphia*, then boarding a train and crossing northern New Jersey to Perth Amboy, where he changed trains to New York City.[24] The pace and schedule in New York were just as frenzied as in Philadelphia, but this fit with Crockett's solidifying persona of politician, celebrated personality, and author. Crockett's predictions and projections about his tour, and the effect it would have on his book sales, were fairly astute and accurate. While in Philadelphia, he had briefly met his publishers and coordinated a print run of 2,000 copies of his *Narrative*, to which they agreed. Sales were booming.[25]

On arrival in New York, Crockett was met by a knot of young Whigs who boarded the train and treated him like the dignitary he was, shepherding him to his opulent lodgings at the American Hotel, where he would remain comfortably, but breakneck busy, for nearly a week. On his first night in New York he took in a burlesque show, complete with slapstick sketches, dancing, and ribald comedy. The next day, moderately rested, Crockett rose and was brought to the New York Stock Exchange on Wall Street, where he delivered a prearranged speech. The highlight of the day came when he took lunch with Seba Smith, the creator and author of Major Jack Downing. The two men must have shared some amusing banter, agreeing that their literary alter egos would exchange letters in the *Downing Gazette*.[26] Later in the afternoon he visited Peale's Museum of Curiosities and Freaks, where he witnessed scientific specimens the likes of which he had never encountered, and watched a ventriloquist, which dazzled and amazed him. The ventriloquist was also a magician, and he performed a few tricks, including making money disappear and magically reappear. Crockett used the moment to master his own comic timing, as he quipped jokingly, "He can remove the deposits better than Old Hickory." The assemblage erupted with hoots, laughter, and applause.[27]

That evening Crockett was treated to a banquet that included esteemed colleagues and fellow supporters of the United States Bank. Among them was Gulian Verplank, the man who had defended Crockett's conduct, and by extension, his honor, back in 1828 when he wrote the letter assuring Crockett's gentlemanly behavior at the Adams's dinner. Also in attendance was Augustin Smith Clayton, the probable author (though the book was published in Crockett's name) of the spurious *Life of Martin Van Buren, Hair-Apparent to the "Government" and the Appointed Successor of General Jackson*.[28] Clayton gave a short speech, followed by Crockett, who by now must have been a bit travel weary despite the excitement of his surroundings. On May 1 Crockett visited various newspaper offices and met with their editors, then toured the noted Sixth Ward.

Though he knew that the tour was bolstering book sales, his enthusiasm for making canned speeches and serving as puppeteer for Whig party propaganda began to flag, and he balked at a well-advertised and well-attended appearance at the Bowery Theatre. After some coaxing by his hosts, Crockett agreed to a brief visit, after which he abruptly adjourned to his lodging—he may truly not have felt well.[29] A good night's rest revived his spirits, and the next day he participated happily in a shooting match and demonstration in Jersey City, which cheered him up and perhaps reminded him why he was there in the first place—for himself, to elevate and cement his public persona. The Whigs had different ideas, of course, and perhaps through his obstinacy and behavior in the Bowery they began to see that his independence might prove too roguish to rein in. Perhaps he was not as politically or personally pliable as they had hoped. Still, the gunplay and hunting demonstration encouraged Crockett, and in the late afternoon he boarded a steamship bound for Boston, via Newport and Providence, brief stops where Crockett waved and bowed to applauding masses.

It was now time to go through a similar meet-and-greet routine in Boston. Between speaking appearances he also visited factories, including one in Roxborough, where the owner gave him a fine hunting coat manufactured on the premises. He now had a fitted rifle and a new hunting coat, and had recently been shooting, all of which would have reminded him of his home in Tennessee, where he had not set foot in many months. On May 7, Crockett visited Lowell to see the mills and was given a tour by textile tycoon Amos Lawrence, a proud and dignified captain of industry. Lawrence presented Crockett with a finely tailored domestic wool suit fabricated by Mississippi haberdasher Mark Cockral.[30] That evening, Crockett dined with "one hundred" Lowell Whigs and spoke in glowing terms of the cleanliness, quality, and beauty of the manufacturing operation and its products and materials, even "praising the health and happiness of the five thousand women toiling in the mills."[31]

This first phase of the tour was drawing to a close, but as the Whigs wished it to end on a high-profile note, they had arranged for Crockett to dine with Whig luminaries at the lovely home of Lieutenant Governor Armstrong. After dinner, Crockett was taken to a theater, for the purpose, as he put it, "to be looked at."[32] He must have begun to feel like one of the specimens on parade at Peale's Museum of Curiosities and Freaks, with people standing shoulder to shoulder just to get a look at him. It would have been simultaneously flattering and taxing, for Crockett truthfully did value his freedom, and he would have sensed that the Whigs were manipulating him for their own purposes. For now, he was willing to go along with the ruse, since he stood to gain from the media attention.

Crockett had been hosted in first-rate manner throughout the tour, and Whig supporters picked up every dinner tab and bar bill, even paying for his accommodations. He was likely also supplied with spending cash, "handshake money" designed to keep him flush. Despite the accolades, the frenzied book sales, and the star treatment, he would have been re-lieved to be making the return trip toward Washington, with just a couple of mandatory stops along the way. After declining an evening of dining and speaking in Providence, Crockett acquiesced in Camden, New Jersey, where he sermonized for "about half an hour" before a large and appre-ciative gathering, then boarded a boat for Philadelphia.[33] Back again in Baltimore, the tour having come full circle, Crockett met a massive and adoring horde, many of whom followed him to his lodgings at Barnum's Hotel, where he made yet another speech and waved good-bye to his fans, relieved for this leg of the tour to have concluded. He limped back into Washington on May 13, drained from the sheer pace of the trip, and per-haps a bit self-conscious about whether or not he had compromised his own principles. Part of his speech along the way had included the convic-tion that he was "no man's follower; he belonged to no party; he had no interest but the good of the country at heart; he would not stoop to fawn or flatter to gain the favor of any of the political demagogues of the pres-ent time."[34] It would take tremendous denial not to see the irony in such claims, as it certainly appeared that David Crockett was in cahoots with the Whigs, despite claims of being a man bowing to no party. They had auditioned him to see how he might play two years later. If he proved not to be potentially "presidential," that was okay, too. At least he had served to publicly criticize the Jackson administration at every stop. It had been a very clever scheme on the part of the Whigs, with virtually no downside.[35]

Fresh from his whirlwind tour and feeling haggard but still quite full of himself, Crockett agreed to sit for a portrait by the painter John Gadsby Chapman. Crockett had lost one portrait previously, unfortunately leaving it on a steamboat, and the others he had sat for in the past few years had failed to impress him much, or, to his mind, capture his likeness in a convincing and—perhaps more important—memorable fashion. Crockett found the previous portraits too formal, making him appear, as he put it, like a "sort of cross between a clean-shirted member of Congress and a Methodist Preacher."[36] He decided he could help orchestrate the image, in effect becoming the costume designer and art director for the project, and Chapman gave Crockett full rein. Crockett launched enthusiastically into the work, thrilled by the collaborative possibilities: "We'll make the picture between us," he told Chapman, it would be "first rate." Then epiphany hit Crockett like a flash of lightning in a hurricane—the best portrait for posterity, the one he wished to be remembered, was out hunting in a "harricane," dressed in full leathers and regalia, with all his hunting gear, tools, long rifle, and a team of likely hounds. Such a scene would be destined to "make a picture better worth looking at."[37]

Crockett took the task of this image-making very seriously, searching out the best and most authentic props: leather leggings, a worn and faded linsey-woolsey hunting shirt, a battered powder horn, a hatchet or tomahawk, a butcher knife, and a pack of scurvy-looking dogs that appeared worn from the hunt. Finally, Crockett coordinated the pose itself, choosing one of action, the hunt about to begin: his felt hat in his right hand, the dogs dashing and yelping underfoot, one looking up expectantly for the word to go ahead, Crockett's gun cradled confidently in the crook of his left arm.[38] It was the Crockett his adoring public wanted to see, not a stuffy, clean-shirted member of Congress, not a fancy gentleman dressed

*Congressman David Crockett in full hunting regalia and
with bear-hunting dogs, immortalized in the image he
helped to create. (David Crockett. Portrait by John
Gadsby Chapman, 1834. Oil on canvas. Harry Ransom
Humanities Research Center, Austin.)*

for an evening of society, but a rough-and-ready backwoodsman, the
man who had years before poked his inquisitive head out of the Tennessee
canebrakes "to see what discoveries I could make among the white folks."
He had discovered much, not the least of which was the uncanny ability

to participate in the making of his own mythology. The image would complement his book, and the publicity from the tour, quite nicely.

Between sittings, Crockett went through the motions of his congressional duties with an animosity toward Jackson that was reaching maniacal proportions and a bilious disdain for the entire governmental process. His verbal assaults now breached all sense of decorum, and on more than one occasion the Speaker of the House was forced to call the fuming Crockett to order.[39] To make matters worse, the land bill, on which Crockett had hung practically his entire political reputation and life, was dead in the water. As the session drew near a close, on June 9 he scribbled an angry and disillusioned letter to William Hack, revealing that what little hope he had possessed now flagged. "We will adjourn on the 30 of June So I fear I will have a Bad Chance to get up my land Bill I have Been trying for some time and if I Could get it up I have no doubt of its passage."[40] He was right about that.

He would be thwarted for the remainder of his term, until he remained nothing but a raging cipher in Congress. In late June he erupted, calling Jackson's advisors

> a set of imps of famine, that are as hungry as the flies that we have read of in Aesop's Fables, that came after the fox and sucked his blood . . . Let us all go home, and let the people live one year on glory, and it will bring them to their senses . . . Sir, the people will let him know that he is not the government. I hope to live to see better times.[41]

He had unraveled completely. Seeing him leaving the Capitol for home one day, Chapman, who had been painting him for weeks, remarked that he appeared "very much fagged" (exhausted).[42] Adding salt to his wounds were the growing criticisms of his absence from Congress for those weeks during the tour, which he attempted to salve by claiming chest pains. "I had been for some time," he wrote in a lame defense, "labouring under a Complaint with a pain in my breast and I Concluded to take a travel a Couple of weeks for my health."[43] But no one was fooled, as his movements and appearances across the eastern seaboard had been widely published in the *Niles Register* and in many other papers across the country. His constituency began demanding answers, and without the passage of his vaunted land bill, he had nothing but excuses to offer them.

Flabbergasted and clearly at his wits' end, Crockett exclaimed, "I now look forward toward our adjournment with as much interest as ever did a poor convict in the penitentiary to see his last day come."[44] So anxious to escape his prison without bars was Crockett, he bolted even before the official adjournment of the session, determining to head back to Philadelphia to visit Carey & Hart, hawk a few more books along the way, pick up the rifle he had been fitted for, and surround himself once again in a cocoon of adulation, where his popularity knew no bounds.

THIRTEEN

"That *Fickle, Flirting* Goddess" Fame

RIDING THE STAGECOACH from Washington to Baltimore, bound for Philadelphia once more, David Crockett had a lot on his mind. He was anxious, even thrilled, for the forthcoming festivities, which included hobnobbing with statesmen like Daniel Webster, with whom he would share the stage in a few days at a scheduled Independence Day fête for political speeches. As the coach jounced along and he looked out the window, he surely thought of home, his friends and family in Weakley County, which now seemed worlds away. And he would have been ambivalent about his return there. His relationship with Elizabeth had all but disintegrated, and while they remained civil, he rarely communicated with her directly. Now that he had been gone from home nearly a year, she qualified as estranged. Even worse, his eldest son John Wesley, who made him proud by following in his political footsteps, had recently given him pause. John Wesley had written to say that he'd undergone a full-fledged religious conversion. Perhaps remembering his own short-lived foray into sobriety and righteousness, Crockett scoffed at the news. "Thinks he's off to Paradise on a streak of lightning," he mumbled. "Pitches into me, pretty considerable."[1]

That, coupled with the burning questions of an unfulfilled and disgruntled constituency, kept Crockett traipsing around the East for the time being. And he could justify it with some legitimate business he had there, including a meeting with his publishers. The rifle that he'd been fitted for would be presented to him on July 1, and ahead of his visit he had sent a letter addressing some shooting specifications: "I am much pleased to see that she Bunches her Balls," he wrote, no doubt daydreaming of the time when her shot would ring true on a bear or deer, but he added that some sighting adjustments were still necessary. "She shoots too low, but that will be altered by Raising the hind sight."[2] Crockett figured he could get a number of details taken care of, and he intended to pick up many tins of superior gunpowder, a variety not available in his county, to be packed in with a shipment of books he would retrieve at Carey & Hart's.

On the first of July, Crockett officially received the handcrafted weapon in a ceremony presided over by Mr. J. M. Sanderson. Crockett grinned as he accepted the gift, marveling at the workmanship and detail. On the barrel of the gun, by the sight, was inscribed his motto GO AHEAD; the stock was inlaid with a silver plate portraying a deer, an opossum, and an alligator, all lifelong quarry of the famed hunter.[3] Into the muzzle the clever gunsmith had also inlaid a gold hunting arrow, conjuring Crockett's time spent in Indian country. Along with the fine hand-hewn hunting rifle, Crockett received some tools and cleaning accessories, a shot pouch, a tomahawk, and an ornate liquor flask that would come in handy for taking horns with hunting compatriots. Crockett graciously accepted the haul, making a short speech in which he vowed to employ his newly dubbed "Pretty Betsey" in defense of his country if forced to, and to pass it down to his able sons when the time came, and they would do the same.[4]

The Fourth of July festivities upon him, Crockett rallied his spirits and perhaps a bit of his theatrical expertise to arrive in fine form, mingling and appearing with some of the nation's significant figures, among them Daniel Webster, whom Ralph Waldo Emerson had recently heralded as "a true genius."[5] The staunch federalist Webster shared the vitriol that Crockett was expected to sling, though in his attacks on Jackson, Webster spoke with more refined cadence and elocution, with a kind of "majesty of oratory."[6] Crockett certainly understood that he was in the presence of true political greatness, but he was rarely intimidated, and the ceremony, the formality of the situation, would hardly have prevented him from being himself. Bolstered by senators Webster, Poindexter, Ewing, and others, Crockett took the stage and bellowed a thundering and inspired oration bewailing the tyranny of Jackson's leadership, its despotism and danger.[7] He underscored his own devout patriotism, his deep and unbending love of land and country, his fierce independence. It was vintage Crockett, even if many in the audience had heard it before.

Crockett and the rest of the retinue were featured later that day, first at the Hermitage in the First District, and later at the Chestnut Street Theatre, both to large and appreciative audiences.[8] Crockett apparently brought only one canned speech with him, or at any rate cared not to alter his first remarks much, and he set forth with much the same hackneyed address, though no one seemed to mind.

The next day Crockett received a visit from a major captain of industry, the aging (and failing, for he would die later in the year) gunpowder maker Éleuthère Irénée Du Pont. The noted Du Pont was the first true chemical industrialist and a renowned businessman, and Crockett later acknowledged how pleased and awed he was at the visit: "He had been examining my fine gun, and . . . wished to make me a present of half a dozen canisters of his best sportsman's powder. I thanked him, and he went off, and in a short time returned with a dozen, nicely boxed up and directed to me."[9] Crockett thanked him again, no doubt excited by now with the prospect of trying out Pretty Betsey, with its novel "cap and ball" firing mechanism, and the high-octane powder.[10] He collected a few more gifts, including a fine imported China pitcher he intended to give to Elizabeth, and then rested for his journey home.

It was finally time to head home, such as it was. He boarded a train and transected Pennsylvania heading for Pittsburgh, where he loaded a steamer aptly named the *Hunter* and chugged down the Ohio all the way to Wheeling, West Virginia.[11] At the few stops along the route fans waited expectantly, hoping to see the famed "Lion of the West," resplendent in his full hunting regalia. A newspaper account records what they actually saw when he consented to step out onto the deck and down a horn or two:

> He talked warmly on politics, and did not seem pleased with the Jackson men of Lancaster, for putting up a hickory pole. He went 'ahead,' after a delay of fifteen minutes, and leaving persons who expected to see a wild man of the woods, clothed in a hunting shirt and covered with hair, a good deal surprised at having viewed a respectable looking personage, dressed decently and wearing his locks much the fashion of our German farmers.[12]

Some might have been disappointed to realize that the legend they'd come to see was a man after all. But they had witnessed David Crockett in the flesh, had seen that he was certainly no ordinary man, and those who did manage a glimpse of the star would tell their children of it, and their grandchildren, relating the sighting of him to anyone and everyone they knew.

Crockett's second son, William, met him on July 22 at Mill's Point for the final thirty-five-mile horseback ride to Weakley County. The ride, the reunion with family, and the old familiar sights and smells of home would certainly have conjured mixed emotions in the national celebrity, and he had hardly dismounted and tied up his horse before the fallout from his eastern tour began to echo across the county, in the papers and through word-of-mouth gossip. Perhaps this lukewarm reception contributed to his short-lived stay at home, where he would linger less than three months. Already he was growing restless. His life had become routine, and routine never sat well with Crockett.

In September, John Crockett, David's father, died. He had followed his son's westward travels and must certainly have been proud to see what his industrious boy had achieved. David was made administrator of the estate, which did not amount to much, and was definitely not enough to solve the younger Crockett's perpetual money problem. David Crockett had the uncanny ability to always spend more than he had, and despite strong book sales, the status of a U.S. Congressman, international celebrity, and friends in the highest echelons of the U.S. government, industries, and financial circles, debt haunted him to the grave. He simply did not possess the ability to properly manage his own accounts.

The bittersweet homecoming included dealing with some old debts, the marks for which had been called in, including one seven years old. A local judge threatened to sell Crockett's property if he did not pay up. In early October he was so strapped that he was forced to sign a promissory note to one of his creditors, William Tucker, for $312.49, and he had outstanding notes at the bank under Nicholas Biddle. Though he hated to do it, Crockett was forced to write Biddle for an extension, saying "I know of no other way that I can do but that to pay you when I get to Washington I am more distressed . . . then anything in the world." Always up-front about his money matters, Crockett added that he'd be leaving for Washington the first week of November, and "I expect to come through Philadelphia at which time I will see you and I will try and have matters arranged."[13] Crockett must have been confused and frustrated that all his efforts at making a name for himself, and the expense and time of his eastern tour, had yet to alleviate his financial woes.

Again, it would get worse before it improved.

Arriving in Philadelphia, Crockett sought a draw against royalties from Carey & Hart, hoping that book sales had been brisk enough to warrant the advance. They were unable to honor his request for $500. His pride bruised considerably, Crockett turned to Nicholas Biddle again. Biddle frequently loaned or backed the nation's top politicians and businessmen with amounts much greater than the $500 Crockett needed, so he immediately agreed to the loan, helping Crockett settle his bill at the Nashville branch and offering to remove his name from the Protest Book, a generous gesture, since having one's name registered under protest was the modern equivalent of a bad credit report, and such a personal blemish could be political fodder for enemies and opponents in the coming election.[14]

Crockett was in dire need of cash. Having been denied an advance by his publishers, he knew he could not merely rely on the sales from the *Narrative*. He would need another source to supplement that and the eight dollars a day he received during the congressional session. Late in the autumn, Crockett had met with fellow boarder William Clark, a Pennsylvanian congressman, to discuss the possibility of writing up an account of his eastern tour and selling that as a stand-alone book. It made a lot of sense, would be relatively easy to collaborate on, and would serve the dual purpose of generating income on its own, plus rekindling sales of the *Narrative*. By the time Crockett reached Washington, his publishers Carey & Hart had agreed to publish the book about the tour, and Crockett finalized his agreement with Clark. Crockett's job would be to provide notes, a few sketches and anecdotes, plus originals and newspaper accounts of his many speeches and the printed details of his tour to Clark, who in turn would edit and organize it all into book form.[15] If they worked quickly and the book sold well, his financial woes might be alleviated. He was painfully aware of his predicament, having written Biddle a letter in mid-December thanking him for the assistance, and adding that the loan would "give me much relief and I hope will not be any disadvantage to the Bank I hope never again to be so hard pressed as I have said poverty is no crime but it is attended with many inconveniences."[16]

Spurred by the prospect of another money-making venture, Crockett tore into his responsibilities on the new book with much more enthusiasm and attention than he gave his congressional duties, churning out more than forty pages of the manuscript in the first three weeks of the session. He delivered the bulk of these to Clark for editing, and Clark was initially optimistic about Crockett's work, expressing confidence that he could turn the pages into a "most interesting book."[17] Encouraged and badly needing more money, Crockett wrote and compiled like a man possessed, contacting everyone he knew and asking them to provide him with newspaper articles of his speeches and notes on his travels, and he wrote with such vigor that he feared Clark would be unable to keep up with him.[18] Clark busied himself with the revisions and with writing the preface, and Crockett expected that at this pace, they would complete the book by late January 1835. Clearly hoping his publishers would be confident in the quick delivery of the book, Crockett then asked them for an advance of $300, to take care of yet another debt, this one due in a matter of weeks. He was forever robbing Peter to pay Paul.

While Crockett hurried to compile the central text for the book and continued dumping it on Clark for editing, only one political certainty remained clear to him: any reelection chances he might have for the coming August hinged entirely on his ability to bring forward, and then pass, the notorious land bill. On December 27, he announced with empty optimism that

> I expect in a few days to be able to Convey the good news to my District of the passage of my occupant land Bill it is the first Bill that will Come up and I have no fears of its passage every member from Tennessee that I have talked to Says that it will pass if So it will Bless many a poor man with a home.[19]

This hollow claim proved insincere, for though on December 9 Crockett had in fact put forth a motion to make his land bill the first order of business for the following day, long speeches on prior matters kept discussion of his bill from reaching the floor. On January 7, Crockett pleaded urgently in a last-ditch effort to get his land bill on the docket, knowing that the end of the term loomed just a few short months away, and nothing in the slow-turning wheels of Congress should have given him confidence.

Frustrated and disgusted, he turned his complete attentions to finishing his portion of the tour book, and this he delivered by January 21, remarkably quickly. Although Clark worked fairly quickly as well, Crockett had been right in his prediction that his editor would not be able to keep up. To further slow the process, just after receiving Crockett's materials Clark fell dreadfully ill, but even in his sickly state he assured Crockett that he would finish his work as soon as he was physically able to sit up. In the meantime, Crockett wrote to Carey & Hart suggesting the title *An Account of Col. Crockett's Tour to the North and Down East in the Year of Our Lord One Thousand Eight Hundred and Thirty Four.* At the same time, Crockett hedged a bit on claiming personal authorship of the book, and instead wondered if a disclaimer of sorts might be appropriate, suggesting that the title page state "written from notes furnished by my self" rather than their original suggestion "written by my self."[20] Crockett showed a good bit of conscience here, as he realized that many careful readers would know that the book was ghostwritten and heavily supplemented by reproductions of previously published materials. In the end, Carey & Hart ignored his request, no doubt driven by the potential of better book sales if it included, as did his *Narrative,* "Written by Himself."

While he waited nervously for Clark to deliver and for Carey & Hart to hurry the book to press, Crockett schemed up yet another book idea. He certainly preferred his role as author, traveling celebrity, and notorious backwoodsman to the terminal tedium of the legislature, with which he was now beyond disenchanted. He wrote a quick letter to his publishers proposing a book on the sly fox himself, Martin Van Buren. Carey & Hart were rightly skeptical, fearing Crockett's known wrath toward the man might lead him to write something overly scandalous. The last thing they needed was a lawsuit brought against them by someone as powerful as Van Buren—that would be very bad for business. But Crockett assured them he would stick to the truth. He determined to spend the winter writing "little vans life" and promised "what I write will be true." But he also added with foreshadowing that the work would be venomous: "I'll do it; and if when you read it, you don't say I've used him up, I'm mistaken, that's all."[21]

The project was ambitious if foolhardy, but by now Crockett believed he could profit from writing, which would now give him an opportunity to rail against the very man he might conceivably face in a presidential election in 1836. Why not start the sparring now? There was at least some residual anti–Van Buren sentiment, for as a party they viewed him as dangerous and potentially harmful to the country. He represented sprawling government, but worse, "lawlessness and violence that bred fear and anger around the country."[22] Crockett echoed their sentiments even louder, exclaiming "I have sworn for the last four years that if Vanburen is our next President I will leave the United States I will not live under his kingdom."[23] Then he added, alluding to a move he'd been thinking about since his conversation with Sam Houston back in April, that rather than submit to a government run by Little Van, the sly fox, Crockett would escape "to the wildes of Texes," where living under foreign Mexican dictates would offer "a Paradice to what this will be."[24]

But politically, Crockett was grasping at straws. He tried numerous times to get his land bill on the floor, failing miserably. He was reduced, as he had been during the previous session, to wild rants and digressions, violent outbursts concerning the despotic administration. His efforts to bring his pet bill to the floor bordered on desperation. He had forwarded a bill to improve navigation on his district's rivers, and that too summarily disintegrated. Even his Whig supporters who had courted him during the tour and contemplated running him for president, cooled toward Crockett. No doubt Crockett's instability, his failure to prove malleable, and his constant debts concerned them. Still, they had yet to settle on a nominee, and Crockett hadn't been entirely ruled out. His anti-Jackson rants would continue to serve them, and it pleased them when he swamped his district with anti-Jackson writings. Crockett kept the heat on, smearing both Jackson and Van Buren as he could, futilely struggling to have his land bill heard, and contacting Augustin Clayton about collaborating on the Van Buren book. It was a busy, desperate winter.

In March, *An Account of Col. Crockett's Tour . . .* hit the bookshelves. The book had none of the wit, charm, or authentic voice Crockett had achieved in his *Narrative*, and though the Whig press lauded the work, the general public, and more particularly, Crockett's growing readership, saw the book for what it was: political propaganda.[25] Sometimes satirical and reading like a travelogue, the work failed to strike the necessary chord in its audience precisely because it lacked Crockett's true voice. Though in their original agreement William Clark was to have assumed the role that Chilton took in writing the *Narrative*,[26] in the end Crockett's narrative voice became subsumed by Clark's and by the replication of news articles and speeches, resulting in an unimpressive political tract that Carey & Hart would have difficulty unloading.[27] Clark proved to be but a shadow of the ghostwriter that Chilton was; Chilton saw the virtue and nuance in letting Crockett do the talking. The sales Crockett had dreamed would alleviate his financial woes would remain just that, a dream.

But he had suffered worse setbacks, and there was still the scathing Van Buren book to come, so Crockett held out a glimmer of hope. Even in the face of disintegrating support from the inside (certain Whigs who had sided with Crockett previously began to jump ship, leaving him marooned in this session), Crockett retained a degree of bravado as to his own prospects. Although by now he privately doubted that anyone would have the strength to defeat Van Buren in 1836,[28] that did not mean he couldn't be defeated four years later. In a tongue-in-cheek letter conceding that the next president would likely be Van Buren, Crockett wrote: "Let the next president come from the North; and then I go with all my heart for a Southwest president, the time after; and that president shall be myself."[29] He wasn't ready to give up just yet, and both recent books, financially and politically motivated, indicated his intention to remain in the game. With an eye on the future, Crockett signed a letter with much of the rest of the Tennessee delegation, asking Senator Hugh Lawson White to run for the Democratic nomination against Van Buren. It made sense, since White was a popular and powerful Whig, and as a fellow Tennessean, his candidacy stood to embarrass Jackson.[30] Believing Van Buren unbeatable, Crockett must have figured White was an ideal scapegoat, the sacrificial lamb.

The first order of business would be to retain his congressional seat, and that was no guarantee. Though his fame would secure him a decent number of votes in the coming August elections, his activities in the session had yielded him nothing to hang a campaign on. He continued to pen open letters to constituents in his district, using the forum to proffer anti-Jackson slurs which, though by now redundant, still had an impact on voters.

By now Crockett knew that his opponent would once again be Adam Huntsman, the shrewd fellow Creek War veteran. Huntsman was a formidable foe, a bright and clever man with a decent sense of humor and sharp political savvy. Crockett figured the race would be tough, but he remained confident, as he always did, in his chances at victory, and he certainly liked politicking a lot more than politics. "I see they have got out A. Huntsman," he wrote, leveling his competitive gaze on his opponent, "I [am] of the opinion I will beat him."[31] The fiery yet sensible Huntsman had his own feelings on the subject, which he shared in a letter to his friend and confidant James Polk, mockingly referring to Crockett, as he had in his *Chronicles,* as "Davy of the River Country":

> I begin to believe I can beat Davy . . . I have been in all the counties but one in this District and Crockett is evidently losing ground or otherwise he never was as strong as I supposed him to be. Perhaps it is both. If my friends take anything of a lively interest in it I think my prospects are as good as usual. He is eternally sending Anti Jackson documents here and it has its effect. If he carries his land Bill it will give him strength. Otherwise, the conflict will not be a difficult one.[32]

Almost as though he could hear those words, Crockett made one last-ditch effort to secure his coveted bill. Four times during the session he attempted to have it heard, and each time he was denied. He endured the same old rhetoric, the same politicking, the same excruciatingly protracted speeches that he had submitted to time and time again, and it ultimately became more than he could bear. On February 4 he tried vainly to terminate a long discussion regarding the Alexandria Canal in order to bring up his land bill, concluding from the painful length of the speeches that Washington was "a better place to manufacture orators than to dispatch business."[33] For the next two weeks he rose again and again, disgusted and almost pleading, but always some other business took precedence. On February 20, Crockett delivered his last recorded speech in the halls of Congress, and fittingly, it was a final stab at passing his doomed bill. It failed to even rise to discussion.[34] Disillusioned, even disgusted, Crockett would have been quite happy to see the session come to a close so that he could leave Washington and its pontificators and head back to Tennessee, then out onto the campaign circuit for one more go-round. Though even electioneering was becoming rote and redundant, he still preferred it to the charade that he considered Washington to be.

But heading home in June, Crockett must have been restless and uneasy. His political independence, his proclamations that "I am no man's man" and that "I bark at no man's bid. I will never come and go, and fetch and carry, at the whistle of the great man in the white house no matter who he is,"[35] had succeeded in ostracizing him in Washington, and even if such protestations were true (for indeed, to the very end he did vote his conscience), they had begun to ring a bit hollow in the expectant ears of his Tennessee brethren. He had less than three months to win over a dubious voting public, one that would seek explanations for his blank congressional record. The one trump card Crockett hoped might gain purchase was an allegiance he had formed with Seba Smith, perhaps cemented at their meal together during Crockett's book and speaking tour. Smith started a new magazine called the *Downing Gazette*, a single-sheet news weekly featuring the missives of Major Jack Downing discussing political issues of the day.[36]

Throughout the summer, the *Downing Gazette* published a series of letters offering political banter between Major Jack and Crockett, with the hope of giving Crockett a campaign bounce from their content, which echoed sentiments, themes, and commentary found elsewhere in Crockett's writings.[37] But the *Downing Gazette* was published in Portland, Maine, and its distribution was limited to the Northeast, plus any copies managing to trickle west. The exchanges probably failed to find readership as far southwest as Crockett's district.[38]

At about the same time *The Life of Martin Van Buren, Hair-Apparent to the "Government" and the Appointed Successor of General Jackson* hit the shelves. Augustin Clayton, initially a vehement opponent of the Second Bank (he later flip-flopped when he managed to procure a $3,000 loan from the bank)[39] wrote the bulk of the book, with Crockett lending very little, mainly his name to the text and a shared scorn for the subject. The book lacked even the humor of the *Tour,* and Carey & Hart found its content questionable enough to publish it under a spurious imprint called Robert Wright, keeping their own names well out of it. The extended, venomous rant abused Little Van viciously, accusing him, among many other things, of being a dandy and a fop: "He is laced up in corsets such as women in town wear, and, if possible, tighter than the best of them. It would be difficult to say, from his personal appearance, whether he was a man or a woman, but for his large *red* and grey whiskers."[40]

The book possessed none of Crockett's mischievousness or fun, its tone instead violent and mean-spirited, and though the Whigs found it devilishly droll, it failed to have much of an impact on the Crockett campaign. In the end he was left to do what he did best, go out amongst his people and tell them what he thought they wanted to hear. But by now he was becoming slightly unsure of just who they expected to see, and perhaps more troubling, he may have begun to experience a crisis of identity. The brash and outspoken champion-of-the-downtrodden approach had been played out, and with his own dalliances among the country's elite well known, his "I'm one of ya'll" claim would be a hard sell. He had said in the opening lines of his *Narrative,* "Most of authors seek fame, but I seek for justice." Perhaps now he had cause to wonder. Having achieved no justice through legislature, what was it that he still sought? What drove him to continue electioneering, keeping himself in the limelight? Could it be the delicious, addictive drive toward *fame,* which he called "that *fickle, flirting* goddess"?

Crockett understood that Adam Huntsman was no slouch as a campaigner, and that it would require a strong effort to defeat him. Huntsman also came into the race with the public backing of both Polk and Jackson. The Jacksonians kept Huntsman's campaigning coffers flush, while Crockett stumped on a minuscule budget. The Jackson camp plied the press with negative stories about Crockett, including charges, not all false, that he had exaggerated his mileage expenses in his trips to and from

Washington, had used franking for personal gain, and most damning of all, that he had failed to achieve any significant legislation in three terms in Congress.[41]

Crockett had stumped and politicked enough not to go down without a scrap, and one trickster ploy, clever and pure Crockett, nearly ruined Huntsman and showed that Crockett never lost his sense of humor. During the Creek War, Huntsman had been badly wounded, one of his lower legs requiring amputation, and from then on he had worn a wooden leg, which served as a reminder of his devotion to his country and allowed him to run on his war record. As often happened, rival candidates billeted together while campaigning, and Crockett and Huntsman spent a night together at the home of a devout Jackson man who just happened to have a beautiful daughter. Late in the evening, with everyone sound asleep, Crockett grabbed a wooden chair and clomped noisily to the daughter's door, which he rattled and knocked on. When she awoke screaming, Crockett placed one foot on the lower rung of the chair, and, holding its backrest, hopped loudly across the wooden floorboards, clomping loudly back to the room he shared with Huntsman, a known rake. Crockett dove into bed, pulled the covers to his chin, and fell into a deep, feigned snore. Having heard the commotion, the farmer rushed in, immediately assuming that Huntsman's peg leg had made the stamping noise across the breezeway. The farmer threatened to kill Huntsman, until Crockett finally managed to calm the enraged father. The ploy won Crockett the man's vote and some of his friends', and completely embarrassed Huntsman.[42]

The ploy allowed Crockett to remain optimistic, even overconfident. With little more than a month to go in the election, Crockett exclaimed of his opponent: "I have him bad plagued for he don't know as much as me about the Government,"[43] adding that he felt confident he would glean twice as many votes as his competitor. Crockett politicked in a frenzied fashion, accepting offers to every stomp-down, dinner, or reaping in the region, maintaining his infectious grin and patented jargon everywhere he went. Near election day he harkened back to an early threat, stating unequivocally "If I don't beat my competitor I will go to Texes."[44]

Crockett promised to write his publishers and his Whig supporters as soon as the results of the August 6 elections were known, and he honored his claim with a long and telling letter on August 11, by which time the final tally was in. The race was tight, with Crockett picking up 4,400 votes to Huntsman's 4,652. Sour, even bitter, and suspicious that the voting had been rigged, Crockett accused bank managers of offering a healthy $25 per Huntsman vote (a rumor Crockett had heard going round). "I have no doubt that I was Completely Raskeled out of my Election," he wrote, adding, as was his style, a high-minded commentary on justice and righteousness, which he may well have believed: "I will be rewarded for letting my tongue Speake what my hart thinks . . . I have Suffered my Self to be politically Sacrafised to Save my Country from ruin and disgrace and if I am never again elected I will have the gratification to know that I have done my duty."[45]

The loss burned into Crockett like a brand searing a cow's flank, and, a sore loser in the best of times and now smarting from an election he considered fixed, he was nearly out of options. Washington no longer wanted him, and now it seemed, shifty vote or no, neither did West Tennessee. His familial relations were civil, but he no longer shared a bed with Elizabeth, and to add biting insult to the painful injury of election loss, her relatives accused him of misconduct in the administration of her father's will, which hurt his feelings deeply and festered into a familial falling-out, though nothing came of legal consequences. Still, he likely felt doubly rejected by both friends and family.[46]

Then the arrogant and boasting press began to flow in from the side of the victors, proving more than Crockett could stomach. A wealthy businessman and ardent Jackson man wrote giddily to Polk, exclaiming, "We

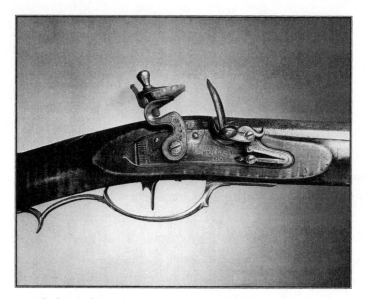

Rifle found after the battle, the kind many of the defenders, including
Crockett, used during the entire siege and battle of the Alamo.
(Dickert rifle, detail photograph. Daughters of the Republic
of Texas Library, San Antonio.)

have killd blacguard Crockett at last."[47] A local building contractor ex-
claimed joyously, "It gives me great pleasure to say . . . that the great
Hunter one Davy has been beaten by a Hunstman."[48] The *Charleston*
Courier appeared giddy with elation, printing on August 31:

> *Col. Davy Crockett,* hitherto regarded as the *Nimerod of the West,* has
> been beaten for Congress by a *Mr. Huntsman.* The Colonel has lately
> suffered himself to be made a lion, or some other wild beast, *tamed,* if
> not caged, for public shew—and it is no wonder that he should have
> yielded to the prowess of a Huntsman, *when again let loose in his native*
> *wilds.* We fear that 'Go ahead' will no longer be either the Colonel's
> motto or destiny.[49]

The Arkansas *Gazette* jumped aboard as well, hitting the man while he was down and referring to him as "the buffoon, Davy Crockett."

It was time to cut and run. At forty-nine years of age, Crockett still had some living to do. Perhaps he recalled the conversation with Sam Houston and felt the pull of Texas. But for now, Tennessee was spent, and there wasn't much to keep him there. He remained a celebrity in the East, but playing the role of the backwoodsman had worn thin. Perhaps it was time to actually *be* a backwoodsman again, to mount a horse, cradle a long rifle in his arms, and trot into a stiffening breeze. He knew that bison still roamed the plains of Texas, and fellows with enough grit and determination could make a go of it on the new frontier. He'd heard stories of how it was bigger than anything you'd ever imagined, plains rolling on and on into the sunset and beyond, the dirt blood-red as the sky. Maybe now might be the right time to see for himself.

He was a man of principle and a man of his word. He had said what he would do if he lost, and now he held himself accountable. He had done everything in his power to win the election, but he'd been rejected for another. Well then, that was that. They could all go to hell, and he would go to Texas.

FOURTEEN

Lone Star
on the Horizon

THOUGH IT WAS NOT THE FIRST TIME David Crockett had lost an election, he took this rejection harder than ever, no doubt because in a very real way his defeat by Huntsman was also a victory for Jackson. Any presidential dreams or aspirations Crockett may have still harbored for 1836 were now dashed, so it was time to look to the future, quite literally toward that flaming western horizon that always tugged at him. Crockett knew, as did most people in his region and certainly everyone involved at high levels of United States government, about the growing skirmish in Texas, which even now was escalating from rebellion to revolution among the colonists, yet his attentions and motivations appeared personal at the moment. He needed, as later Westerners would put it, to "get out of Dodge."

But he was headed toward a turbulent place. The political situation in Texas was complicated, the dominion and "ownership" of the nebulous region controversial. Spanish conquistadores arrived on the shores as early as 1519, seeking the storied "cities of gold." Spain continued to attempt to colonize the region by setting up missions in the western and southern boundaries, maintaining this system through the eighteenth and into the early nineteenth century. But the governing seat of Spain was too far away to effectively maintain order, and more important, control a vital and growing population. Texas was simply too big a holding to manage. In the meantime, there were other claims to the territory, from both within and without. Andrew Jackson himself believed that Texas belonged to the United States as part of the Louisiana Purchase,[1] though in 1825 Jackson offered to purchase the entire territory from Mexico for 5 million dollars, but was refused.

By 1821, Moses Austin and his son, Stephen F. Austin, had negotiated a deal with Spain to set up the first authorized Anglo colony in Texas, and a clause allowed a grant to bring in 300 families to settle on the Colorado River within two miles of the ocean.[2] Later that same year, Mexico declared independence and Stephen F. Austin took on the mantle of colonization alone. His father Moses fell ill, most likely to pneumonia, and his dying wish was that his son would continue their colonization plan.[3] By 1824, Austin was able to lure prospective colonists with sweet land enticements—granting up to a full league (4,428.4 acres) of land to those willing to convert to Catholicism and sign an oath of allegiance.[4] Free land, or virtually free land was sufficient temptation, and settlers began to pour across the Red and Sabine Rivers—eventually by the thousands—carrying what little money they might have, hope for a better life, and not a lot else.

Wide-ranging and mobile bands of Apaches, Kiowas, and Comanches often attacked settlers in night raids, "sweeping down from their camps west of the Balcones Escarpment, . . . stealing horses, burning ranches, killing men, and carrying off terrified women and children."[5] Texas remained a dangerous and inhospitable land that would need better incentives to entice the right kind of men to settle there, those willing to risk their own lives as well as the lives of their families. The land itself would ultimately prove that lure.

Initally resident Mexican settlers known as Tejanos were content with the influx of Anglo settlers, as it buffered them against the hostile Indians and provided potential for commerce and trade.[6] Over time laws were enacted to restrict further immigration from the United States, but many downtrodden U.S. settlers ignored the laws and bolted for Texas anyway, creating tension among the Tejanos and drawing the ire of President-General Antonio Lopez de Santa Anna. As early as 1830, Santa Anna ordered the expulsion of all illegal settlers, "and all Texians (as they now preferred to call themselves) disarmed."[7] The power-hungry Santa Anna went so far as to dismantle the constitutional government and Federal Constitution of 1824, effectively taking over as dictator of Mexico. Austin, watching his dream of settlement begin to disintegrate, struck out for Mexico City to lobby for Texas statehood.[8] Austin was imprisoned shortly after his arrival in early January 1834, and would have to work toward an independent Texas state from the confines of the very same prison cell once used during the Mexican Inquisition.[9]

Such was the maelstrom into which Crockett had determined to ride.

NOT ONE TO SLINK AWAY from a defeat in silence, Crockett planned to depart with flying colors, making a feast of the occasion and throwing a "going-away" barbecue for himself and the others who had agreed to join him.[10] Family and friends convened at his farm in Gibson County, the late October air sweet and cool, the scent of adventure and opportunity on the wind. Crockett dug barbecue pits, and hired men tended the spitted meats while "the boys" were competing at logrolling and other games of strength and agility, and, of course, draining horns of whiskey. As the day wore on it turned into a full-fledged frolic, with dancing, more drinking, and fiddle-playing on into the evening, even through a pouring rain.[11] They reveled late into the night, with Crockett talking up Texas, convinced it was the right place to go. He could scout the land and report back to his family, and if he liked it there as much as he hoped to, perhaps he could convince them, including Elizabeth and her family, to follow him west once more. It was certainly worth a shot, perhaps the last such shot he would ever have.

On the first of November Crockett loaded the horses, packing as he would for an extended autumn-long hunt. It promised to be an expedition, like many of his scouting forays in the past, riding out to new and unknown country, the familiar thud of hoofbeats on the roadway, the acrid scent of horse sweat in his nose, saddle leather squeaking as they trotted along. He'd salted down as much meat as he could carry in saddlebags and packed plenty of powder and ammunition for the hunting, no doubt including as many canisters of the fine Du Pont powder. He must have been happier than he had been in years, finally about to embark on what he loved more than anything else in the world—a journey into a new frontier, with a few friends and his trusty hunting rifle Betsey.[12] He could hardly contain his anticipation of the journey ahead, writing with optimism to his brother-in-law George Patton, "I am on the eve of Starting to the Texes . . . we will go through Arkinsaw and I want to explore the Texes well before I return."[13] It promised to be a trip of a lifetime, and Crockett had no set schedule for his return; it all depended on what he found when he got there.

Crockett would not be traveling alone, a fact that would have pleased the stoic Elizabeth, for she and David remained amicable if separated. Accompanying him for the long ride to the Southwest would be his nephew, William Patton, with whom Crockett got on well. Also saddled up were two friends, Abner Burgin and Lindsey Tinkle.[14] A small party was better than going solo, especially once they shook free of civilization and headed into open range and Indian country. On the morning of November 1, 1835, the four men swung onto their mounts, heeled their spurs into the flanks of their horses, and waved good-bye to their families and friends.

They rode steadily, reining their horses south to Bolivar, then onto the well-traveled road heading west toward Memphis, where they planned to hole up for a few days for a series of unofficial sendoffs. Crockett's celebrity preceded him, as usual, so that even without a Whig-tailored itinerary, the word-of-mouth buzz was that Crockett was coming. He took his time to visit with old acquaintances along the way, and some, having heard that a small band was heading toward Texas, took it as a muster-call and were packed up and ready to join as he passed through their towns. Riders joined their party along the way, some with real intentions of sticking it out, others just for the bragging rights—to say they had ridden the trail in the company of the great David Crockett.

While Crockett's intentions had been clear at the outset—this was an extended scouting and hunting expedition—news of the uprisings in Texas had some men's dander up, and certainly some of those who strung along the military road from Jackson to Bolivar believed they were heading south to fight for freedom. On October 5, Sam Houston had written an appeal from Texas to the American citizens, and it appeared with remarkable celerity just two days later in the *Red River Herald*, which printed the following near-panicked exclamation: HIGHLY IMPORTANT FROM TEXAS!!!! WAR IN TEXAS—*General Cos landed near the mouth of the Brazos with 400 men.*[15] The story received a great deal of attention and wide circulation, appearing also in the *Arkansas Gazette* and filtering around the region to many papers, including the *Lexington Observer*, the *Kentucky Reporter*, and the *Commonwealth*, most including Houston's personal appeal:

> *War in defence of our rights, our oaths, and our constitutions is inevitable, in Texas!* If volunteers from the United States will join their brethren in this section, they will receive liberal bounties of land. We have millions of acres of our best lands unchosen and unappropriated. Let each man come with a good rifle, and one hundred rounds of ammunition, and come soon.[16]

The references to "liberal bounties of land" piqued the interest of many and the allusions to "millions of acres" of essentially free land were not lost on the entrepreneurial mind of David Crockett. Whether he intended to or not, Crockett had become the de facto leader of what resembled a small military band, and as one onlooker reported, seeing Crockett and the men depart Jackson, "Col. Crockett went on some time ago at the head of 30 men well armed and equipped."[17] The natural-born leader of men now traveled with an entourage.

Crockett and company trotted into Bolivar, where Crockett was hosted by his friend Dr. Calvin Jones, the very man who had given him such equitable terms in leasing him his Gibson County farm.[18] Dr. Jones could not help but be impressed by the bustling crowds that poured onto the streets in advance of Crockett's arrival, and he noted that "every eye was strained to catch a glimpse of him."[19] Jones added that as Crockett rode through town "every hand extended either in courtesy or regard," some reaching out to pat him on the back or brush against his shoulder. The treatment Crockett received from complete strangers, the awe, the cheers and shouts of good luck, proved to Jones that David Crockett was no ordinary man, he was a full-blown legend in the flesh. Dr. Jones later admitted that he was "more of a Lion than I had supposed."[20]

As they rode on toward Memphis, some of the group begged off, perhaps realizing the gravity of their potential journey, so that by the time they reached Memphis on November 10 they were a small hunting party again. Crockett looked forward to dismounting and sidling up to the bar with a few of his old cronies, including his good friend and patron Marcus Winchester. Crockett liveried his chestnut and checked into the City Hotel, freshened up a bit, then spent the day walking about the town, reconnecting with old friends and gathering a kind of posse as he went. By nightfall the boys were in a reveling mood, piling into the half-brick, half-frame Union Hotel bar.[21] Their numbers bursting to the walls of the smallish establishment, the crew decided they needed better comfort to take a social horn, so they backed out and headed to a proper emporium, Hart's Saloon on Market Street, where the drinking began in earnest. The men ordered round after round, and soon the place was load and smoky, with shouting over the bar tab and proprietor Royal Hart worried that he was going to get stiffed, as Gus Young, who had done most of the ordering, assured Hart he would pay for the drinks the next day.[22] Hart wasn't keen on the idea, and was close to drubbing the intoxicated Young when Crockett intervened, offering to pay for the liquor himself. Soon the lot of them were arguing over who would pay, and in the end the tab was taken care of and the rowdy gang now hoisted Crockett onto their shoulders and carried him down the street to the next venue, McCool's.

There, the boisterous band of brothers hoisted Crockett right onto the bar and demanded a speech from the legendary man. He knew what they wanted to hear, and he'd made this short speech more than once. He hushed the group as they raised their glasses, and offered up this rendition:

> My friends, I suppose you are all aware that I was recently a candidate for Congress in an adjoining district. I told the voters that if they would elect me I would serve them to the best of my ability; but if they did not, they might go to hell, and I would go to Texas. I am on my way now.[23]

With that, the theatrical Crockett leapt from the bar, and into the shouting and cheering mass. Owner and barkeep Neil McCool lost his cool when he saw Crockett's grimy boots staining the linen on his bar top, and he flew into a rage, demanding that the rowdy bunch leave. A scuffle commenced, with items like sugar crushers and tumblers flying through the air, some broken glass, and most embarrassing of all, McCool's wig being yanked from his head and tossed about from person to person, his shiny bald dome coming as a delicious surprise to the locals.[24]

The sensible Crockett suggested they disperse and hit the sack, for he had a long journey ahead of him, and as they had already been booted from one bar, perhaps they should cut their losses. But the momentum had them rolling, and the diehards of the group dragged Crockett to Jo Cooper's on Main. Here Crockett submitted to a couple more impromptu speeches, his words by now slurring. Cooper liked having Crockett in his place, and he happily "brought out liquors in quantities. He had the largest supply and the best quality on the bluff, but only sold by the barrel or cask."[25] The men partied for hours, drinking themselves into a staggering stupor which they finally took home to their beds at an hour closer to morning than night.

Crockett was no stranger to the odd hangover, but the one that greeted him on November 11 must have been memorable; still, Crockett managed to roust himself, shake off the cobwebs, gather his boys, and head down to the Catfish Bay ferry landing, where he would cross the "American Nile" and step onto Arkansas soil. Winchester and some other Memphis old timers like Edwin Hickman and C. D. McLean escorted Crockett and his traveling companions onto a large flatboat used to ferry folks across the river. An aspiring young journalist named James D. Davis followed the historic walk "in silent admiration" down to the water, with no way of knowing that those would be the final steps that David Crockett would ever take in his home state of Tennessee. Davis recounted the scene, claiming to remember it "as if it were yesterday":

He wore that same veritable coon-skin cap and hunting shirt, bearing upon his shoulder his ever faithful rifle. No other equipment, save his shot-pouch and powder-horn, do I remember seeing. I witnessed the last parting salutations between him and those few devoted friends. He stepped into the boat. The chain untied from the stob, and thrown with a rattle by old Limus into the bow of the boat, it pushed away from the shore, and floating lazily down the little Wolf, out into the big river, and rowed across to the other side, bearing that remarkable man away from his State and kindred forever.[26]

Knowing he would have an audience, Crockett may well have been wearing his Nimrod Wildfire regalia for effect, the consummate showman giving his audience what they wanted to see. He'd stuffed his dress attire deep in his saddle bags, figuring a formal fête or dinner might offer itself along the way to Texas.[27] The hoots and hollers diminished as they entered the bigger water and finally there was just a knot of men waving good-bye from the banks. They were waving good-bye to more than a man. The onlookers stood and saluted the person who had become the legend, the self-made man who, lore had it, Old Hickory had commissioned to scale the Alleghenies and personally wring off the tail of Halley's Comet.[28] That night, and for the remainder of the nights of Crockett's journey, those who paused to gaze skyward would have seen the languid but fiery luminescence of Halley's Comet scoring its path across the southern sky and into the people's memory, almost as if the conjuror Crockett had orchestrated the timing of his departure and the return of the feared and famous comet, to coincide.

Having crossed the river and disembarked in the Arkansas territory, Crockett and his company struck west, following the military road roughly 130 miles toward Little Rock. Crockett would likely have pondered, with some bitterness, that the road they traveled was part of the "Government's" (aka Jackson's) grand plan, used primarily to carry out the removal of eastern Indian tribes to the western territories.[29] That ironic (and to him, unfortunate) fact would not have been lost on Crockett as he rode along. He was essentially following the Trail of Tears.

The men rode with purpose, and two long days in the saddle brought them to Little Rock, a young capital city now serving as a thoroughfare for people emigrating to the Red River country. The quiet community had perhaps heard rumors that Colonel Crockett was on the move and heading west, and some were already out lining the streets. Crockett had a deer slung over the saddle behind him, the limp carcass slapping at the flanks of his horse.

The group boarded at the Jeffries Hotel, hoping to rest for a night and then strike due south the next morning, but that plan was derailed when a small group of excited civic leaders paid a visit to the hotel to invite David Crockett to a banquet in his honor. The men could not find Crockett about his room or in the bar, but one spotted him out behind the hotel, where he bent over to butcher his recent kill, his knife and tomahawk bloody. One of the citizen leaders was a Colonel Robert Childers, an old acquaintance, and he barked out Crockett's name. Pleased, Crockett lifted his head from his work, "Robertson Childers, as I'm alive," he quipped. Crockett quickly took the opportunity to brag about the shot he'd made on the buck, just outside of Little Rock. Nodding to his trusty Old Bet, Crockett grinned, reminiscing about the shot. "Made him turn ends at two hundred yards."[30] They talked of the hunt, and Crockett realized that though he was tired, he would have no chance to escape the dinner party.

Knowing at least one of the community leaders, Crockett shifted into performance mode, stepping up for a patented anti-Jackson harangue, recalling his recent election defeat and his reasons for being there, and the predominantly anti-Jackson audience ate it up, stomping and cheering wildly.[31] He was heading to Texas, he told them, with no intention of coming back. The evening festivities proved a grand success, and his remarks were met with general enthusiasm, as evidenced by an article that appeared a few days later in the *Arkansas Gazette:*

A rare treat. Among the distinguished characters who have honored our City with their presence, within the last week was no less a personage than Col. David Crockett . . . who arrived . . . with some 6 or 8 followers, from the Western District of Tennessee, on their way to Texas . . . Hundreds flocked to see the wonderful man. In the evening, a supper was given him, at Jeffries' Hotel, by several Anti-Jacksonmen, merely for the sport of hearing him abuse the administration, in his out-landish style.[32]

In public forums such as these, especially if he performed impromptu, Crockett rarely disappointed his audiences. The hundreds who lined the streets and riverbanks to watch the charismatic man would remember him always, and tell their children, and their children's children, that they had seen "the real critter himself." Some would make up their own tall tales of their experiences with him. One surfaced soon after he left, that in a Little Rock drinking establishment, Crockett was offered a shot of "Ozark corn," a crude and discolored form of grain alcohol. Not wanting to offend the offering host, Crockett eyeballed the stuff, then belted it back in one quick swoop, grimacing mightily. The story goes that Crockett later admitted, "Gentlemen, I et my victuals raw for two months afterwards. My gizzard so all-fired hot, that the grub was cooked afore it got settled in my innards."[33]

Another story held that while in Little Rock, Crockett had agreed to a friendly shooting competition against Arkansas's finest marksmen. He upstaged the locals by sending a ball dead center of the target, a shot of such accuracy that it was hard to believe, and some even called it lucky. Crockett smirked, walked back to his place, leveled Old Betsy again, and fired. A quick inspection revealed no other hole in the target, and everyone assumed that the noted marksman had inexplicably missed. The clever Crockett simply smiled, then pointed out that he had not missed, but rather had shot with such precision that the second ball had followed exactly the trajectory of the first, passing through and exiting the very same hole! Mouths agape in awe and disbelief, everyone headed to the tavern to talk it over.[34]

Early the next morning Crockett arose, took some breakfast, then stopped by a local carpenter's shop to sharpen his tomahawk's blade, no doubt dulled in the butchering and cleaning of the deer.[35] Crockett didn't know when he would have the luxury of a grinder, workshop, and tools again, so it made sense to head out with tools whetted sharp.

At mid-morning he rounded up his party and nosed his horse south. He wanted to get out into the open country, the likely river bottoms flush with game. Little Rock had been a pleasant diversion, but it was a long ride to Texas. As they left town, they rode past curious and admiring on-lookers, many of them cheering and shouting words of encouragement and good luck. Many assumed, as did the local papers, that Crockett was leading his men to the revolution. The *Gazette* described the scene of his leaving with a nod toward that purpose:

> The Colonel and his party, all completely armed and well mounted, took their departure on Friday morning, for Texas, in which country, we understand, they intend establishing their future abode, and in de-fence of which, we hope they may cover themselves with glory.[36]

It is true that Crockett and his men were well armed, for they did not know when, or if, they would ever return to their native Tennessee. Crockett and other men on long hunts typically traveled with more than one rifle, providing for loss, something valuable with which to barter, as well as not uncommon mechanical failure. It was easy to assume that Crockett headed south with military intentions, but nothing so far in his language about the trip had indicated as much. Still, he certainly was not beyond letting people attribute noble thoughts to him if it suited his pub-lic relations purposes. The migration to the Southwest to aid the revolu-tion was obviously on everyone's minds and tongues around this area, close as the skirmish was to their border.

They continued south, pushing hard and riding long hours, scaring up game as they drove along. The country began to show great promise, with dense stands of pin oaks, good cover for game, shrouding the banks of the Red River. Somewhere along the river here, near the little town of Lost Prairie, David Crockett rode across the river and into Texas.[37] That night, no doubt elated to be in Texas at last and encouraged by the terrain, Crockett accepted an offer to spend the night at the home of Isaac Jones. He could use the free food and billet, for once again, in what must have seemed to Crockett a perturbing and pesky perpetual state, he was completely broke. What little money he had started with had gone to lodgings, food, provisions, and a few horns, and now he rode with empty pockets and purse.

Though he no doubt hated to do it, Crockett needed to sell his engraved watch, the timepiece given to him by the Philadelphia Whigs during his book tour, which Isaac Jones purchased for thirty dollars and another, less ornate watch.[38] Content that it was a fair deal, Crockett consented. Despite being humbled and embarrassed by his predicament, Crockett nevertheless impressed Jones, who later commented on his chance but memorable meeting with him, and on the deal they struck:

> With his open frankness, his natural honesty of expression, his perfect want of concealment, I could not but be very much pleased. And with a hope that it might be an accommodation to him, I was gratified at the exchange, as it gave me a keepsake which would often remind me of an honest man, a good citizen and a pioneer in the cause of liberty, amongst his suffering brethren in Texas.[39]

Crockett would have been grinning like a wildcat to see the country underfoot, the great prairie rolling to the south, the dense stands of timber along the rivers where animals could hole up to cool themselves during the heat of the day, and sleep safely at night. They rode miles of level ground to a place called Big Prairie. They spent the night before continuing on to Clarksville, where they took refuge at the Becknell home and determined that this would be the very place to serve as a staging point for a big hunt. Crockett was referred to a man named Captain Henry Stout, a tough, knowledgeable woodsman who was known about the area as a phenomenal hunter and "one of the most remarkable guides on any frontier."[40]

Stout took them west, toward a remarkable region which, to Crockett's great delight, was entirely uncivilized. The towns had receded into memory, and there were no houses or settlements of any kind, just endless land unfurling in all directions, wild and free. To the west the ground was open, dry, sun-parched and cracked, but easing to the east the land soaked up moisture from the rivers, the canopy of trees cooling the ground, fueling the moist grasses and woodlands. The wildness of the place also brought the specter of potential danger, and it was rumored that aggressive Indians rode the very region into which they were heading. In fact, a band of Comanches were at that very moment "on the warpath."[41]

Henry Stout knew where he was going and he kept them out of harm's way as he led them through stirrup-high prairie grasses, riding some eighty idyllic miles west into pristine wilderness the likes of which Crockett had not seen in decades, since his scouting days in the Creek War. They finally arrived at the lush land separating Bois d'Arc Creek and what Stout called Choctaw Bayou, the two gorgeous waterways draining into the Red River. Crockett surveyed the flowing meadows and prairies sprawling every direction but north, where the land skirting the Red River grew dark, choked with thick timber and extending southward nearly 300 miles. This was it; this was the sort of place he had dreamed of all his life, an Eden of his own. Crockett could see himself living here; there would be no need to move back to Tennessee or revisit his troubles there; he would only have to go back to retrieve the family, those who still had faith in him, those willing to follow him and his western dream.[42]

Crockett's elation poured forth in the letter he wrote the family some weeks later, after he had discovered not only some of the best hunting ground in the world, but that the land was practically being given away, with qualified settlers handed over 4,428 acres each. He could barely contain his enthusiasm as he reported his incredible discoveries to his family:

> It's not required here to pay down for your League of land. Every
> man is entitled to his head right of 400-428 [4,428] acres. They may
> make the money to pay for it on the land. I expect in all probability to
> settle on the Border or the Chactaw Bro of Red River that I have no
> doubt is the richest country in the world. Good land and plenty of
> timber and the best springs and will [wild] mill streams, good range,
> clear water, and every appearance of good health and game aplenty. It
> is the pass where the buffalo passes from north to south and back twice
> a year, and bees and honey plenty. I have a great hope of getting the
> agency to settle that county and I would be glad to see every friend I
> have settled thare. It would be a fortune to them all.[43]

Crockett was so impressed, so utterly enamored of the place, that he is said to have carved the words "Honey Grove" into a tree in celebration of a quaint little tree-lined grove where his hunting party had camped and dined on wild honey. He essentially named the place, for it is known as Honey Grove to this day.[44] By now, Crockett must have been nearly frothing, for he had heard that men like Stephen Austin and his friend Sam Houston were setting up land agencies, through which, if they played things right, and Texas became a part of the United States, as was surely inevitable, the land agents or *empresarios* (akin to modern realtors or developers) stood to become immensely wealthy men. Crockett was feeling superb physically, and the stings from his recent emotional wounds were now a distant memory as the land and his current situation showed nothing but opportunity and promise. If he kept his head about him, looked for and seized the chances as they came to him, David Crockett was on the cusp of finally making his fortune, in a magnificent wilderness where he could hunt practically year-round, catching the buffalo on two migrations per year and bears in the autumn as they foraged in preparation for hibernation, in their dens in winter, and once again when they awoke and reemerged in the spring.

He continued hunting, in a state of euphoria, right through Christmas, missing a rendezvous he had planned with other members of his party, which had split up, at the "falls of the Brazos."[45] The hunting was simply too good, the outriding, sleeping under the explosion of stars in the immense Texian sky, too enjoyable for Crockett to leave just yet. He traveled a leisurely pace, hooking up with the Trammel's Trace, the main link connecting Red River country and Texas, by New Year's and heading south, in the direction of Nacogdoches.[46] Crockett had heard that his old friend Sam Houston was in Nacogdoches, once again practicing law and now setting up land agencies, and in fact Houston was at the time the "newly named commander in chief of the forces of the provisional government of Texas"[47] and he would likely be able to set Crockett up with an agency of his own in the Red River country that had so mesmerized him.

Even out on the open prairie and sparse plain, news traveled with fair speed by word of mouth via horseback, so when Crockett rode into Nacogdoches on January 5, word of his coming had beaten him there, and he was heartily welcomed by scores of people, including his old friend and protégé Ben McCulloch.[48] It was good to see some familiar faces in the bustling little town that now served as the gateway to the South. Prominent townsfolk hosted the national celebrity at a large dinner, where Crockett had no choice but to trot out his requisite "go to hell speech" to thunderous applause.

During his few days in Nacogdoches he learned of some crucial developments that may have shifted his attentions and refocused his goals for the future. Word was afoot that a Constitutional Convention was to be held, designed to make a formal declaration of independence for Texas and compose a constitution, essentially creating a new republic.[49] Though before leaving Tennessee Crockett had soured on politics, this was different. Here no one seemed to know of his recent failures, or if they did, they didn't care—he was treated like a celebrity and frontier hero, titles he had earned. As he knew from jealously regarding the meteoric rise of his nemesis Andrew Jackson, military fame equaled political success, and now there was news that the Mexican armies had been driven south of the Rio Grande, and that their leader Santa Anna, the feared "Napoleon of the West," rode hard from the south with a large force of men. With a military skirmish looming, and nearly free land for any man willing to fight for Texas statehood, the stars seemed to be intentionally aligning in Crockett's favor once again.

The ladies of Nacogdoches invited Crockett and company to a grand dinner a few days hence, which he graciously accepted; then he gathered a few of his men and rode east, to the town of San Augustine, where he was exuberantly greeted by booming cannon fire, then invited to a dinner in his honor. Crockett stopped to deliver one of his "corner speeches," which impressed resident James Gaines deeply, prompting him to conclude the next day: "David Crockett gave one of his Corner Speeches yesterday in San Augustine and is To Represent them in the Convention on the first of March."[50] Later that evening Crockett attended the opulent dinner in his honor, then spent the night at the home of Judge Shelby Corzine, whose daughter wrote that she would never forget that day when David Crockett visited and stayed in their home.[51]

Though he had been practically invisible and anonymous while out hunting in the Choctaw Bayou, news of the great Crockett once again spread in all directions, even as far back east as New York, where it was reported that Crockett was "urged to become a candidate for the Convention; but the Colonel told the Texians that he came to fight for them and not seek office; but as he took care at the same time to tell them that he had rather be a member of the Convention than the Senate of the United

States, we dare say he will be elected."[52] Of course, his claim that he came to fight is suspect and illustrates his shrewd political savvy and ability to respond to a situation as well as the desire of an audience. He had come to hunt and scout turf, but this potential windfall was simply too good to pass up. Brimming with hope and enthusiasm, Crockett found the time in San Augustine to begin a letter to his oldest daughter, Margaret, and her husband, Wiley Flowers, his final surviving correspondence:

My Dear Sone and daughter
This is the first I have had an opportunity to write you with convenience. I
am now blessed with excellent health and am in high spirits, although I
have had many difficulties to encounter. I have got through safe and have
been received by everyone with open cerimony of friendship. I am hailed
with hearty welcome to this country . . . I must say what I have seen of
Texas it is the garden spot of the world. The best land and best prospects
for health I ever saw . . . There is a world of country here to settle . . .[53]

Crockett appears not to have finished the letter in San Augustine,[54] but instead packed it away in his satchel and ridden back to Nacogdoches, where he honored his acceptance to appear at a dinner celebration and party with the town's prominent women and other notable citizens. That out of the way, flush with his rekindled fame and notoriety, he made his way to the office of Judge John Forbes at the Old Stone Fort on January 12. There Crockett and those who had ridden with him read over the "oath of allegiance to the provisional government of Texas," which they had come to sign. Doing so would allow them to vote, and be voted for, in the coming constitutional convention, but also, of course, required that they fight for Texian liberty, apparently a price Crockett was more than willing to pay given the potential upside of land, leadership, military fame, and high governmental station. He would be a fool not to sign up.

But before he did, Crockett took his time, reading over the document carefully. It began, "I do solemnly swear that I will bear true allegiance to the provisional government of Texas, or any future government that may be hereafter declared." Crockett stopped right there, read it over again, and looked up at Forbes. This would simply not do, as he was unwilling to support "any future government." That could easily include a dictator-ship, and as he'd shown before, he refused to be yoked to any individual man. In a defiant move, no doubt accompanied by murmurs and chatter in line behind him, Crockett refused to sign unless Forbes agreed to insert the word "republican" just ahead of "government." Impressed at Crock-ett's intense scrutiny, Forbes willingly consented, and with a stroke of the quill Crockett had signed on as a volunteer, come what may. More than twenty years since he had last carried a firearm against an enemy, Crock-ett had once again joined the army. His future was now.[55]

They would be riding out in just a few days, and Crockett revisited the letter that he had begun in San Augustine. His tone remained confident, reflecting his thrill at the coming adventure and the incredible promise that his future in Texas held. He told them of his taking the oath, and said that "We will set out for the Rio Grande in a few days with the volunteers from the United States," and then he pointed to his newfound political chance: "I have but little doubt of being elected a member to form a con-stitution for this province. I am rejoiced at my fate. I had rather be in my present situation than to be elected to a seat in Congress for life." That last comment illustrated how his short-term memory operated, for not long before he had claimed he was completely finished with politics of any kind. He had not anticipated the reception he would receive in Texas, and Crockett was ever an opportunist. He added the firm indication that he fully intended to prosper, then bring his family to Texas to share the wealth of his bounty: "I am in hopes of making a fortune yet for myself and my family," he wrote proudly, "bad as my prospect has been."[56]

David Crockett stood on the cusp of fulfilling his dreams, for himself, for his family, and perhaps most important of all, for his ego. He would show those doubters back in Tennessee what he was really made of, winning the wealth he had always craved, winning his family back, and in the offing, reclaiming his own identity, so long subsumed by everyone else's desires about who he should be.

FIFTEEN

"Victory or Death"

I T WAS TIME TO RIDE, to muster and mount and begin the long march—some 300 miles—toward the Rio Grande. For the last few days, ever since signing the oath that made him a soldier once again, Crockett had seen others follow suit, some inflamed by the call to arms, some, as he was, lured by the land and the freedom it symbolized. The land that stretched out before them appeared vast, subtly undulating grass prairie ground, so limitless that Sam Houston had written of it three years before, commenting in a letter to Andrew Jackson, "I have traveled five-hundred miles across Texas, and there can be little doubt but the country east of the Grand River . . . would sustain a population of ten millions of souls."[1] Now a steady stream of those souls poured through Nacogdoches, and the steadfast and the hearty took the pledge and armed for inevitable battle.

Officially, David Crockett held no military rank, but that did not keep the small band of volunteers who began to huddle around him from appropriating him as their de facto leader. Abner Burgin and Lindsey Tinkle, with him at the start, appear to have begged off and headed home back to Tennessee, but flanking Crockett were his loyal nephew William Patton, his cousin John Harris, his buddy Ben McCulloch, and other men including Daniel Cloud, Jesse Benton, and Peter Harper. Perhaps to honor their adopted leader, they nicknamed themselves the Tennessee Mounted Volunteers.[2] There was much to do, and Crockett took charge, drawing on his expertise, still there after lying dormant for twenty-odd years, in planning to lead a small band of scouts into hostile and foreign wilderness. He procured a canvas tent to shelter his men from the biting winds and rain they might encounter, though he personally preferred to sleep under the stars whenever possible.[3] Broke as usual, perhaps as the result of buying extra rifles for the Choctaw Bayou hunt,[4] Crockett struck a deal with the government to purchase for $240 two of his long guns, some of his on-hand equipage, and the chestnut he rode, though only a very small percentage of the money was given him in cash—the remainder due him scribbled on a promissory voucher.[5] He organized what further provisions he could, and by January 16 the mustered Tennessee Mounted Volunteers were ready to ride.

Perhaps sensing that it would be his last chance for a good long time, before Crockett left Nacogdoches he had stolen some private time to finish his letter to his daughter, his prose imbued with tenderness and hope, and yet his final words reflect his understanding that there might be cause for his relatives to be concerned about him. He tried to assure them that everything would be fine: "I hope you will do the best you can and I will do the same. Do not be uneasy about me. I am among friends. I will close with great respects. Your affectionate father. Farwell"[6]

And with that he slid his boot into the stirrup, slung his forty-nine-year-old frame once more into the saddle, reined his horse tight and clucked the tall steed forward. True to his own motto, he was going ahead, this time to the Texian revolution, riding headlong toward destiny.

CROCKETT AND HIS COMPANY rode La Bahia Road unhurriedly, south toward Washington-on-the-Brazos, stopping to hunt when game flushed from cover or broke from the timber, which now grew sparser and diminished behind them. Some of the men decided to detour and go gander at the rumbling Falls of the Brazos, rumored to be magnificent.[7] Crockett kept on, agreeing to rendezvous with the other boys in Washington, and the marshy terrain they soon encountered would have reminded him of the bogs and swamps he had scouted in Florida. The horses lurched and squelched through miles of mucky pools, the sulfurous stench rising like steam around them, until they finally broke onto the banks of the Rio de Brazos de Dios, the far-reaching River of the Arms of God.[8]

When Crockett and the four men still with him crossed the muddy Brazos and rode into town, they found a frontier outpost literally hatcheted from river woods, immense stands of towering oaks and hickories; the newly hewn town of some 100 residents still riddled with the stumps of recent cuttings.[9] Crockett may well have expected to find Houston there, but their paths failed to cross, as Houston was off negotiating a deal with the Comanche not to interfere with the colonists,[10] and he would not arrive in Washington until March 2.[11] They had taken their time getting here, meandering as did the riverbanks they rode. He would hole up in Washington for a couple of days to rest and see what he could learn about the military situation, and find out where he might be needed.

What he learned upon arrival, and what Houston had recently discovered as well, was that the situation in San Antonio de Béxar had become grave. Colonel James C. Neill, who had been left with just a hundred or so men to guard San Antonio, which they had secured in a brief skirmish December 5, scratched out an urgent message to Houston on January 14. He explained that the conditions at the garrison were worsening, and he had received reports that Santa Anna moved north toward the Rio Grande with a large army, and that he could be attacked in as few as eight days.[12] Given the news, Houston had quickly dispatched James Bowie and a modest company of men to Béxar to shore up Neill if he could. Houston also made it clear that he wanted "the old Mexican fortifications in the town demolished so they would be of no use to the enemy,"[13] and that in-

Notorious James Bowie of Louisiana led
the volunteers at the Alamo until illness confined
him to his quarters. (Portrait of James Bowie
from glass plate negative. Lucy Leigh Bowie papers,
Daughters of the Republic of Texas Library,
San Antonio.)

cluded the Alamo, an old Spanish mission being used as a fort, if necessary. But when Bowie reached Béxar, he found that Neill had done a superb job fortifying the garrison, buttressing the walls of the Alamo,
strengthening the gun emplacements, so that upon reviewing the compound with Neill, the two men decided that in fact Béxar could be held,
especially with the cannons seized in December.[14] With an injection of

fresh volunteer troops, they reckoned, San Antonio could be defended for a time, anyway.

Crockett was not the kind of man to panic or shirk danger, though upon hearing about the likely convergence of Mexican forces from the north, and Houston's recently dispatched units heading south, his dander would have been up. He did not rush from Washington, and perhaps awaited specific orders with his small company, including John Harris, his cousin, and fellows Daniel Cloud, B. Archer Thomas, and Micajah Autry, the rest having not arrived from their split as yet.

Crockett rode out to Gay Hill, not far from town, on the afternoon of January 24, and on reaching the homestead of James Swisher he saw a man on horseback arriving with a deer slung behind his saddle, a familiar and intriguing sight for Crockett. It was Swisher's son, John, then just seventeen but already quite skilled with his rifle. Crockett assisted the youngster in heaving the deer from the horse, complimenting the boy on his handsome trophy and asking to know the details of the shot and kill, the sorts of woodsy stories which always interested him. Impressed with the young man, who perhaps reminded him of his own boyhood, Crockett began calling John Swisher his "young hunter," and in fun, he even challenged the lad to a shooting contest.[15] The young man was so taken by the attentions that he claimed he "would not have changed places with the president himself."[16]

Crockett spent a few days there, and his hosts recalled that during that time they never let him get to bed before midnight or one in the morning, so enthralled were they with his stories and his manner. "He conversed about himself in the most unaffected manner without the slightest attempt to display any genius or even smartness," John recalled fondly, adding, "He told us a great many anecdotes, many of which were common place and amounted to nothing within themselves, but his inimitable way of telling them would convulse one with laughter."[17] The Swisher family was quite honored to have the distinguished man in their midst, if only for a short time: "Although his early education had been neglected, he had acquired such a polish from his contact with good society, that few men could eclipse him in conversation."[18] As he did with nearly every person he ever met, David Crockett left an indelible impression on the Swishers before it was time to saddle up and ride again.

The Swishers came out to watch Crockett and B. Archer Thomas ride away, feeling a mixture of admiration for the legend and regret that he had to go. The man they waved to from their home seemed more mortal than legend: "He was stout and muscular, about six feet in height, and weighing 180 to 200 pounds. He was of florid complexion, with intelligent gray eyes. He had small side whiskers inclining to sandy. His countenance, although firm and determined, wore a pleasant and genial expression."[19] Despite heading into the unknown, which very likely included being in harm's way, Crockett maintained that infectious conviviality, that joy in being alive.

DAVID CROCKETT did not look like much of a soldier as he made the final leg of his journey south, and neither did his riding companions. None of them had official uniforms, instead riding in what civilian clothes they had, some in tanned leather leggings and "buckskins," traditional utilitarian frontier garb or "leatherstockings."[20] The men traveled with all their belongings tied behind their saddles, extra clothes and a bedroll and perhaps some scant provisions in saddlebags, heading into biting winds and driving winter rains, their fur hunting hats pulled down over their ears in the cold mornings and evenings.[21] The terrain grew ominous, and about three days' ride from Washington the men would have passed through the massive, eerie forest of Lost Pines.[22] They rode through Bastrop[23] and Gonzales, finally arriving in San Antonio de Béxar and dismounting under a steady drizzle in a Mexican graveyard west of the main town, where they took shelter.[24] Before long, someone sent word to James

Bowie that a small knot of riders was at the graveyard, and Bowie himself, accompanied by Antonio Menchacha, rode out to find out who had arrived, hopeful of reinforcements.[25] They found David Crockett and his little band of Tennessee Mounted Volunteers, their number now reduced to just five. Bowie and Menchacha escorted Crockett and his boys into town, taking him directly to the home of Don Erasmo Seguín, one of San Antonio's most prominent citizens.[26] Crockett would stay there, hosted warmly and treated well, until he took lodgings off the main plaza.

Crockett's arrival obviously created a buzz around the township and the garrison, both his celebrity status and his military experience as a scout boosting morale. Though he likely had no desire to be incognito anyway, shortly Crockett was asked to make a speech and he consented, and by the time he arrived at the main plaza an expectant audience awaited. Colonel James Clinton Neill had rounded up men from the garrison[27] and locals flocked curiously around as Crockett mounted a dry-goods box that had been placed for him to stand on as the applause rose. According to Dr. John Sutherland, who recorded the events of that day, after the initial cheering died down and the assembled crowd realized it was really the flesh-and-blood Crockett standing before them, a "profound silence" fell over the crowd as they waited for him to speak. At last he spoke, opening with light yarns and transitioning into his patented "you can go to hell" anecdote, then becoming serious once the laughter subsided. "Fellow citizens," he assured those he had ridden so far to join, "I am among you." He must have meant this figuratively as well as literally, even spiritually. According to Dr. Sutherland, Crockett went on in this vein: "I have come to aid you all that I can in your noble cause. I shall identify myself with your interests, and all the honor that I desire is that of defending as a high private, in common with my fellow citizens, the liberties of our common country."[28] Crockett closed with the assurance that he would do whatever it took to help, and that he expected no special treatment or honors: "Me and my Tennessee boys, have come here to Help Texas as privates," he told them with honesty and conviction, "and will try to do our duty."[29] It was all anyone could have asked of the man.

Two nights later, a bona fide shindig was organized, in good part to honor the arrival of the famous Tennessean David Crockett. The affair was well-attended, including several prominent Tejanos, among them Antonio Menchacha, who had been kindly urged to bring with him "all the principal ladies in the City."[30] William Barrett Travis, James Bowie, and other officers were there as well, enjoying the entertainment which included the seductive fandango, a style of dance more provocative than the Americans volunteers would have been accustomed to. They were riveted by the pulsing beat, the foot stomping, the swirling dresses of the exotic women. The party blended into a mixture of frontier stomp-down and Mexican fandango inside the ballroom, with everyone feasting and drinking with relish. Around 1 a.m., a lone horseman thundered into town, the clatter of hoofbeats mixing with the music as he skidded to a halt and brought forth the most recent courier report from the south of the Rio Grande. The envoy, sent by Placido Benavides, "the Alcade [mayor and magistrate] of Victoria and now employed by the Seguíns as a spy, arrived at the ballroom requesting to speak with Captain Seguín."[31] Learning that Seguín was not available, Menchacha agreed to receive the message.

Interested, Bowie approached Menchacha, who pored over the contents of the letter. His eyes narrowed with concern, Menchacha passed the missive to Bowie, who scanned it quickly. Bowie tried to hand the letter to the passing Travis, but Travis quipped that he was otherwise engaged, currently dancing with the most gorgeous woman in San Antonio, and he had no time for reading letters. Bowie frowned, insisting that he might be interested enough to hold off on the dance. With others, including Crockett, huddled excitedly around, Travis read the contents aloud. Ten thousand men, led by their chief, Antonio Lopez de Santa Anna, were marching on San Antonio, with the sole intention of seizing it. The note was four days old, which meant that, depending on their pace over the roughly 150 miles remaining, the Mexicans would be there in less than two weeks.[32]

It was a fantastic party, and it was by now quite late. Many of the men were already drunk. There was no point in breaking up the festivities. "Let us dance to-night," Travis hollered, perhaps hoping to rally the men and keep morale high, "and to-morrow we will make provisions for our defense."[33] The men returned to the ladies, and the dancing went on until sunrise.

Although J. C. Neill had done a remarkable job of maintaining order, morale, and a semblance of military discipline around the garrison, there were still rumblings about the camp—disgruntlement over lack of pay and provisions—and some men were planning to bolt if things did not improve soon. Neill's abilities and leadership moved Bowie to write, "I cannot eulogise the conduct and character of Col. Neill too brightly," he said, adding that "no other man in the army could have kept men at this post, under the neglect they have experienced."[34] His skills and competence made the news of his departure tough for Bowie to take; on February 11, Neill departed abruptly, citing a sudden illness in the family and a special mission to procure defense funds.[35] He requested a "twenty day's leave," and officers and volunteers alike pleaded with him to stay, but his mind was made up. As he readied to ride off, Neill assigned William Barrett Travis the command of the garrison.

Travis, who had arrived only a week or so before and was a mere twenty-six-year-old stripling, did not immediately command the respect of the troops. In fact, many felt that the older, more experienced local Jim Bowie to be the obvious choice. Bowie had deep ties to San Antonio, having taken full citizenship back in 1831 and married the daughter of the town's richest family—the Veramendis.[36] As a result, Bowie was well known about the place, and the men liked his festive side, too. A hard drinker and storyteller (he was rumored to have wrestled alligators in the

Louisiana of his youth), Bowie assumed that the command of the Alamo would be his. The volunteers and the mercenaries preferred Bowie's command, while the regulars—what few there were of them—opted for Travis. Travis saw that he was in a precarious situation, and immediately called for an impromptu company election. Some of the volunteers actually suggested that Crockett should be included because of his obvious war experience and clear leadership abilities, but he diplomatically declined, citing his intention only in assisting Travis.[37]

The ballots were quickly cast, with only two volunteer companies voting. Bowie was elected,[38] but as it was barely a majority, and allegiances were clearly split between him and Travis, the reality was that no one was technically in command, the camp now divided in two. Bowie decided to celebrate his "victory" by launching into a powerful two-day drunk, carousing wildly about the town. He stumbled to the jail and released Mexican prisoners, then commanded his followers to halt a massive, ox-drawn cart filled with fleeing civilians, afraid of the advancing Santa Anna forces. Violently asserting his control, Bowie crazily ordered the Tejanos to return to town.[39]

Travis was disgusted by the despicable behavior. He wrote to Governor Henry Smith, complaining of the situation: "Since the election [Bowie] has been roaring drunk all the time. If I did not feel my honor & that of my country compromitted I would leave here instantly for some other point with the troops under my immediate command—I am unwilling to be responsible for the drunken irregularities of any man."[40] In fact, seeing that Bowie's behavior was beginning to infect the other men as well, as many of the garrison were now drunk, too, Travis made a shrewd decision and ordered the regulars to follow him to an encampment on the Medina River a few miles from town where order could be restored.[41]

His sensible tactic worked, for two days later, on February 14, a sober and contrite Bowie offered apologies for his erratic behavior, though by now he was falling feverishly ill, his head throbbing. The two came to a compromise: Bowie would lead the volunteers of the garrison and Travis would remain in command of the regulars, plus the volunteer cavalry, a joint command, with all correspondence and orders signed by both of them.[42] They wrote Governor Smith urgently requesting money, supplies, and munitions, and expressing hope that they would get them soon. Though they did not know exactly when Santa Anna and his troops would arrive, they could practically feel the force's hoofbeats rumbling their way. "There is no doubt that the enemy will shortly advance upon this place," they wrote together. "We must therefore urge the necessity of sending reinforcements as speedily as possible to our aid."[43] Travis moved back into lodgings inside town, and Bowie and his volunteers boarded at the Alamo compound. They were committed to the fight, and had silently agreed that they would die fighting for Texas if necessary.

Crockett moved into the Alamo with the rest of the volunteers, busying himself by helping as he could to shore up the defenses of the abandoned mission. When time permitted, he visited with volunteers, told jokes and stories, trying to keep morale high, even when the mood among the famished and ill-provisioned camp was low. Crockett had felt want as a soldier before, remembering all too well those anguished days plodding near dead through the Florida swamps. He would cheer up the men with his witty and outrageous stories. If Crockett had known what was coming, he might have been less jovial.

On February 16, Santa Anna crossed the Rio Grande at Paso de Francia, immediately predicting that the Texians anticipated his arrival from the south, by way of the Laredo Road.[44] Instead, he would swing around to converge on San Antonio de Béxar from the west. During the journey north, Santa Anna's army had grown, and when he had met Cós's retreating force of 815 poorly armed and poorly clothed soldiers, he annexed them straight away, ordering them to turn around and head toward San Antonio once more. Then Santa Anna "angrily ordered Cós to violate the terms of his parole, that is, that he would not bear arms against the Anglo-Americans."[45] These haggard men, as well as those of General José Urrea, whose 550 men had crossed the Rio Grande at Matamoros on February 17,[46] would converge on Béxar and catch the Texians by surprise. They rode hard through plunging temperatures and a threatening sky filled with pounding hail and snow. José Enrique de la Pena, an officer in Santa Anna's army, described the macabre scene, swathed as their men were in "torment and cold": "What a bewitching scene! As far as one could see, all was snow. The trees, totally covered, formed an amazing variety of cones and pyramids, which seemed to be made of alabaster."[47] The weary men pressed on, riding through the bizarre spectacle riddled with dead and dying mules, horses, and men, the snow "covered with the blood of these beasts, contrasting with the whiteness."[48] The cold and violent spring storm darkened the skies of Texas, looming like a false front before a violent thunder burst.

Despite a number of warnings by scouts that the enemy was fast approaching, Travis remained calm and dismissed the reports as exaggerations. Conflicting intelligence passed through Béxar like prairie fires, so that no one knew quite what to believe. There was heightened tension about town, with some of the Tejano population beginning to pack what they could of their belongings. Still, on February 22, 1836, Travis and Bowie agreed to an impromptu celebration of George Washington's birthday, held at Domingo Bustillo's establishment on Soledad Street. Barbecues crackled in the cold air, and people roasted beef and feasted on tamales, enchiladas, and strong grain liquor. As the night wore on the guitars and fiddles came out and the volunteers and conscripts danced, even attempting the fandango by whirling smiling Mexican girls awkwardly around the place. Crockett, never one to miss a party, held forth with the ladies, told hunting stories to the men, and dazzled onlookers with jigs on his fiddle for a few songs.[49] Like the earlier fandango held in Crockett's honor, this one raged on through the night, the mood festive rather than foreboding, the men perhaps sensing that it was the last chance for fun in the foreseeable future.

Neither Crockett nor Travis would have had much time to sleep. By early morning the town was bustling with activity, with the sounds of squeaking oxcarts, of horses neighing, chickens squawking across the busy streets. People were scurrying away from Béxar in droves, scattering with their entire families out into the country. However many of Santa Anna's forces were coming their way, they wanted no part of them, and would rather take their chances out on the plains.[50] When Travis finally roused and noted the exodus, he detained a few Tejanos for questioning, and when none offered anything of use, explaining deceptively that they were merely getting a head start on their spring planting.[51] Frustrated, and sensing that all these frightened-looking Tejanos knew something that he did not, Travis appealed to a trusted local merchant named Nathaniel Lewis, who reluctantly gave him the grim news: just five miles southwest of Béxar, at Leon Creek, the Mexican army had been sighted, and they were on the move.[52] Sometime in the night the Tejanos had received the intelligence, and they'd been streaming out of town ever since.

In fact, Santa Anna had intended to mount a surprise attack during the fandango, but the storm, snows, and heavy rains had swollen the rivers, thwarting his chances for smooth, efficient crossings. He would have to wait for more cooperative weather, even a full moon.

Travis wanted confirmation of the news, so he positioned a man in the belfry of the San Fernando Church to keep lookout toward the southwest. At mid-afternoon, there sounded the desperate clanging bell from the San Fernando watchtower. Travis and some others hurried to the tower, barely able to hear the watchman shouting "the enemy are in view!" over the din of the bell and their own labored breathing.[53] Travis himself scrambled to the lookout, and he anxiously gazed across the horizon, but there was nothing. No men, no horses, no movement. It must surely have been a false alarm. The sentinel swore adamantly that just moments before he had seen hundreds of mounted cavalry, but now they had hidden behind the brushwood.[54] Travis was inclined to believe the sentinel, but wished he had seen them himself. A moment later Dr. Sutherland suggested that he would ride out and confirm the sentinel's sighting, if he could take along someone knowledgeable of the area; John Smith, a local carpenter known affectionately as "El Colorado," volunteered for the detail.[55] They would ride out slowly and signal to Travis in this way: a return at anything other than a "slow gait," would indicate that the sentinel had seen true.

Sutherland and Smith rode easily but attentively south-southwest, likely trotting along the Laredo Road for a mile and a half or so before they ascended the slope cresting the Alazan hills.[56] The wide flat vista afforded them a dreadful sight, and they reined up hard. They had ridden directly into the head of Santa Anna's advance guard, hundreds of "well-mounted and equipped" cavalry, and some 1,500 troops at the ready.[57] Sutherland and Smith wheeled their horses around, loosed their reins and spurred hard, whipping their animals quickly to a gallop. Driving rains had slicked the hoof-worn road, and Sutherland's horse lost footing, skidding and finally crashing down on its side, Sutherland's leg crushed in the violent roll. Smith returned just as the horse shook itself back up from the ground, and he helped the injured Sutherland as they galloped again toward Béxar.

Their return speed told the grim news, confirming the sentinel's report, and Travis launched into action, barking orders, evacuating the town and sending everyone inside the walls of the Alamo. Crockett rode out on his own reconnaissance and met Sutherland and Smith near the vacant main plaza, informing them of the orders to take refuge inside the Alamo. Crockett escorted them inside helping Sutherland down from his horse and, grabbing him up under the shoulder, assisted the limping, shaken man into Travis's office.[58] Travis was frantically scribbling a letter to Judge Andrew Ponton in Gonzales: "The enemy in large force is in sight. We want men and provisions. Send them to us. We have 150 men and are determined to defend the Alamo to the last. Give us assistance."[59] He scrawled a similar plea to Fannin in Goliad, reiterating his dire needs: "We have removed all our men into the Alamo . . . We have one hundred and forty-six men, who are determined *never to retreat*. We have but little provisions, but enough to serve us till you and your men arrive . . ."[60] Travis handed the first missive to Sutherland, who, practically on one leg, agreed to carry the message to Gonzales. He gave a young messenger named Johnson the note for Fannin. Crockett immediately spoke up, offering his services and those of his men. "Colonel, here I am. Assign me a position, and me and my twelve boys will try to defend it."[61] Sutherland noted, as he readied to leave, that Crockett and his boys were assigned to "the picket wall extending from the end of the barracks, on the south side, to the corner of the Church."[62] As a sign to his enemy, Travis raised the national tricolor flag, bearing two stars signifying the two states of Coahuila and Texas.[63]

Sutherland met up with Smith again on his departure, and as they rode they could see Santa Anna's cavalry and foot soldiers marching directly into the main plaza, storming the town without a single shot of resistance. The sight, and the sheer numbers, would have chilled the men as they headed quickly out of town and onto the open plain. Sutherland would later recall that the pain in his knee was so excruciating that he considered turning back, returning to the Alamo, for fear he would not be able to bear the long ride to Gonzales. But then the single echoing boom of cannon fire drove him onward.[64]

Travis had witnessed the unnerving spectacle, too, the rumbling hoofbeats entering town, then watched in bitterness as Santa Anna ordered the blood-red flag of "no quarter" hoisted, signaling his intentions to show no mercy, and the promise of death to any man who dared oppose him, where it waved threateningly above the San Fernando church.[65] In defiant response, Travis ordered the single blast from his eighteen-pounder, a dull and exclamatory report. Insulted, Santa Anna lobbed back a brief volley of four grenades aimed into the compound, but none caused damage or casualties. Word traveled that at the same time the four cannons were fired, the faint sound of a bugle had gone up, indicating the desire to meet and talk.

Travis and Bowie discussed their options, at odds over the next move. Travis preferred to wait, to see what Santa Anna would do, while Bowie thought a discussion, a "parley," was in order.[66] Though feverish and weakening minute by minute with fever, Bowie still had a brash and independent, even rogue, character, acting on his own as he tore a page from a child's schoolbook and dictated a message to be written in Spanish. He wished to know if in fact a parley had been called for by the Mexicans. Bowie made certain to end the brief message with words of defiance: "God and Texas." Without consulting Travis, he handed the message to the Alamo's engineer, Green Jameson, and sent him off bearing a white truce flag. The cannon fire ceased as he emerged from the garrison.[67]

Santa Anna considered the men in the garrison rebels and foreigners, in violation of Mexican law, and he had no intention of negotiating. He sent Jameson back with a clipped message: "The Mexican army cannot come to terms under any conditions with rebellious foreigners to whom there is no other recourse left, if they wish to save their lives, than to place themselves immediately at the disposal of the Supreme Government from whom alone they may expect clemency after some considerations are taken up. God and Liberty!"[68] Though the response was ripe with interpretive possibilities, Travis figured that at the very least, he and Bowie would be executed if they surrendered, and if they would not be allowed to leave their garrison with standard "honors of war," such as those that had been afforded Cós when he was allowed to leave Béxar, then there would be no deal.[69]

Travis decided to dispatch his own emissary, Albert Martin, who rode out and spoke directly with Colonel Almonte, who had been educated in the United States, and spoke fluent English, so would perhaps prove reasonable.[70] Almonte simply replied that he could not presume to speak for the general, and that in fact, Santa Anna had already offered his reply, and his terms, to Bowie. The discussion was over. Travis added that he would soon let them know if he accepted their terms, and if not, he would discharge another single round from his cannon.[71] Travis had no intention of negotiating, and after a brief and animated rallying of the troops, he let fly the cannon shot.

The Mexicans replied immediately with a sustained volley of bombardment, and Travis could do nothing but retreat to his quarters and wait. Bowie did the same, his condition worsening with some combination of pneumonia, malaria, or typhoid, and with the Mexican artillery fire shaking the Alamo walls, he was barely able to rise from his bunk.

The shelling continued the next morning and into the afternoon of the following day, with Travis now in sole command of the garrison. The men did what they could, which was little, other than remain out of harm's way. Finally, unconvinced that his and Bowie's appeals to Gonzales and Goliad had been received, or were explicit enough, Travis stole time in his quarters to pen an eloquent and rousing missive addressed to "The People of Texas & All Americans in the World":

> I am besieged, by a thousand or more of the Mexicans under Santa Anna—I have sustained a continual Bombardment & cannonade for 24 hours & have not lost a man.—The enemy has demanded a surrender at discretion, otherwise the garrison are to be put to the sword if the fort is taken—I have answered the demand with a cannon shot, & our flag still waves proudly from the walls—*I shall never surrender or retreat. Then,* I call on you in the name of Liberty, patriotism, & everything dear to the American character, to come to our aid, with all dispatch—The enemy is receiving reinforcements daily & will no

doubt increase to three or four thousand in four or five days. If this call is neglected, I am determined to sustain myself as long as possible & die like a soldier who never forgets what is due to his own honor & that of his country—*Victory or Death.*[72]

Travis understood his predicament, knew the odds were stacked against them, and now all he and the men could do was hope for some manner of reinforcements. Despite imminent defeat, surrender was simply not an option for the headstrong Travis and the proud men. Like it or not, they were committed to the stand, attempting to defend a relatively indefensible structure against staggeringly overwhelming odds. Bowie lay quivering and shaking in his bunk. Hundreds of miles away, Sam Houston sat sharing a peace pipe with Chief Tewulle, their collaborative efforts having produced a treaty with the Cherokees and assuring they would stay out of the Mexican-American skirmish.[73]

Crockett, peering over the wall and squinting out at the swarms of soldiers amassing around the flaking adobe compound, would have wondered just what in the hell he had signed up for, and whether the bear he was about to grapple with was a sight bigger than he had reckoned.

SIXTEEN

Smoke from a Funeral Pyre

CROCKETT WOULD HAVE RELISHED his detail at the southern wall, firing his long rifle at enemies a great distance away in the manner of a sharpshooter, his legendary marksmanship boosting the mood of the men. Of the 146-odd men inside the compound, nearly forty were sick and weak with dysentery, run down from lack of rations, exposure to the elements, and the abysmal condition of food and water stores. On the morning of February 25, the enemy artillery served as an early reveille, and Travis soon witnessed more than 200 Mexicans crossing the San Antonio and brashly setting up just 100 yards from the southwest corner of the Alamo, right where Crockett stood leveling his weapon.[1] Travis quickly ordered his crack riflemen, including Crockett, to fire on the Mexicans by opening "a heavy discharge of grape and canister on them,"[2] scattering them into confusion and pinning them down in the brushy-roofed huts or *jacales*.

The firefight continued through the cold pelting rain of a descending norther, with many of the defender's shots hitting their mark, Crockett's sure and experienced blasts among them. The exchange lasted for hours, during which time Travis noted that his riflemen brought down eight or ten of the enemy, who were dragged off under continuous fire.[3]

Crockett continued to blaze away, and while reloading, he ran about excitedly, rallying the other riflemen to shoot true. His enthusiasm and valor impressed Travis a great deal, and he later remarked that "The Hon. David Crockett was seen at all points, animating the men to do their duty."[4] The sniping was exactly Crockett's brand of sport, and he covered his comrades as the south gate was briefly opened at Travis's order and two men slipped silently out on horseback to set fire to the dry *jacales* that the enemy had been using as cover. The tactic worked, and without the close cover, the frontal assault was forced to retreat, at least for the moment. But the offensive proved to Travis that a full and sustained attack was imminent.

John Sutherland had ridden the seventy miles from Béxar to Goliad through mind-numbing pain, but he knew the situation at the compound and faithfully delivered his message to Colonel Fannin. Fannin, himself in a delicate frame of mind and uncertain of his own abilities to lead, made a quick, definitive decision, leaving 100 men at Goliad to defend what they had dubbed Fort Defiance, and take the other 320 to Béxar.[5] Fannin's aide-de-camp at Goliad was a man named John Brooks, who wrote of Fannin's orders and decision, "We will start tonight or tomorrow morning at the dawn of day in order to relieve that gallant little garrison, who have so nobly resolved to sustain themselves until our arrival."[6] It was a glimmer of hopefulness that the besieged at Béxar would never know about, for the relief effort, while noble and well-intentioned, soon foundered. They were threadbare, near-starved, with scant provisions, and an inauspicious start doomed the mission at the outset. One of the ox-drawn wagons broke a few hundred yards into the journey, and crossing the rain-swollen San Antonio proved tedious and time consuming. The muddy track made the going excruciatingly slow, and several of the oxen managed to wander off in the night.[7] They were a ragged and unprepared army, devoid of winter clothing, their boots rotting off their feet, and almost out of ammunition. Fannin determined that his troops were in no condition to rescue anyone—they needed reinforcements themselves. His heroic rescue mission was dead in the water before it even began.

The beleaguered defenders would continue to wait, to pray for troops to come to their aid. Crockett kept up his daily sharpshooting to pass the time, and some reports suggest that his rifle was the one to bring down the first of the enemy soldiers. Late in the day on February 27, as long, muted light began to whiten the walls of the Alamo, a cocky Santa Anna rode toward the mission at the head of his men, almost as if calling Crockett and his boys out. They were happy to oblige, and a rumor went round that a bullet fired from Crockett's rifle sent the arrogant general clambering for cover, the shot nearly killing the famed Napoleon of the West.[8]

In the early morning hours of March 1, in the cold blackness on the other side of midnight, the hopes of the defenders were answered, if only in a small way. Thirty-two brave men of Gonzales had responded to Travis's dramatic plea and ridden the dangerous road. They arrived at the gates of the Alamo under cover of darkness, wet and cold, their hands frozen to their reins, and after some confusion—the defenders could not be certain they were friendly and even fired on them once—they were hurried inside the walls and welcomed.[9] Though small in number and unlikely to significantly shift the balance of power, the fact that they had been able to ride through enemy lines and sneak inside the fort proved uplifting to Travis and his men, who now believed that more might be en route.

But the arrival of the "Gonzales Ranging Company of Mounted Volunteers," led by "El Colorado" John Smith himself, had been more lucky than skillful. Santa Anna had anticipated Fannin's relief to arrive from the southeast, heading up from La Bahia, and had stationed patrols there. Coming from the northeast, Smith and the volunteers rode right in.[10] Still, the reinforcements lifted spirits inside the garrison, and though the day dawned freezing cold, men scurried about with a renewed cheerfulness.

Crockett took out his fiddle for a jig or two, joined by the Scotsman John McGregor, and the two of them played tunes together, a huddle of men humming along, clapping and laughing when the two competed to see who could create the most noise with his instrument.[11] Crockett's grin, good humor, and storytelling buoyed the cold, hungry, and lonely men during the long days under siege by an army whose numbers grew to frightening proportions. Travis, feeling spry with the arrivals, ordered his gunners to launch two cannonballs from his twelve-pounders, one crashing into the military plaza, the other exploding on its target in a direct hit, tearing through the timber roof of a house suspected to be the headquarters of Santa Anna himself and sending Mexicans scattering for cover.[12]

Travis and the men were unaware of most of the goings-on outside their immediate surroundings. It was probably best that Travis was ignorant of Sam Houston's behavior and state of mind, for the notorious Raven was in Washington-on-the-Brazos at the constitutional convention, where, rather than acting like a general and future president of Texas, he was engaged in a raging drunk. His drinking was so severe that his friends had to physically subdue him and carry him from the grogshops to his bed. When, on March 2, the *Brazoria Texas Republican* published Travis's "Victory or Death" letter, Houston balked, doubting the veracity of the letter and calling it "a damned lie," then adding that the reports by both Travis and Fannin were schemes to bolster their popularity.[13] The resulting doubt about the claims from Béxar slowed immediate action from Washington-on-the-Brazos.

Meanwhile, on March 2, Santa Anna resumed his shelling of the compound, and even began slowly inching his artillery forward, pinching in closer and closer to the Alamo walls.[14] Beneath his veneer of hope and optimism, Travis would have been feeling exasperated frustration, noting that his appeals had gone mostly unanswered, and that thirty-two men was hardly enough. He had expected Fannin and hundreds.

The next day Travis witnessed a harrowing sight: long, serpentine lines of enemy soldiers streamed into Béxar, numbering over a thousand strong by the looks of them. Even more disconcerting, the arrival of this regiment, a well-armed cavalry in full-dress regalia, was heralded by music, boisterous singing, drums, firing weapons, and fanfare, so that he concluded (wrongly, it turned out, since Santa Anna had actually been there since the siege began) that the hoopla signaled the arrival of Santa Anna himself. As he stared grimly across the river and the plaza, Travis surveyed a force of some 2,500 troops.[15]

But Travis also witnessed something else, something nearly miraculous considering it was broad daylight: James Butler Bonham galloped up, having managed to squirt directly between the Mexican-seized powder house and cavalry commander General Ramirez y Sesma's troops. It was a daring move: after hiding in the thicket and brush, he had bolted for open ground and spurred hard, swinging low on his mount to minimize himself as a target, but no fire came. At around 11 a.m. Bonham arrived inside the Alamo walls.[16] He quickly reached into his saddlebags and produced a letter from R. M. Williamson in San Felipe, addressed to William Barrett Travis, dated March 1, 1836. The words could not have been more welcomed, suggesting that even as Bonham read, Texians were hastening to their defense. It was precisely the kind of positive news the garrison had long awaited:

Sixty men have set out from this municipality and in all human probability they are with you at this date. Colonel Fannin, with three hundred men and four pieces of artillery, has been on the march toward Bejar for three days. Tonight we expect some three hundred reinforcements . . . and no time will be wasted in seeking their help for you . . . PS. For God's sake, hold out until we can help you.[17]

Travis took Bonham's unscathed arrival as a prompt that he might also succeed in getting a messenger out, and he retired to his quarters to write the convention in Washington. He would choose his words and tone carefully, resulting in a most detailed, informative, and patriotic document, one that reiterated his intention to fight to the death, reinforcements or none. He coldly and clearly assessed his military situation and laid out his military needs. "Colonel Fannin is said to be on the march to this place," he wrote, adding his dubious appraisal, "but I fear it is not true." He reiterated that despite incessant shelling since February 25, they had managed to hold the fort down without losing a single man. Travis told the men of the convention that he was completely surrounded by the enemy, yet despite the continual bombardment, he had been able to fortify "this place, that the walls are generally proof against canon balls." He then turned to the condition and mental state of his brave defenders. "The spirits of my men are still high, though they have had much to depress them." He went on to estimate that the enemy encircling him was between 1,500 and 6,000, including the thousand marching in as he wrote.[18]

He needed help, and he needed it now. He carefully outlined his desires: 500 pounds of cannon powder, 200 rounds of cannonballs in six-, nine-, twelve-, and eighteen-pound balls, ten kegs of rifle powder, and a healthy supply of lead, all sent with no further delay, under heavy guard.[19] If these requests were quickly met, he and the defenders might just have a chance. But if the relief did not arrive expeditiously, Travis would have no alternative but to "fight the enemy on his own terms," and those terms were to the death, with a "no prisoners" provision from the enemy. "A blood-red banner waves from the church of Bejar, and in the camp above us, in token that the war is one of vengeance against rebels. They have declared us as such, and demanded that we should surrender at discretion, or that this garrison should be put to the sword."

Travis closed with defiance, pointing out that the red flags of "no quarter" did not faze him, nor his men. "Their threats have had no influence on me, or my men, but to make all fight with desperation, and that high souled courage which characterizes the patriot, who is willing to die in defence of his country's liberty and his own honor."[20] In a cryptic and grim postscript, Travis underscored that the enemy reinforcements continued to pour in, and their numbers would soon mount to two or three thousand. He signed off—"God and Texas—Victory or Death." He pressed the long letter into his courier's hand and sent him toward Washington, where the delegates were busy framing the Texian Declaration of Independence, lifting most of it directly from that of the United States of 1776.

Perhaps sensing that the end was drawing near, Travis penned two more letters during the day, these shorter and more personal, one to his friend Jesse Grimes, the other a brief note to friend David Ayers, guardian of Travis's son. Perhaps fearing that his first letter would fail to make it through the enemy lines, Travis reiterated some of that correspondence, then added

> Let the Convention go on and make a declaration of independence; and we will then understand and the world will understand what we are fighting for. If independence is not declared, I shall lay down my arms and so will the men under my command. But under the flag of independence, we are ready to peril our lives a hundred times a day, and to dare the monster who is fighting us under a blood-red flag, threatening to make Texas a waste desert . . . If my countrymen do not rally to my relief, I am determined to perish in the defence of this place, and my bones shall reproach my country for her neglect.[21]

He had made his case, politically and militarily, so that now all that was left was to write a note regarding his son, which echoes some of the sentiment found in Crockett's letter to his family back in January. Both mention that securing Texas would result in a "fortune" for themselves and their families. Travis procured a ripped scrap of yellowing paper and scribbled the following:

> Take care of my little boy. If the country should be saved I may make him a splendid fortune. But if the country should be lost, and I should perish, he will have nothing but the proud recollection that he is the son of a man who died for his country.[22]

Thinking of his son and certainly doubtful that he would ever see the boy again, Travis handed the letters to his trusted envoy, "El Colorado" John Smith, and sent him on his way.

Ironically, the same day, March 3, in Washington-on-the-Brazos, the declaration of independence was read aloud to the assembly and signed by everyone present, officially ratifying the Republic of Texas.[23] The next day, Sam Houston was made commander in chief of the army, and it would be his job to rescue the defenders if he could gather enough troops and get there in time.

The next morning, Santa Anna began bombarding the fort and he kept the pressure on throughout the day, pointing the bulk of his efforts on the north wall. Dismally low on powder, Travis could do no more than shrug and hold off with any retaliation, which would be token at best. He would need all ammunition and powder for the major assault, which he must have sensed looming. The only shots Travis is said to have fired that day or the next were three signal shots, aimed at any aid en route, denoting that he was still holding down the fort.[24] A few days earlier, Bowie had felt good enough to be lifted on his cot and brought out into the open air of the courtyard, and had even encouraged some of the men to stand strong and proud. But by now he was back in his quarters, his ailments gripping him to the core, clutching him in feverish shakes.

David Crockett may have been thinking of the hunting grounds he had discovered on the Red River, or favorite old haunts back home, as he looked out at the overwhelming odds they were about to face. He had done what he could to shore up the morale of the men, playing music, telling jokes and tall tales, but even his optimism would have been tested by the spectacle of being surrounded by thousands of men, the constant strain of watching the horizon and hoping for recruits to arrive. Crockett wished to be out on the open plain again, and a claustrophobic feeling overtook him as he pondered the walls of the fort now penning them in like cattle herded to slaughter. "I think we had better march out and die in the open air," he said aloud. "I don't like to be hemmed up."[25] But it was only the wishful thinking of a man who longed for the freedom of open country once more, who dreamed of outriding, perhaps conjuring that idyllic Honey Grove, the twice-yearly passing of buffalo, the sweet smell of blossoms and hives dripping with honey.

Santa Anna convened a war council on the eve of March 4. A few of his officers suggested that, if the general were willing to wait for even more artillery to arrive, then the Alamo could be taken with very little loss of Mexican troops.[26] But the tactical Santa Anna craved drama, and more than that, he wished to send a message to both the rebellious "pirates" and his own troops. Attacking now, in great force, "would infuse our soldiers with that enthusiasm of the first triumph that would make them superior in the future to those of the enemy."[27] He had already said that the attack would serve as a necessary example to Béxar and all of Texas, of the price of rebellion, "in order that those adventurers may be duly warned, and the nation be delivered . . ."[28] His mind was made up, and when the topic of how to treat prisoners of war was broached, Santa Anna scoffed and waved his officers away. His army would take no prisoners.[29]

On March 5, the observant hunter Crockett would have noticed that the Mexican camp, its troops and guns, was eerily silent, the menacing electric tension of a calm before a storm. The crumbling fortress had endured twelve consecutive days of near-constant shelling, and Crockett and the rest of the men would have welcomed the respite, a chance for the ringing in their ears to cease. The quiet would give them a chance to think about their families, their goals and dreams for the future, the many trails that had led them here, and, for those who believed, what the afterlife might bring. And the tranquil air would give some of them a chance to sleep, especially those who had been trading watch for nearly two weeks, their eyes burning with sleep deprivation. Travis would send out one last messenger, a youngster named James Allen, with a last-ditch appeal to Fannin to come fast.[30] Travis then made the rounds of the garrison, posting sentries outside the walls and on guard, and then ascertaining that all the men on watch had multiple "loaded rifles, muskets or pistols," at their immediate reach.[31] Finally, convinced he had done all he could up to now and certainly for today, Travis slumped into bed sometime after midnight.

About the time Travis was being overtaken by exhaustion, Santa Anna and his officers began rousting his men with severe whispers, poking them with staffs or kicking them awake with boots, fingers pressed to their lips, ordering complete silence for the dawn attack.[32] Crowbars and ladders were distributed, and officers made certain that all men in the attack wore shoes or sandals for ascending the walls, to assure they did not give away their positions by yelping out in agony as their bare feet met sharp rocks and thorns or prickly cactus.[33] On his command, which would be given at 5 a.m. March 6, the men were to assault in linear formation, and those in the first waves would have known they would be cut to pieces by musket fire and cannonballs tearing dreadfully at the columns of men.[34] Resolute and following orders of their supreme commander, the men shook from sleep and formed lengthy columns, their sharpened bayonets gleaming in the moonlight. Simultaneously, Sesma saddled his cavalry, their job to survey the perimeter of the Alamo and make certain that no one escaped the attack once it was under way. Though the temperatures had warmed slightly the day before, it was still cold, and the horses and men huffed cottony plumes of breath that mingled with the shimmering moonglow. The men stood shivering, holding weapons or tools, their long moon shadows ghoulish, waiting for the command to move. By 3 a.m. they stood like zombies, waiting for orders in the snap-still air. At 5:30, Santa Anna ordered Jose Maria Gonzalez to sound the call to arms, a sound inspiring the men to "scorn life and welcome death." Other trumpeters picked up "that terrible bugle call of death," and the columns began the assault.[35]

Travis's sentries, exhausted from weeks at their posts, stood or sat dozing, leaning uncomfortably against walls or their muskets. None detected Santa Anna's stealthy death march, the sound of hundreds of horse

March 6, 1836, Santa Anna's army storms the Alamo.
(FALL OF THE ALAMO. *Theodore Gentilz. Gentilz-Fretelliere Family Papers, Daughters of the Republic of Texas Library, San Antonio.*)

hooves, or their whinnies and exhalations, the metronomic clank of metal and arms, the panicked voices of frightened foot soldiers reciting their last prayers, until it was too late. Long skeins of light tore across the embattled sky as night fought to become day, the weird moonlight lingering on the plain, bathing the fort in a surreal glow. Santa Anna's men were upon the Alamo.

The attackers responded to the bugles and surged forward, shouting "Viva Santa Anna" and "Viva Mexico," and then, spurred by blood lust and their own code of honor, they also began to chant *"Muerte* [death] *a los Americanos!!"*[36]

Officer John J. Baugh finally woke to the commotion and sprinted to Travis's quarters, hollering "The Mexicans are coming!" Travis instinctively clutched saber and shotgun and dashed for the north wall, his slave Joe at his heels as he reached the gun emplacement amid the horrible and confused flashes of enemy gunfire from without and the lowing and baying of terrified horses and cattle from within.[37] Inside, the Alamo awakened to the nightmare; half-dressed men streaked from their cots in the long barracks and scrambled to positions, shooting rifles randomly, igniting cannons and aiming them vaguely at the gray-black lines of men they could make out in the half-dark. The blazing, orange-yellow arcs of cannons whistled and spit skyward, then died out in the distance as the ordnances fell to the ground. Travis climbed quickly to the emplacement and looked down, seeing soldiers leaning ladders against the walls. He turned back to his men in the fort and shouted, *"Come on, Boys, the Mexicans are upon us and we'll give them Hell!"*

For a few minutes, they did. Without proper canister shot, Travis had made do, ordering the men to stuff their shotguns with "chopped up horseshoes, links of chain, nails, bits of door hinges—every piece of jagged scrap metal they could scavenge," firing these deadly shotgun blasts on the huddled masses of men below.[38] A violent hail of fiery shards sliced down on the columnar waves of charging Mexicans, cutting many to pieces in their tracks. Travis peered over the wall at the surging onslaught, shouting encouragement and ordering another volley of shotgun blasts and a first surge of round shot in the form of nine-pound iron, when his head snapped back, a leaden ball from a Mexican Brown Bess striking him in the forehead and hurling him backward into a motionless heap against one of his own cannons, his gun still clasped in his hands.[39]

Crockett was somewhere in the frenzied rush to defend, amidst the cacophony of cries from comrades taking lead balls from volleys thrown by the onrushing waves of the enemy. The inside of the fort flickered, illuminated by gunfire and cannon flare. He would have fought for all he was worth, galvanizing his knowledge of warfare and defense into one last-ditch effort to survive. Crockett no doubt clambered to a post and started shooting, helping expel the initial surge which fell back, taking heavy casualties, but then resurged. Mexican sergeants and officers flogged any recruits trying to retreat, herding new formations on ahead.[40] With a second formation hammering hard at the north wall, forces also pinched like talons from the south and the east, while Santa Anna's reserves, and his band, lay in wait by the northern battery.[41] Desperate columns, taking incessant grapeshot and ducking under the dreadful whir and whistle of flaming metal flying overhead, convened near the north wall. Crockett and his riflemen fired and reloaded as fast as they could work, grabbing rifle after rifle until all their pieces were empty and they were forced to stop and reload once more, their efforts forcing the oncoming column to angle out and away, toward the southwest corner.[42]

A third advance came, and now the Mexicans were mounting the ladders, redoubling their efforts. Two other ragged lines at the east and northwest had breached and reformed, and now all merged into a single swarming mass at the base of the north wall. They were too close for cannon fire, but shotgun spray and rifle bullets peppered them from above. Still, they came, now scaling the rough woodwork repairs that latticed the outer walls. They placed ladders, and into the face of direct fire, up and over they went, droves upon droves of men hoisting each other from the bottom, climbing over one another, stepping on each other's arms and hands and heads. Soon, the defenders at the top could no longer reload fast enough to repel the sheer numbers mounting the parapet, and they found themselves engaged in hand-to-hand combat, stabbing viciously with bayonets and knives. José Enrique de la Pena was there under Santa Anna's command, and he remembered the scene vividly:

> The sharp reports of the rifles, the whistling of bullets, the groans of the wounded, the cursing of the men, the sighs and anguished cries of the dying . . . the noise of the instruments of war, and the insubordinate shouts of the attackers, who climbed vigorously, bewildered all . . . The shouting of those being attacked was no less loud and from the beginning had pierced our ears with desperate, terrible cries of alarm in a language we did not understand.[43]

The Alamo had been breached.

As the north wall fell and the Texians retreated under the onslaught, the fight turned inward, with defenders shooting anything that resembled a Mexican uniform, brandishing tomahawks and long knives, hacking and stabbing wildly with bayonets. Mexicans poured over the south wall as defenders retreated to the open courtyard, while some, hemmed in on two sides now and staring down certain death, leapt from their positions on the palisade or squirted through the corner of the cattle pen.[44] Those who managed to escape were summarily ridden down and slain point-blank in the ditches and chaparral surrounding the fort by Ramirez y Sesma's men, who killed them with lances.[45] Crockett's desire to die out in the open air may have crossed his mind, but he had his hands full fending off the newly breached south wall and the hundreds of Mexicans streaming in. Now soldiers outside used massive timber to bash and ramrod the gates, also breaking through any and all windows and doors. Crockett and his riflemen stood in defiance as long as they could, "then withdrew into the chapel."[46]

The Mexicans moved room to room, blasting doors apart with the defenders' own cannons, entering with bayonets brandished. Reaching the hospital rooms they found the sickly, weak, and debilitated men feebly attempting to defend themselves, the once-strong and fierce knife fighter Jim Bowie among them. He lay in his cot, beneath the covers, perhaps already unconscious, and he offered no resistance as the Mexicans stabbed him repeatedly, then fired on him at point-blank range, spattering his brains across the wall.[47]

By now there remained only a handful of defenders still alive inside the Alamo walls, and the Mexicans had but to round them up and slaughter them one at a time. The chapel held the last defenders. The Mexicans blew the chapel open with cannon fire and pressed in, enveloping a small knot of six men who were now surrounded. David Crockett was among the last standing.[48]

Santa Anna received news that the Alamo was secured, and soon he entered, scanning the dreadful slaughter in the first pink-orange embers of daylight. Perhaps forgetting the previous chant of *Degüello*, no quarter and no mercy, General Manuel Fernandez Castrillion brought forward Crockett and the others, whom he had ordered his reluctant soldiers to spare. Santa Anna took no time at all to scoff at Castrillion, waving him away "with a gesture of indignation," and order the immediate execution of David Crockett and those who stood with him that cold morning. Nothing happened for a moment, and it appeared that the men might actually disobey their commander. They had seen enough killing, and these helpless men now posed no immediate threat. But in the dim twilight, the sky and air gunmetal cold, officers hoping to ingratiate themselves with their leader leapt forward, "and with swords in hand, fell upon these unfortunate, defenseless men just as a tiger leaps upon his prey. Though tortured before they were killed, these unfortunates died without complaining and without humiliating themselves before their torturers."[49]

David Crockett was dead.

BY THE TIME all the smoke had cleared and the bodies were counted, Santa Anna's one-sided victory proved to have come at a very high cost—nearly 600 of his men had been wounded or killed. Commander in Chief Sam Houston marched toward the Alamo, realizing that the pleas from the fort had been legitimate, but by now of course it was too late. Houston took his own sweet time moving south, spending five entire days on a ride that should have taken just two, during which time he camped two nights on the Colorado.[50] On March 11, Fannin received two missives from Houston, the first confirming that the Alamo had fallen, the second ordering Fannin to withdraw, repositioning for defense at Victoria, on the Guadalupe.[51] He was also instructed to blow up the fortress before departing.

Fannin dallied, and his indolence cost him and his men dearly. Mexican General José de Urrea closed in quickly, catching Fannin in retreat on March 18 and surrounding him a day later out on the open plain. By the end of a daylong skirmish Fannin had suffered sixty losses compared to 200 Mexicans, but by the next morning Urrea received significant reinforcements, rendering Fannin and his men defenseless. When Urrea, a humane and decent general, called a ceasefire, Fannin believed he might convince his opponent to offer reasonable terms of surrender, but he had not reckoned on the wrath of Santa Anna, who reiterated his order that rebels and traitors be executed on the spot.[52] Urrea hated to do it, but after seizing all of Fannin's weapons and ammunition, the sickened Mexican general marched Fannin and his men in four columns out onto the road under the guise of wood-gathering and a journey to Matamoros, and summarily leveled them with musket fire, finishing them off with bayonets and knives until 342 men were slain. A few dozen escaped to report the horrific event.[53]

On April 21, 1836, Houston finally entered the fray, advancing on Santa Anna's fatigued army which, with two recent decisive victories and blood still drying on their hands, understood Houston to be in full retreat mode. Instead, Houston marched two parallel but roughshod columns totaling some 900 men inflamed by the battle cries "Remember the Alamo!" and "Remember Goliad!" The surprise attack stunned Santa Anna and his exhausted troops, who were unprepared to defend themselves in soldierly fashion, and lapsed into panic and confusion.[54] Even Santa Anna himself—who had been sleeping—became disoriented, unable to give useful orders as the Texians advanced in battle frenzy. They continued to chant "Remember the Alamo, remember Goliad"; some were even said to cry out "Remember Crockett!" The attack was so sudden and unexpected that many of the Mexicans simply ran for their lives, but were thwarted by the bayou and the lines of Texians, who gunned them down.[55]

The Battle of San Jacinto was really more of a slaughter, a revenge massacre for Santa Anna's "no quarter" victories at the Alamo and Goliad. Men were shot attempting to swim away in the Buffalo Bayou, others ridden down and impaled with bayonets, and many were shot point-blank in the head. One Texian participant called it "the most awful slaughter"[56] he ever witnessed. It was over in just eighteen minutes. Houston had two horses shot from under him and his ankle shattered by a rifle ball, yet he could take solace in the fact that he'd captured the Napoleon of the West, when Santa Anna was finally rounded up and taken prisoner. Shrewdly realizing that the great general was more useful alive than dead, Houston would hold on to his prize until he could get what he wanted, which was the rest of Santa Anna's army back in Mexico, on the other side of the Rio Grande.[57] As a result of his success at San Jacinto, Sam Houston joined his old friend from Tennessee, David Crockett, as a hero of Texian independence. Houston would live to be elected twice as the president of the new Republic of Texas and ultimately governor of the state—Crockett would live on as a legend.[58]

Back home in Tennessee, it did not take long for the rumors of Crockett's demise to arrive. In mid-April the *Niles Register*, quoting from the *New Orleans True American*, listed Crockett as having fallen with the fort: "Colonel David Crockett, his companion Jesse Benton, and Colonel Bonham of South Carolina, were among the number slain."[59] Elizabeth would certainly not have been surprised: he had nearly died afield more than once, had tricked death time and again—she well knew the Christmas gunpowder story, the barrel-staves scrape, all the close calls. The stalwart, now twice-widowed woman knew how to keep scrapping when things got tough, and she would certainly have lowered her head and pressed forward. By early summer, tender and heartfelt letters of condolence began to find their way to her, canonizing the man she knew as well as anyone had—and knew as a man, not a legend. She had known his love for the outdoors, known him to be happiest when in nature, and she would have been especially moved by the letter she received from Isaac Jones of Lost Prairie, Arkansas, the man to whom Crockett had sold his watch, who returned the timepiece out of respect. Jones offered his sympathies, adding that with Crockett's loss, "freedom has been deprived of one of her bravest sons . . . To bemoan his fate, is to pay tribute of greatful respect to nature—he seemed to be her son."[60]

Although Crockett failed to garner the coveted "league of land" or fortune for his family, Elizabeth was eventually granted his soldier's share, and in 1854 she and a handful of family members and children followed his tracks from Tennessee to Texas, where they would live out their lives, and Crockett's dream, on the vast frontier.[61] Robert Patton Crockett, eldest son by Elizabeth, went earlier, heading to Texas in 1838 to volunteer his services in the army as his father had done. Elizabeth remained true to the memory of her husband, and was said to wear black until her own death, in 1860.[62]

John Wesley Crockett followed his father's trail to the United States Congress, where he served two consecutive terms beginning in 1837, winning the seat left open by the retired Adam Huntsman. John Wesley Crockett picked up where his obstinate father had left off, and, fittingly and ironically, in February of 1841, John Wesley drove through the passage of a land bill in many ways comparable to that which his father and Polk had compromised on back in 1829.[63] Apparently content with that

Ruins of the Church of the Alamo, San Antonio de Bexar. (Lithograph by C. B. Graham, after a drawing by Edward Everett. In government report by George W. Hughes, 1846, published as Senate Executive Document 32, 31st Congress. Daughters of the Republic of Texas Library, San Antonio.)

punctuation mark on his father's congressional career, John Wesley opted to retire at the end of his term in 1843.

SANTA ANNA WOULD FINALLY SAY of the storming and subduing of the Alamo, which took just a single hour, "it was but a small affair." He perused the carnage, hundreds of bodies strewn and smoldering, their "blackened and bloody faces disfigured by desperate death."[64] After briefly praising his troops for their courage, he ordered the dead defenders piled into three heaps, two smallish mounds outside the grounds, and one large central pyre for those slain within the Alamo walls.[65] Soldiers then scoured the countryside to collect dry wood, lugging it back in carts. With sufficient wood gathered, soldiers mounded men and wood in piles, scattered smaller pieces of kindling about, doused the mass with flammable fluids, and pyre by pyre, set the Alamo defenders ablaze. The flames rose high and the fires burned all through the day and then into night, spitting and smoldering for three full days, until vultures began circling over the mission and crowds gathered around the ashes and embers.[66] Fragments of bones and the curling remnants of charred flesh lay among the ashes, and "grease that had exuded from the bodies saturated the earth for several feet beyond the ashes and smoldering mesquite faggots."[67]

Somewhere high above, David Crockett's spirit drifted freely on the Texas wind, lofted away to immortality by the smoke of his funeral pyre.

Epilogue

D AVID CROCKETT'S DEATH AT THE ALAMO made him a martyr. In dying there and in that way, it was almost as if Crockett had said, "Well then, if I'm not going to make a fortune in this life—I might just as well become immortal and make my fortune in the next." And that's exactly what he did. Facts were shrouded in mythology almost immediately following the siege, as bogus reports began to circulate around Texas and abroad that Crockett had not fallen, but had been captured, taken prisoner, and brought to Mexico, where he was toiling away in a mine somewhere.[1]

Crockett's own publishers, Carey & Hart, were quick to capitalize on the fascination and uncertainty regarding the controversial frontiersman. Just two months after the fall of the Alamo, Philadelphia writer Richard Penn Smith wrote, and Carey & Hart published, the wholly fictional and anonymously written *Col. Crockett's Exploits and Adventures in Texas.* The first-person narrative, ostensibly penned by Crockett, included a very convincing preface, signed by Alex J. Dumas, claiming that the contents were the "authentic diary" of David Crockett discovered among the ruins at the Alamo by a Mexican general who subsequently died at San Jacinto.[2] Staring at an unsold pile of Crockett's legitimate (if cobbled together and poorly written) *Tour to the North and Down East,* Carey & Hart hurried *Texas Exploits* off to press, and it was considered genuine for many years, selling thousands of copies.[3] It was not until 1884 that the fabrication was exposed in print, but by that time generations had swallowed the diary as authentic, accepting and incorporating the tales and exploits into lore. A gullible public appeared more than ready to devour these fictions as memoir, and the farce became a virtual keystone on which the Crockett legend would be built.

Simultaneously, fuel arrived in the bound copies of the *Crockett Almanacs,* which first appeared in 1835, under Crockett's aegis.[4] Badly in need of money and reduced to hawking his own books for cash, the new author Crockett had produced the first two almanacs to coincide with his *Narrative* in 1834 and his *Tour* book in 1835, and the almanac contents were essentially reprints and reproductions drawn directly from that material. *The Almanacs* were therefore a fast and easy publishing venture, selling between 20,000 and 60,000 copies, and a clever foray into mass marketing.[5] Unfortunately for Crockett, while the sales sounded impressive and did advance his reputation, he failed to get rich from them. The high numbers were not lost on unscrupulous opportunists, either, who continued publishing counterfeits and imitations from the year of Crockett's death until 1856. The tales, presumably told by Crockett himself, became more and more outrageous, crude, bawdy, and downright offensive as the years went by, helping to buttress his legendary folk status.[6]

There were also the theatrical renditions and images of Crockett which created clear and identifiable images of the mythological figure. James Hackett had portrayed Nimrod Wildfire beginning in 1831, and by 1837, a woodcut made from a portrait by Ambrose Andrews, depicting Hackett as Wildfire, appeared on the cover of that year's *Davy Crockett Almanack of Wild Sports in the West.* The image shows Wildfire wearing

The Crockett Almanacs, *first published in 1834,*
contributed significantly to the Crockett legend and
mythology for many decades. (DAVID CROCKETT,
FRONTIERSMAN. *Unidentified artist, woodcut, 1837.*
Published in Davy Crockett's Almanack for 1837,
Nashville, 1837. Smithsonian National Portrait
Gallery, Washington, DC.)

the wildcat-skin hat we all associate with his image, complete with the tail on[7] (what appears to be a bobcat would eventually change, thanks to Disney, into a raccoon).

In 1872, another significant play appeared, this one called *Davy Crockett; Or, Be Sure You're Right, Then Go Ahead*. Written by Frank Murdock expressly for the actor Frank Mayo, the play became "probably the best known of the American frontier melodramas,"[8] and enjoyed a stupendous twenty-four-year run of more than 2,000 performances, including stints in New York, England, and as far west as Denver, where it finished in 1896, closing only when its lead actor died.[9]

For the next sixty years or so "Davy," both man and myth, hibernated, though the advent of motion pictures offered a new medium in which the legendary figure could appear. In 1909, a silent film entitled *Davy Crockett—in Hearts United* was released, starring Charles K. French as "Davy Crockett." A year later, Selig Polyscope brought out a film called *Davy Crockett*, and from 1911 to 1953 another half-dozen films were produced depicting Crockett as a hero of the Alamo or as an Indian fighter/ scout.[10]

In 1934 Constance Rourke wrote *Davy Crockett*, a clever and fascinating biography of Crockett that incorporated old yarns, folklore, and essentials of the fictitious almanacs into the historical facts of his life. One result of her book was to propel "Davy" into even greater "mythic status,"[11] further blurring the distinctions between the real man and the legendary character he was becoming.

The real paradigm shift arrived in 1954, however, when the profound medium of television ensured that lasting, even indelible images of Crockett would be forever branded into the American consciousness. Needing a heroic American character for initial episodes of the *Frontierland* series, executive producer and entrepreneurial visionary Walt Disney turned to screenwriter Tom Blackburn and ABC network producer Bill Walsh to fashion a three-episode life of their chosen vehicle—Crockett. The trilogy would take the form of "Davy Crockett, Indian Fighter," "Davy Crockett Goes to Congress," and "Davy Crockett at the Alamo." Fess Parker, a relatively unknown but handsome, clean-cut, and affable actor, took the role of Crockett, and on three otherwise obscure Wednesday evenings, December 15, 1954, January 26, 1955, and February 23, 1955, Davy Crockett strode into living rooms across America and neither he, nor the audiences who viewed him, would ever be the same.[12] Had Disney possessed even the vaguest notion of the phenomenon he was about to create, he certainly would never have killed off his hero in only the third episode.

Fess Parker became an instantaneous star (as well as the most enduring Crockett image—for millions of people, Fess Parker's face *is* the face of Davy Crockett), and by the end of the third show, Crockett was easily the most famous and recognizable pioneer in the annals of American history, eclipsing even his great frontier predecessor, Daniel Boone.[13] The unexpected success of the show created a windfall for Walt Disney and his new concept company and theme park, for in Crockett he had his first marketable, merchandisable, buckskin-wearing and tomahawk-toting action figure, and his marketing folks worked themselves, and the American public, into a frenzy that came to be called the Davy Crockett Craze. Every red-blooded American boy (and many girls, too) wanted to be Davy Crockett or act out scenes from the shows fighting Indians, and at its height nearly every kind of item imaginable (and some unimaginable) was on sale and associated with Davy Crockett: buckskin-fringed jackets, pants, even Davy Crockett underwear. The tools of Crockett's hunting trade were available, with wooden "Betsey" replicas, holstered pistols, and the trusty powder horn, and those were just the fashion accessories.[14]

Literally everything went Crockett—dining sets, lunchboxes, thermoses, and ice cream cartons, pajamas and bear rugs and chairs, puzzles and game boards and tricycles and bicycles, guitars and fiddles and even barbaque grills "for Frontier Living"—there was nothing the merchandisers wouldn't put the Crockett name or picture on.[15] Then came the biggest hit of all, that enduring symbol of the frontier, the coonskin cap. Many frontiersmen, including Daniel Boone, had worn the practical hat, and "in 1776, when Benjamin Franklin had journeyed to France he donned a coonskin cap instead of a powdered wig,"[16] presumably to illustrate the significant class distinction between title-conscious Europe and pioneering, up-from-your-bootstraps America. Disney made an excellent choice, and of all the merchandise, the coonskin cap became the biggest-selling item of them all—practically every kid in America wanted one, and a large percentage of them got one.

The economic tally was even more impressive than the 105 bears the real Crockett said he killed in a single year. By May 1955, the American consumer had dropped more than $100 million on Davy Crockett paraphernalia, and by the end of the initial craze (which was relatively short—not much more than a year) the number surpassed $300 million, a staggering figure equivalent to over $3 billion in today's dollars).[17] During the run, the humble "gentleman from the cane" rose to megastardom, becoming the most commercially lucrative individual figure in history, bigger even than GI Joe, Superman, and Spider-Man.[18]

Crockett himself would have chuckled heartily, and with great personal satisfaction, to see what a stir his image created more than a century after his death. But he had already known there was a public yearning for his image back in 1834 when he posed for John Gadsby Chapman. What neither Crockett nor even Disney could ever have predicted was that Davy Crockett himself would become the very vehicle to deliver what has come to be known as the "television generation."[19] It took the media magic of Crockett and everything he represented—duty, patriotism, the hope and desire for freedom, heroism—to usher in the confluence of entertainment, commercial products, advertising, and the selling and buying, whole-hog, of Walt Disney's version (and vision) of the American dream. So what if Disney blended fact and fiction? This was, after all, just entertainment. It didn't matter whether Crockett ever actually wore a coonskin cap, whether he went down swinging at the Alamo, taking thirty or so Mexicans with him as he bashed wildly with his rifle butt. What mattered was that America now had a certifiable, clearly identifiable, enduring, and irrefutable symbol of the frontier, of the past, of the quintessential American story.

Even when alternative "endings" to Crockett's life surfaced, through biographies and scholarly research, it was far too late for the mainstream to consider them, much less embrace them. The simultaneous enlarging mythology of the Alamo itself required heroes, brave defenders, and underdogs, dying together for the common cause of freedom.[20] And the timing could not have been better to reinforce such patriotic notions; just a decade removed from World War II,[21] Americans sought stories and heroic figures that underscored their inherent rightness and gave them a version of America they wanted to believe in while at the same time self-promoting the myth being created.

In 1960 John Wayne took his shot at Crockett, producing and directing *The Alamo*, a longtime dream and one that cost over $7 million to make, a gargantuan budget for that time. It was worth every penny, for his three-plus hour epic delivers a much more real and complicated Crockett than Disney managed. In essence, to metamorphose into Crockett all John Wayne needed to do was play himself, for the Duke was "an American legend in his own right."[22] Wayne, a political conservative, saw in the tale of the Alamo the story of America itself, replete with plenty of clichés: good triumphing over evil, the inherent rightness of Manifest Destiny, black-and-white notions of right and wrong, and real men doing manly things. His Crockett is paternal, patriotic, and prudent, possessing a raw wisdom that can only be wrought in a rugged life outdoors, not in a schoolroom. Like Wayne himself, his rendition of Crockett is of a straight-shooter and a no-nonsense straight-talker, brashly independent, even possessing—as Crockett did himself—a sharp sense of humor. In the film, Travis questions Crockett's motivations for coming to Texas in the first place, to which Wayne has him reply, "My Tennesseans . . . think they came to Texas to hunt and get drunk." Of course, Wayne then has Crockett explain that he is at the Alamo to fight for liberty and justice.[23] To deal with Crockett's last minutes on earth, Wayne has the noble patriot, pierced by several Mexican swords, running with an ignited torch and leaping in to detonate the powder supply, gloriously taking a bunch of the enemy with him.

The most recent cinematic incarnation is actor Billy Bob Thornton's 2004 Crockett in the Imagine Entertainment (interestingly, a Disney Company) film *The Alamo*. Thornton conveys a believable, likable, raw Crockett who is keenly aware of his internal dilemma, that of being trapped within the confines of his own legend. Director John Lee Hancock also intimates that Crockett's rationale for coming to Texas in the first place has more to do with land-grabbing and a political future than freedom-fighting. An early scene places Crockett with Houston in 1835, where the two men are at a theater with other politicians and society folks to watch a production of *The Lion of the West*. Crockett toasts Tennessee, and the hard-drinking Houston says, "to hell with Tennessee, here's to Texas." He then goes on to urge Crockett to come see for himself, that the new republic of Texas is like Tennessee was before it was settled, that there is more land available than one can possibly imagine. Crockett smiles as Houston leaves, then asks wryly, "Hey Sam—you figure this new republic's gonna need a president?" The light moment underscores, accurately, that while Tennessee appeared played-out politically for Crockett, Texas was all about opportunity.

In a poignant scene inside the Alamo, Crockett and the ailing Bowie meet one night, standing by the palisade wall, Crockett staring out at the open land. Bowie teases him about his wildcat-skin hat, asking him why he isn't wearing it and whether it "crawled off," to which Crockett admits he only started wearing it when it became popularized by the Nimrod Wildfire character. He then pauses and points out, quite seriously, "The truth is, people expect things." He's been giving them what they want for so long that it has begun to weigh on him. Bowie nods, but goads him further, showing that he, too, is familiar with the fictions. "Which was tougher," he asks, grinning, "jumping the Mississippi or riding that lightning bolt?" Cannon fire startles them both, and they flinch, prompting Bowie to ask, "Can you catch a cannon ball?"

Billy Bob Thornton's Crockett pauses beautifully, a man completely aware of his own ironies and paradoxes, of his own mortality, a man who can no longer exist outside his own legend. He looks toward the walls and speaks with moving honesty to Bowie. "If it was just me, simple ol' David from Tennessee, I might drop over that wall some night and take my chances—But that 'Davy Crockett' feller . . . They're all watching him."

The finest Crockett moment of the film comes on the eve of the attack, as the band from the Mexican army continues to torment the besieged men with the incessant playing of *Degüello*, the "no quarter" death march that signifies the act of beheading or throat-cutting. The dirge is unnerving the defenders, but suddenly David Crockett knows exactly what to do. He grabs his fiddle, ascends the wall, and proceeds to answer the band with a sweetly whimsical harmonizing that is just discordant enough to sound slightly irreverent. It's a magnificent performance, Crockett alone on the wall, utterly exposed yet unafraid and defiant, keenly aware of his performance yet simultaneously natural, honest, and true to himself. The man and the legend merge into one figure, silhouetted there on the wall, against a fiery Texas sunset, playing his fiddle, entertaining people. All eyes and ears are upon him as he finishes the song, quieting the Mexican band. Columns and columns of orderly soldiers stare back in amazement at the singular man on the wall who has managed to command the attention of all present, each and every defender and the entire Mexican army. Finally, an older soldier knowingly nudges a younger compatriot next to him on the shoulder. He smiles and nods, whispering to him a single word like a gift, telling him who he has just been fortunate enough to witness, as if with the very utterance of his name he will live forever in memory, immortalized:

"*Crockett!*"

No doubt Thornton's Crockett will not be the last. Such is the nature of men who become legends, and especially the nature of

Frank Mayo starred as Crockett in an amazing twenty-four-year run
of the play Davy Crockett; Or, Be Sure You're Right, Then
Go Ahead, *by Frank Murdock and Frank Mayo. (Score from*
"Davy Crockett March." Rose Music Collection, Tennessee
State Library and Archives, Nashville.)

David Crockett of the state of Tennessee, who wrestled bears, spun yarns, managed to get himself elected to offices for which he was only dubiously qualified, and perished, achieving martyrdom and immortality. His is an image and a story that refuses to die. Crockett, in the end, transcends the facts of his own mortal life to become an enduring symbol of possibility, remembered not for his deeds or his greatness as a head of state but for the sheer tenacity of his spirit, for what he came to represent. Benjamin Franklin became a model of the self-made man, his life the "classic American success story—the story of a man rising from the most obscure of origins to wealth and international preeminence."[24] Crockett knew the story well (among the few personal possessions he took to Texas is thought to have been Franklin's *Autobiography*),[25] and he attempted to live it himself and very nearly did, and one can only speculate on what he might have achieved had things turned out differently that cold morning of March 6, 1836. He never achieved the wealth, and in that respect he failed, but he managed the international prominence, at least in name and in memory. In the end David Crockett's importance lives on, not in what he achieved but because he never stopped trying, he never quit and he never lost hope. He kept his eye on that western horizon, pulled his hat down tight, gritted his teeth, and rode on into the blazing sunset, come what may.

NOTES

Prologue

1. David Crockett, *A Narrative of the Life of David Crockett of the State of Tennessee: A Facsimile Edition with Annotations and an Introduction by James A. Shackford and Stanley J. Folmsbee* (Knoxville, 1973), 11.

Chapter 1: Origins

Direct Crockett quotes in this chapter are taken from his *Narrative*, unless otherwise noted.

1. There remains ongoing discussion regarding Crockett's heritage, including the possibility that he is the descendant of a French Huguenot named Antoine de Crocketagne, who immigrated to England, then Ireland, in the seventeenth century. For a detailed discussion of this uncertain lineage, see James A. Shackford, *David Crockett: The Man and the Legend* (Chapel Hill, NC, 1956), 293n. Also see Crockett, *Narrative*, 14; Stanley J. Folmsbee and Anna Grace Catron, "The Early Career of David Crockett," *East Tennessee Historical Society's Publications* 28 (1956): 59–60; William C. Davis, *Three Roads to the Alamo* (New York, 1998), 9; and Robert V. Remini, *Andrew Jackson and His Indian Wars* (New York, 2001), 11.

2. Quoted in Folmsbee and Catron, "Early Career," 59.

3. Richard Boyd Hauck, *Crockett: A Bio-Bibliography* (Westport, CT, 1982), 9.

4. Ibid, 9. Shackford, *Man and Legend*, 3–5.

5. Davis, *Three Roads*, 10. Hauck, *Bio-Bibliography*, 9. Folmsbee and Catron, "Early Career," 59–60.

6. Shackford, *Man and Legend*, 4.

7. Hauck, *Bio-Bibliography*, 9. Shackford, *Man and Legend*, 5.

8. Davis, *Three Roads*, 12. Mark Derr, *The Frontiersman: The Real Life and the Many Legends of Davy Crockett* (New York, 1993), 40. Folmsbee and Catron, "Early Career," 60.

9. Derr, *Frontiersman*, 40–41.

10. Shackford, *Man and Legend*, 7.

11. Ibid, 5.

12. Derr, *Frontiersman*, 41.

13. Ibid. Shackford, *Man and Legend*, 6.

14. Davis, *Three Roads*, 13.

15. Folmsbee and Catron, "Early Career," 61–62. Hauck, *Bio-Bibliography*, 11.

16. Crockett, *Narrative*, 22.

17. Shackford, *Man and Legend*, 6.

18. Hauck, *Bio-Bibliography*, 12. H. W. Brands, *The First American: The Life and Times of Benjamin Franklin* (New York, 2000), 20.

19. Crockett, *Narrative*, 23.

20. Shackford, *Man and Legend*, 8–9. Davis, *Three Roads*, 16.

21. Crockett, *Narrative*, 24.

22. Davis, *Three Roads*, 16–17. Joseph J. Arpad, *David Crockett: An Original Legendary Eccentricity and Early American Character* (Duke University, 1968), 171–72. Folmsbee and Catron, "Early Career," 62.

23. Derr, *Frontiersman*, 46. Davis, *Three Roads*, 17.

24. Crockett, *Narrative*, 29.

25. Ibid, 31.

26. Ibid, 34.

Chapter 2: Runaway

Direct Crockett quotes in this chapter are taken from his *Narrative*, unless otherwise noted.

1. Arpad, *Original Legendary*, 130.

2. Shackford, *Man and Legend*, 10.

3. Crockett, *Narrative*, 35.

4. Ibid, 36.

5. Ibid, 37.

6. Ibid.

7. Ibid, 38.

8. Ibid.

9. Ibid, 38–39.

10. Ibid, 40.

11. Shackford, *Man and Legend*, 10–11.

12. Crockett, *Narrative*, 41.

13. Ibid, 42.
14. Ibid, 9.
15. Shackford, *Man and Legend*, 11. Crockett, *Narrative*, 42.
16. Crockett, *Narrative*, 43.
17. Crockett appears to have dropped a year in his narrative, claiming that he was "almost fifteen" at this point, when actually he would have been nearly sixteen. See Crockett's *Narrative*, 43, 22n. See also Shackford, *Man and Legend*, 11 and 294n.

Chapter 3: The Dutiful Son Becomes a Man

Direct Crockett quotes in this chapter are taken from his *Narrative*, unless otherwise noted.

1. Crockett, *Narrative*, 45.
2. Ibid.
3. Ibid, 47.
4. Ibid.
5. Ibid, 47–48.
6. Stanley Folmsbee, in his marginal annotations of Crockett's *Narrative*, points out in note 12 on page 49 that Crockett exaggerates his ignorance for political reasons. Time and again, Crockett illustrates that he was an incredibly adaptable, sharp, and inquisitive learner and astute student of human nature. His later letters show that he significantly increased his early education over time, and especially his writing skill, almost exclusively through self-study.
7. *Marriage License and Bond Book 1792–1840* (Jefferson County, TN). Crockett, *Narrative*, 49–50, 14n.
8. Shackford, *Man and Legend*, 13. Hauck, *Bio-Bibliography*, 14.
9. Crockett, *Narrative*, 62, 10n. Folmsbee notes the many references to Crockett's presence when wolf scalps were brought in, recorded, and purchased, in *Lawrence County Minutes* 1818–1823. Shackford, *Man and Legend*, 39, 298n.
10. Crockett, *Narrative*, 65, 16n.
11. Ibid, 67. Folmsbee and Catron. "Early Career," 63n. Two days have passed between the Finley altercation and the actual performance of the ceremony.
12. Crockett, *Narrative*, 68.
13. Ibid, 20n. Folmsbee and Catron. "Early Career," 64.
14. Shackford, *Man and Legend*, 295n.
15. Davis, *Three Roads*, 25.
16. Hauck, *Bio-Bibliography*, 17.

Chapter 4: "My Dander Was Up"

Direct Crockett quotes in this chapter are taken from his *Narrative,* unless otherwise noted.

1. Davis, *Three Roads,* 25.
2. Robert V. Remini, *Andrew Jackson and His Indian Wars* (New York, 2001), 5–6.
3. Davis, *Three Roads,* 25. Derr, *Frontiersman,* 59–60.
4. Hauck, *Bio-Bibliography,* 19. Remini, *Indian Wars,* 50. John Sugden, *Tecumseh: A Life* (New York, 1997), 352.
5. Shackford, *Man and Legend,* 18–19.
6. Remini, *Indian Wars,* 6.
7. Ibid, 3–4.
8. Ibid, 1. Sugden, *Tecumseh: A Life,* 237.
9. H. S. Halbert and T. S. Ball, *The Creek War of 1813 and 1814* (Tuscaloosa, AL, Alabama Press, 1895), 156–57. The actual number dead was 275, not the 500 or "half a thousand" quoted by Halbert and Ball.
10. Remini, *Indian Wars,* 6.
11. Crockett, *Narrative,* 72.
12. Ibid, 73.
13. Andrew Burstein, *The Passions of Andrew Jackson* (New York, 2003), 94–97.
14. Remini, *Indian Wars,* 15.
15. Crockett, *Narrative,* 74.
16. Folmsbee and Catron, "Early Career," 64.
17. Crockett, *Narrative,* 75.
18. The account of this expedition is drawn primarily from Crockett's *Narrative,* 71–82, and Halbert and Ball, *Creek War,* 266–78.
19. Hauck, *Bio-Bibliography,* 21–22.
20. Remini, *Indian Wars,* 61.
21. Ibid.
22. Ibid, 60. John Buchanan, *Jackson's Way: Andrew Jackson and the People of the Western Waters* (New York, 2001), 203. S. Putnam Waldo, *Memoirs of Andrew Jackson* (Hartford, CT, 1820), 1–69.
23. Quoted in Remini, *Indian Wars,* 64.
24. Crockett, *Narrative,* 90.
25. Halbert and Ball, *Creek War,* 269–70.
26. Quoted in Shackford, *Man and Legend,* 26.
27. Ibid. Halbert and Ball, *Creek War,* 270.
28. Crockett, *Narrative,* 94.
29. Hauck, *Bio-Bibliography,* 25. John Reid and John Henry Eaton, *Life of Andrew Jackson* (Tuscaloosa, AL, 1974), 89–91. Folmsbee and Catron, "Early Career," 64.

30. Remini, *Indian Wars*, 70.

31. Burstein, *Passions of Andrew Jackson*, 102. James Parton, *The Life of Andrew Jackson* (New York, 1862), vol. 1, 463.

32. Crockett, *Narrative*, 96, 31n.

33. Remini, *Indian Wars*, 74.

34. Ibid.

Chapter 5: "Mounted Gunman"

Direct Crockett quotes in this chapter are taken from his *Narrative*, unless otherwise noted.

1. Remini, *Indian Wars*, 75.

2. Responding to the severity of his fighting tactics in battles such as Horseshoe Bend, and his unyielding nature as a negotiator, the Indians nicknamed Jackson "Sharp Knife" or "Pointed Arrow."

3. Remini, *Indian Wars*, 75.

4. Ibid. A detailed description of the "Holy Ground" is provided in Halbert and Ball, *Creek War*, 246–49.

5. Quoted in Remini, *Indian Wars*, 75.

6. Ibid, 76.

7. Buchanan, *Jackson's Way*, 287–88.

8. Ibid, 77. Sean Michael O'Brien, *In Bitterness and Tears: Andrew Jackson's Destruction of the Creeks and Seminoles* (Westport, CT, 2003), 146.

9. James L. Haley, *Sam Houston* (Norman, OK, 2002), 15.

10. Ibid, 15. Buchanan, *Jackson's Way*, 289.

11. Haley, *Sam Houston*, 15.

12. Quoted in Burstein, *Passions of Andrew Jackson*, 105. Parton, *Life of Andrew Jackson*, vol. 1, 512–20.

13. O'Brien, *Bitterness and Tears*, 150.

14. Ibid. Buchanan, *Jackson's Way*, 291.

15. Quoted in O'Brien, *Bitterness and Tears*, 150. Frank Owsley, Jr. *Struggle for the Gulf Borderlands: The Creek War and the Battle of New Orleans* (Gainsville, FL, 1981), 81–82.

16. On August 9, 1814, Jackson imposed the Treaty of Fort Jackson on the Creek Nation. On September 14 to October 4, 1816, he signed a provisional treaty with the Cherokees, and on September 20, 1816, he signed a treaty with the Chickasaws. There would be a string of such subjugations and treaty signings through 1820, the treaty with the Choctaws.

17. Remini, *Indian Wars*, 81.

18. The Florida expedition is largely based on Crockett, *Narrative*, 101–13. Halbert and Ball, *Creek War*, 143–76, 280–84, also offers an extensive and detailed account of the entire campaign.

19. Folmsbee and Catron, "Early Career," 70.
20. The expedition into the swamps of the Escambia River is based largely on Crockett, *Narrative*, 115–24.
21. Hauck, *Bio-Bibliography*, 26–27. Halbert and Ball, *Creek War*, 280.
22. Shackford, *Man and Legend*, 30.
23. Hauck, *Bio-Bibliography*, 27.
24. Though Crockett calls it "The old expression," the origin of the phrase is actually attributed to him in more than one place. See the *Dictionary of American English*, Charles E. Funk, *A Hog on Ice and Other Expressions* (New York, 1948), 36, and Folmsbee annotation, *Narrative*, 118.
25. It is unclear why the men would not eat the horses, which, even in their emaciated condition, would have offered a good deal of meat. Taboo against the practice may have prevented them from consuming their own mounts.
26. See Crockett, *Narrative*, 124, 17n, for a discussion of the discrepancy in his rank. Also, Folmsbee and Catron, "Early Career," 71n.
27. Davis, *Three Roads*, 34.

Chapter 6: Trials on the Homefront

Direct Crockett quotes in this chapter are taken from his *Narrative*, unless otherwise noted.

1. Shackford, *Man and Legend*, 33. Davis, *Three Roads*, 63, 600n.
2. Ibid.
3. Davis, *Three Roads*, 64. Folmsbee and Catron, "Early Career," 71. Shackford, *Man and Legend*, 34.
4. Derr, *Frontiersman*, 79–80.
5. Ibid, 79. Shackford, *Man and Legend*, 281–82. Descriptions of David Crockett's physical appearance are few and not wholly consistent or reliable. Many are based on one or more of the portraits painted of him, and none of those was done before his entry into Congress. See Shackford, *Man and Legend*, appendix 4, 281–91, for an in-depth analysis. There are numerous references to Crockett's "rosy cheeks," including his own comment in page 59 of his *Narrative*, and in his letter to James Blackburn of February 5, 1828, Tennessee State Library and Archives, Nashville.
6. Shackford, *Man and Legend*, 34–35. Derr, *Frontiersman*, 80.
7. Shackford, *Man and Legend*, 35; Jessie A. Henderson, "Unmarked Historic Spots of Franklin County," *East Tennessee Historical Magazine*, second series, 3 (January 1935): 117–18.
8. Hauck, *Bio-Bibliography*, 30.
9. Crockett, *Narrative*, 132.
10. Ibid.
11. *American State Papers, Indian Affairs* (Washington, DC, 1832–1834). See Shackford, *Man and Legend*, 37, and Folmsbee annotations in Crockett, *Narrative*, 132–33.

12. Torrence, *Crockett*, 12; Crockett, *Narrative*, 127, 8n.
13. Robert M. Torrence and Robert L. Whittenburg, *Colonel Davy Crockett, a Genealogy* (Washington, DC, 1956), 12.
14. Ibid, 89. Derr, *Frontiersman*, 89.
15. Shackford, *Man and Legend*, 38.
16. Crockett, *Narrative*, 135. Folmsbee notes in annotation 25 that Crockett exaggerates here, and that his judgments needed entire court approval.
17. Davis, *Three Roads*, 68.
18. Arpad, *Original Legendary*, 135–39. Davis, *Three Roads*, 68.
19. Derr, *Frontiersman*, 92.
20. Quoted in Derr, *Frontiersman*, 93.
21. Crockett, *Narrative*, 141.

Chapter 7: "The Gentleman from the Cane"

Direct Crockett quotes in this chapter are taken from his *Narrative*, unless otherwise noted.

1. See Crockett, *Narrative*, 143, annotation 11, and Davis, *Three Roads*, 73 and 601n. Crockett milks this story and uses it on more than one occasion.
2. Shackford, *Man and Legend*, 47.
3. Derr, *Frontiersman*, 97.
4. Shackford, *Man and Legend*, 47.
5. Ibid, 48–49. Folmsbee and Catron, "Early Career," 72.
6. Davis, *Three Roads*, 78.
7. Ibid. Shackford, *Man and Legend*, 52–53. Folmsbee and Catron, "Early Career," 73.
8. The origin of this story is the book *Life and Adventures of Colonel David Crockett of West Tennessee*, ghostwritten by Matthew St. Clair Clarke. (Cincinnati, 1833). See also Shackford, *Man and Legend*, 52–53, and Folmsbee and Catron, "Early Career," 73.
9. Crockett, *Narrative*, 145.
10. Quoted in Davis, *Three Roads*, 76, 601n. Also see John Jacobs to editor of *Morristown Gazette*, November 22, 1884, Tennessee State Library and Archives, Nashville. Derr, *Frontiersman*, 93, 276n.
11. Shackford, *Man and Legend*, 48.
12. Davis, *Three Roads*, 72.
13. Crockett, *Narrative*, 147, 1n.
14. Norma Hayes Bagnall, *On Shaky Ground: The New Madrid Earthquakes of 1811–1812* (Columbia, MO, 1996), 28–40. Hauck, *Bio-Bibliography*, 34.
15. Ibid. Hauck provides an interesting discussion on multiple meanings of the terms "canebrake" and "haricane."

16. The account of Crockett's trip upriver to McLemore's Bluff is drawn primarily from Crockett's *Narrative*, 147–54.

17. Derr, *Frontiersman*, 108.

18. Shackford, *Man and Legend*, 55.

19. Ibid, 55–56. Shackford describes the exact minutiae of these judgments. See also Derr, *Frontiersman*, 104.

20. Shackford, *Man and Legend*, 58.

21. Ibid.

22. *Journal of the House of Representatives*, Second Session, Fourteenth General Assembly, 1822, p. 129. Quoted in Shackford, *Man and Legend*, 57.

23. Ibid.

24. Ibid.

25. The "Christmas guns" anecdote is based on Crockett, *Narrative*, 159–60.

26. Hauck, *Bio-Bibliography*, 35. Richard Slotkin, *Regeneration Through Violence: The Mythology of the American Frontier, 1600–1860* (Middletown, CT, 1973), 555–56.

27. Shackford, *Man and Legend*, 63.

28. Crockett, *Narrative*, 166–67.

29. Ibid, 169.

30. Shackford, *Man and Legend*, 64, 300n. Shackford points out in a note that the most accurate authentication for this story comes from a contemporary of Crockett's, one Colonel Robert I. Chester. For Chester's rendition of the story, see H. S. Turner, "Andrew Jackson and David Crockett: Reminiscences of Colonel Chester," *Magazine of American History* 27 (May 1892): 385–87.

31. Shackford, *Man and Legend*, 64. Davis, *Three Roads*, 603n. Davis offers an interesting note that clarifies the traditional ordering of stump speeches, observing that the men often alternated, in which case Crockett may not have had to ask to go first. Also see Turner, "Reminiscences of Colonel Chester," 385–87.

32. Shackford, *Man and Legend*, 66.

33. Ibid.

34. Ibid. Derr, *Frontiersman*, 117–18; Davis, *Three Roads*, 87.

35. Parton, *Life of Andrew Jackson*, vol. 1, 136, quoted in Burstein, *Passions of Andrew Jackson*, 27.

36. Davis, *Three Roads*, 88.

37. Shackford, *Man and Legend*, 69; Davis, *Three Roads*, 88.

38. Quoted in Shackford, *Man and Legend*, 69.

39. Folmsbee and Catron, "Early Career," 78–83.

40. Shackford, *Man and Legend*, 70–71, quoting *National Banner and Nashville Whig*, September 27, 1824.

Chapter 8: "Neck or Nothing"

Direct Crockett quotes in this chapter are taken from his *Narrative*, unless otherwise noted.

1. Stanley J. Folmsbee and Anna Grace Catron, "David Crockett: Congressman," *East Tennessee Historical Society Publications* 28 (1957), 40–41.
2. Circular of 1824, Tennessee Historical Society, Nashville.
3. Folmsbee and Catron, "David Crockett: Congressman," 40.
4. Shackford, *Man and Legend*, 73–74. Hauck, *Bio-Bibliography*, 39.
5. Folmsbee and Catron, "David Crockett: Congressman," 41.
6. Crockett, *Narrative*, 173, 20n.
7. This bear hunting anecdote is based on Crockett, *Narrative*, 185–91.
8. See Shackford, *Man and Legend*, 77 and 301n, for testimonials of Crockett's expertise as a hunter and marksman.
9. Derr, *Frontiersman*, 134.
10. Crockett's rescue and his fortuitous arrival in Memphis is recorded in James D. Davis, *History of the City of Memphis* (Memphis, 1873), 146–50. Crockett, *Narrative*, 195–200.
11. Shackford, *Man and Legend*, 79.
12. Derr, *Frontiersman*, 136.
13. Crockett, *Narrative*, 201–2.
14. Derr, *Frontiersman*, 139.
15. Shackford, *Man and Legend*, 81–83.
16. Davis, *History of Memphis*, 150–51, 176. Shackford, *Man and Legend*, 83, 302n.
17. Shackford, *Man and Legend*, 83.
18. Derr, *Frontiersman*, 140.
19. Crockett, *Narrative*, 204.
20. Stanley, J. Folmsbee, and Anna Grace Catron, "David Crockett and West Tennessee," *West Tennessee Historical Society Papers* 28 (1974): 9n, from election returns of 1827.

Chapter 9: Political Reality

1. Folmsbee and Catron, "David Crockett Congressman," 44. Davis, *Three Roads*, 123. Shackford, *Man and Legend*, 84–86.
2. Shackford, *Man and Legend*, 84. Derr, *Frontiersman*, 143.
3. Shackford, *Man and Legend*, 84–85.
4. Quoted in Shackford, *Man and Legend*, 86 and 303n. For a complete account of this duel, see James A. Shackford, "David Crockett and North Carolina," *North Carolina Historical Review*, 28: 298–315. Also see J. R. Hicklin, "The Carson-Vance Duel," *The State* [North Carolina], 6 (December 10, 1938): 9.
5. Davis, *Three Roads*, 126, 609n. Arpad, *Original Legendary*, 188.

6. David Crockett to James Blackburn, February 5, 1828, Tennessee State Library and Archives.

7. Davis, *Three Roads*, 126.

8. Derr, *Frontiersman*, 144.

9. Quoted in Shackford, *Man and Legend*, 88.

10. Quoted in Shackford, *Man and Legend*, 89 and 303n.

11. Derr, *Frontiersman*, 144–45. James Sterling Young, *The Washington Community: 1800–1828* (New York, 1966): 98–107.

12. Derr, *Frontiersman*, 145. *Jackson* [Tennessee] *Gazette*, January 31, 1829.

13. Shackford, *Man and Legend*, 88. Hauck, *Bio-Bibliography*, 43.

14. Derr, *Frontiersman*, 142.

15. Crockett to James L. Totten, February 11, 1828, Crockett Papers, Special Collections, University of Tennessee.

16. Letter from Crockett to Mr. Seal, March 11, 1828, Crockett Papers, Special Collection, University of Texas. Quoted in Davis, *Three Roads*.

17. Quoted in Davis, *Three Roads*, 129. Folmsbee and Catron, "David Crockett, Congressman," 45. Shackford, *Man and Legend*, 89.

18. Shackford, *Man and Legend*, 89. Folmsbee and Catron, "David Crockett: Congressman," 45.

19. Derr, *Frontiersman*, 147–48. Folmsbee and Catron, "David Crockett: Congressman," 45. Shackford, *Man and Legend*, 87–89, 303n.

20. Duff Green Papers. Southern Historical Collection of the University of North Carolina.

21. Josephine Seaton, *William Winston Seaton of the National Intelligencer: A Biographical Sketch*. (Boston, 1871), 184. Derr, *Frontiersman*, 152.

22. Derr, *Frontiersman*, 123.

23. Hauck, *Bio-Bibliography*, 42. Folmsbee and Catron, "David Crockett: Congressman," 47.

24. Ibid, 47–48. Derr, *Frontiersman*, 150. Shackford, *Man and Legend*, 90–91.

25. Quoted in Folmsbee and Catron, "David Crockett: Congressman," 48. Derr, *Frontiersman*, 150. *Register of Debates in Congress*, vol. 4, part 2 (Washington, DC, 1827–1828): 2,519.

26. *Register of Debates in Congress*, vol. 4, part 2: 2,519.

27. Shackford, *Man and Legend*, 91.

28. Derr, *Frontiersman*, 151.

29. Davis, *Three Roads*, 133–34. Derr, *Frontiersman*, 153. Folmsbee and Catron, "David Crockett and West Tennessee," 11, 11n.

30. Derr, *Frontiersman*, 153. Folmsbee and Catron, "David Crockett, Congressman," 48–49.

31. *Jackson* [Tennessee] *Gazette*, January 31, 1829.

32. Shackford, *Man and Legend*, 125.

33. *Nashville Republican*, March 18, 1828. Quoted in Davis, *Three Roads*, 122. Derr, *Frontiersman*, 146.

34. *Register of Debates in Congress*, vol. 5: 162.

35. Folmsbee and Catron, "David Crockett: Congressman," 55–56. Derr, *Frontiersman*, 155.

36. Letter from James K. Polk to Davison McMillen, January 16, 1829, in Herbert Weaver, ed., *Correspondence of James K. Polk*, vol. 1, 1817–1832 (Nashville, 1969), 229–231, 231n.

37. Ibid, 230.

38. *Register of Debates in Congress*, vol 5: 210.

39. Davis, *Three Roads*, 139.

40. Letter from James K. Polk to Davison McMillen, January 16, 1829, in Weaver, *Correspondence of James K. Polk*, vol. 1, 230.

41. David Crockett in *Jackson* [Tennessee] *Gazette*, March 14, 21, 28, 1829.

42. Crockett to George Patton, January 27, 1829, Miscellaneous Collection, Tennessee Historical Society.

43. Quoted in Burstein, *Passions of Andrew Jackson*, 173.

Chapter 10: Crockett's Declaration of Independence

1. Davis, *Three Roads*, 165. Promissory note, February 24, 1829, Panhandle-Plains Historical Museum Research Center, Canyon, TX.

2. *Jackson* [Tennessee] *Gazette*, March 7, 1829. Folmsbee and Catron, "David Crockett and West Tennessee," 14.

3. Derr, *Frontiersman*, 162. Folmsbee and Catron, "David Crockett and West Tennessee," 14n, quoted in Shackford, *Man and Legend*, 125.

4. Davis, *History of Memphis*, 110–11.

5. Ibid, 111.

6. J. M. Keating, *History of the City of Memphis and Shelby County, Tennessee* (Syracuse, 1880), 175–76.

7. Haley, *Sam Houston*, 60; Crockett to Gales & Seaton, April 18, 1829, Personal Miscellaneous Papers, New York Public Library.

8. Davis, *Three Roads*, 168.

9. Folmsbee and Catron, "David Crockett and West Tennessee," 14. Derr, *Frontiersman*, 163.

10. Arpad, *Original Legendary* 131 and 193–96. Davis, *Three Roads*, 169.

11. Catherine L. Albanese, "Citizen Crockett: Myth, History, and Nature Religion." *Soundings: An Interdisciplinary Journal*, 61 (1978): 89–90.

12. Shackford, *Man and Legend*, 101.

13. Quoted in Shackford, *Man and Legend*, 102. *Register of Debates in Congress*, 7: 391.

14. Shackford, *Man and Legend*, 103.

15. Derr, *Frontiersman*, 168.

16. Crockett to Hugh Nelson, January 24, 1830, Tennessee Historical Society, Miscellaneous Collection, Tennessee State Library and Archives.

17. Folmsbee and Catron, "David Crockett: Congressman," 62.

18. *Register of Debates in Congress,* vol. 6: 583.

19. Ibid, 716–17. Folmsbee and Catron, "David Crockett: Congressman," 60–61.

20. Ibid.

21. Ibid.

22. Davis, *Three Roads,* 174. Shackford, *Man and Legend,* 110.

23. Remini, *Indian Wars,* 115.

24. Ibid, 233.

25. Ibid, 237. Davis, *Three Roads,* 176. Burstein, *Passions of Andrew Jackson,* 186–88.

26. Remini, *Indian Wars,* 234.

27. Ibid, 234. Burstein, *Passions of Andrew Jackson,* 187.

28. Quoted in Remini, *Indian Wars,* 232.

29. Quoted in Remini, *Indian Wars,* 236.

30. Crockett, *Narrative,* 206.

31. Remini, *Indian Wars,* 237.

32. Crockett, *Narrative,* 206.

33. *Speeches on the Passage of the Bill for the Removal of the Indians Delivered in the Congress of the United States* (Boston: 1830). There is controversy over whether the speech was ever actually given—and whether Crockett was the sole author of the speech. But it was published in the above citation under "A Sketch of the Remarks of Hon. David Crockett." For discussion, see Shackford, *Man and Legend,* 116, 304n, and Folmsbee and Catron, "David Crockett" Congressman," 63–64.

34. Folmsbee and Catron, "David Crockett: Congressman," 64.

35. Arpad, *Original Legendary,* 33–34. Davis, *Three Roads,* 177.

36. Alexis de Tocqueville, *Journey to America,* trans. by George Lawrence (Garden City, NY, 1971), 267–68. As a nobleman and French political dignitary, Tocqueville unsurprisingly argued against universal suffrage, remarking with incredulity that the people of Tennessee would have sent as their representative in Congress a man with "no education," who "could read only with difficulty, had no property, no fixed dwelling, but spent his time hunting, selling game for a living, and spending his whole life in the woods." Tocqueville was equally unimpressed with Sam Houston and perplexed that someone who had "risen from his own exertions" would be elected governor of a state. Toqueville's aristocratic mind could not comprehend how on earth voters would "wish to be represented by people of their own sort."

37. Arpad, *Original Legendary* 35–37, 48–49, 73, 193. M. J. Heale, "The Role of the Frontier in Jacksonian Politics: David Crockett and the Myth of the Self-Made Man," *Western Historical Quarterly,* vol. 4 (October 1973): 406.

38. Davis, *Three Roads,* 178.

39. Shackford, *Man and Legend,* 118.

40. Davis, *Three Roads*, 179.

41. Quoted in Shackford, *Man and Legend*, 112.

42. *Jackson* [Tennessee] *Gazette*, March 27, 1830.

43. Quoted in Shackford, *Man and Legend*, 130.

44. Burstein, *Passions of Andrew Jackson*, 173–74.

45. Derr, *Frontiersman*, 178.

46. Quoted in Shackford, *Man and Legend*, 105–6. David Crockett's Circular to the Citizens of the Ninth Congressional District of the State of Tennessee, February 28, 1831. A copy resides in the McClung Collection, Lawson McGhee Library, Knoxville, TN.

47. Quoted in Shackford, *Man and Legend*, 107.

48. Quoted in Davis, *Three Roads*, 181. Jackson to Samuel J. Hays, April 1831, quoted in Emma Inman Williams, *Historic Madison: The Story of Jackson, and Madison County, Tennessee* (Jackson, TN, 1946), 403.

49. Davis, *Three Roads*, 182. Crockett to Michael Sprigg, May 5, 1830 [1831], Philpott Collection, catalog item no. 222.

50. Heale, "Frontier in Jacksonian Politics," 406.

51. Ibid.

52. Weakley County [Tennessee] Court Minutes, 1827–1835, vol. 1, 279. Shackford, *Man and Legend*, 136. Folmsbee and Catron, "David Crockett, Congressman," 67.

53. Shackford, *Man and Legend*, 136.

54. Derr, *Frontiersman*, 182. Shackford, *Man and Legend*, 139–41, 151. Folmsbee and Catron, "David Crockett: Congressman," 69.

55. Derr, *Frontiersman*, 183.

56. Quoted in Shackford, *Man and Legend*, 132–33. This incident is based, according to Shackford, on an anecdote "with substantial basis in fact" characterizing a discrepancy between Crockett and Fitzgerald in Paris, Tennessee, in the summer of 1831.

57. Quoted in Shackford, *Man and Legend*, 133.

58. Crockett to James Davidson, August 18, 1831. Crockett Biographical File, Daughters of the Republic of Texas Library, San Antonio, quoted in Davis, *Three Roads*, 185.

59. Folmsbee and Catron, "David Crockett: Congressman," 67.

Chapter 11: "Nimrod Wildfire" and "The Lion of the West"

1. Albanese, "Citizen Crockett," 88–90. Arpad, *Original Legendary*, 3–4. Slotkin, *Mythology of the American Frontier*, 414–15.

2. Quoted in Arpad, *Original Legendary*, 85.

3. James K. Paulding to John Wesley Jarvis, n.d. [1829–1830], Ralph M. Alderman, ed., *The Letters of James Kirke Paulding* (Madison, WI: 1962), 113.

4. Derr, *Frontiersman*, 189.

5. Quoted in Arpad, *Original Legendary*, 37. James Kirke Paulding, *The Lion of the West*, ed. James N. Tidwell (Stanford, CA, 1954).

6. Arpad, *Original Legendary*, 112.

7. Alderman, *Letters of James Kirke Paulding*, 113.

8. Quoted in Shackford, *Man and Legend*, 254. Arpad, *Original Legendary*, 112–13.

9. Albanese, "Citizen Crockett," 90–91. Arpad, *Original Legendary*, 48, 73–74.

10. Derr, *Frontiersman*, 185.

11. David Crockett letter to Richard Smith, January 7, 1832, Connaroe Collection, Historical Society of Pennsylvania. Folmsbee and Catron, "David Crockett: Congressman," 67.

12. Derr, *Frontiersman*, 186. Letter to Doctor Jones, August 22, 1831, Jones Papers, Southern Historical Collection, University of North Carolina, Chapel Hill. Folmsbee and Catron, "David Crockett: Congressman," 67. Davis, *Three Roads*, 310.

13. Davis, *Three Roads*, 313, 670n. Crockett to Daniel Webster, December 18, 1832, *American Book Prices Current 1987–1991*, Index (Washington, CT, 1992) 167–68.

14. Hauck, *Bio-Bibliography*, 68.

15. Hauck, *Bio-Bibliography*, 66–67. Shackford, *Man and Legend*, 27, 296n.

16. Arpad, *Original Legendary*, 182. Adam Huntsman to William Harris, *Southern Statesman* [Jackson, TN], June 20, 1833.

17. Burstein, *Passions of Andrew Jackson*, 188.

18. Ibid, 194. Parton, *Life of Andrew Jackson*, vol. 3, 447.

19. Burstein, *Passions of Andrew Jackson*, 200–1.

20. Crockett, *Narrative*, 210.

21. V. L. Parrington, *Main Currents in America Thought: The Romantic Revolution in America* (New York, 1927), vol. 2, 166.

22. Hauck, *Bio-Bibliography*, 3–4. The authorship of this work has long been in question. Before Shackford's 1956 biography, the work was thought to have been written by James Strange French of Virginia. Shackford, *Man and Legend*, 258–64, makes a strong case for Mathew St. Clair Clarke. This case is echoed by Hauck, *Bio-Bibliography*, as cited above.

23. Crockett, *Narrative*, 3–4.

24. Parrington, *Main Currents* (New York, 1927), vol. 2, 166.

25. Shackford, *Man and Legend*, 258.

26. Ibid, 261.

27. Arpad, *Original Legendary*, 179. Shackford, *Man and Legend*, 158.

28. Quoted in Arpad, *Original Legendary*, 181. Alan Nevins, ed., *The Diary of John Quincy Adams, 1794–1845*, New York, 1928), 444–45.

29. Heale, "Self-Made Man," 405.

30. Paul Andrew Hutton, *A Narrative of the Life of David Crockett of Tennessee* (Lincoln, NE, 1987), xxi. Arpad, *Original Legendary*, 33–38. Davis, *Three Roads*, 317. Heale, "Self-Made Man," 406.

31. Davis, *Three Roads*, 317, 671n. Letter from David Crockett to Carey & Hart, January 8, 1835, David Crockett Vertical File, Maryland Historical Society, Baltimore.

32. Ralph C. H. Catterall, *The Second Bank of the United States* (Chicago, 1902).

33. Shackford, *Man and Legend*, 147. *The Congressional Globe*, vol. 1: 37. See Shackford, 307n.

34. Quoted in Shackford, *Man and Legend*, 147.

35. Folmsbee and Catron, "David Crockett: Congressman," 69. Crockett to Nicholas Biddle, January 2, 1832, Nicholas Biddle Papers. Crockett to Richard Smith, January 7, 1832, Conarroe Autograph Collection, Historical Society of Pennsylvania.

36. Crockett, *Narrative*, 172.

37. Ibid, 5.

38. Ibid, 7.

39. Hauck, *Bio-Bibliography*, 47. Shackford, *Man and Legend*, 255–6. *Spirit of the Times*, Batavia, NY, December 21, 1833. Also in Arpad, *Original Legendary*, 113.

40. Letter to Carey & Hart, February 23, 1834, in the Boston Public Library. Shackford, *Man and Legend*, 267–68, 315n.

41. Ibid, 267.

42. Crockett, *Narrative*, 8–9.

43. Quoted in Walter Blair, "Six Davy Crocketts," *Southwest Review* 25 (July 1940): 457.

Chapter 12: A Bestseller and a Book Tour

1. Davis, *Three Roads*, 324.

2. Hutton, *Life of David Crockett*, vi. Broadside reproduced in Hutton, *Life of David Crockett*, vi, Beinecke Rare Book and Manuscript Library, Yale University.

3. Blair, "Six Davy Crocketts," 457.

4. Arpad, *Original Legendary*, Shackford, *Man and Legend*, 310.

5. Davis, *Three Roads*, 323.

6. Parrington, *Main Currents in American Thought*, vol. 2: 165.

7. Arpad, *Original Legendary*, 195. Parrington, *Main Currents in American Thought*, vol. 2: 170–71.

8. Quoted in Shackford, *Man and Legend*, 148, 307n. It appears that the original letter has been lost.

9. Arpad, *Original Legendary*, 193–96.

10. Derr, *Frontiersman*, 203.

11. Quoted in Shackford, *Man and Legend*, 148. Arpad, *Original Legendary*, 185.

12. Quoted in Shackford, *Man and Legend*, 148.

13. Arpad, *Original Legendary*, 187–88.

14. Letter to William T. Yeatman, June 15, 1834. quoted in Davis, *History of Memphis*, 155.

15. Shackford, *Man and Legend*, 154. Derr, *Frontiersman*, 203.

16. Haley, *Sam Houston*, 101. Shackford, *Man and Legend*, 308n.

17. Haley, *Sam Houston*, 101. Brands, *Lone Star Nation*, 235.

18. Quoted in Haley, *Sam Houston*, 438n. Sam Houston to John H. Houston, 31 July 1833, in Amelia Williams and Eugene C. Barker, eds. *Writings of Sam Houston* (Austin, TX, 1938–1943), vol. 5: 5–6.

19. Arpad, *Original Legendary*, 187. Shackford, *Man and Legend*, 154, 307n.

20. Arpad, *Original Legendary*, 187.

21. Derr, *Frontiersman*, 205.

22. Shackford, *Man and Legend*, 157.

23. Ibid.

24. Ibid, 158.

25. Crockett to Carey & Hart, May 27, 1834. Carl H. Pforzheimer Collection, New York Public Library. Quoted in Davis, *Three Roads*, 390 and 688n.

26. Derr, *Frontiersman*, 206. Shackford, *Man and Legend*, 158.

27. Quoted in Davis, *Three Roads*, 391. Helen Chapman to Emily Blair, May 1, 1834, William W. Chapman Papers. Center for American History, Austin, TX.

28. Folmsbee and Catron, "David Crockett: Congressman," no. 28 (1957): 69–71.

29. Shackford, *Man and Legend*, 158.

30. Ibid, 159.

31. Derr, *Frontiersman*, 207; Hamlin Garland, *The Autobiography of David Crockett* (New York, 1923), 149.

32. Quoted in Shackford, *Man and Legend*, 159. The book tour is summarized in Shackford, *Man and Legend*, 156–61.

33. Ibid.

34. Ibid, 161. *Niles* [Washington, DC] *Weekly Register*, ed. H. Niles, 4b: 252.

35. Shackford, *Man and Legend*, 161.

36. Quoted in Curtis Carroll Davis, "A Legend at Full-Length: Mr. Chapman Paints Colonel Crockett—and Tells About It," *American Antiquarian Society* (October 1959), 165.

37. Ibid.

38. Ibid, 166.

39. Shackford, *Man and Legend*, 167. Davis, *Three Roads*, 392.

40. Quoted in Shackford, *Man and Legend*, 163, 309n. Letter to William Hack, June 9, 1834, Miscellaneous Collection, Tennessee Historical Society. Also in *American Historical Magazine*, 2, 2 (April 1897): 179–80.

41. *Register of Debates in Congress*, 10: 4,586–88.

42. From Chapman, quoted in Davis, "Mr. Chapman Paints Colonel Crockett," 173.

43. Quoted in Shackford, *Man and Legend*, 164.

44. Davis, *History of Memphis*, 155.

Chapter 13: *"That* Fickle, Flirting *Goddess" Fame*

1. Davis, "Mr. Chapman Paints Colonel Crockett," 171.

2. Quoted in Shackford, *Man and Legend*, 167.

3. Jim Cooper, "A Study of Some David Crockett Firearms," *East Tennessee Historical Society Papers* 8 (1966): 66. Shackford 309–310n. *Attakapas Gazette* [St. Martinville, LA], June 12, 1834. Davis, *Three Roads*, 393.

4. Shackford, *Man and Legend*, 168. For an in-depth discussion of Crockett's numerous rifles, see Cooper, "Crockett Firearms," 62–69.

5. Quoted in Robert V. Remini, *Daniel Webster: The Man and His Times* (New York, 1997), 420.

6. Remini, *Daniel Webster*, 9.

7. Folmsbee and Catron, "David Crockett and West Tennessee," 20.

8. Ibid. Shackford, *Man and Legend*, 168.

9. Quoted in Shackford, *Man and Legend*, 168. David Crockett, *An Account of Col. Crockett's Tour to the North and Down East, in the Year of Our Lord One Thousand Eight Hundred and Thirty-Four* (Philadelphia, 1835).

10. Crockett presumably nicknamed this new gun "Pretty Betsey" to differentiate it from his favored "Betsey." See Shackford, *Man and Legends*, 169. Folmsbee and Catron, "David Crockett and West Tennessee," 20n. Cooper, "Crockett Firearms," 66.

11. Shackford, *Man and Legend*, 169.

12. Quoted by W. Frederick Worner, "David Crockett in Columbia," *Lancaster County Historical Society Papers* 27: 177.

13. Letter from Crockett to Nicholas Biddle, October 7, 1834, Nicholas Biddle Papers, Historical Society of Pennsylvania.

14. Quoted in Derr, *Frontiersman*, 214. Nicholas Biddle to David Crockett, December 13, 1834, in *President's Letter Book*, 279, Library of Congress.

15. Letter from Crockett to Carey & Hart, December 8, 1834, in Houghton Library, Harvard University. Davis, *Three Roads*, 395. Derr, *Frontiersman*, 214.

16. Letter from Crockett to Nicholas Biddle, December 16, 1834. Nicholas Biddle Papers, Historical Society of Pennsylvania.

17. Shackford, *Man and Legend*, 173.

18. Crockett to Carey & Hart, December 21, 1834, Rosenbach Museum and Library.

19. Quoted in Shackford, *Man and Legend*, 174. Crockett to John P. Ash, December 27, 1834, University of the South Archives.

20. Quoted in Derr, *Frontiersman*, 219; Letter from Crockett to Carey & Hart, January 8, 1835, Crockett Vertical File, Maryland Historical Society, and Manuscript Department, New-York Historical Society.

21. Quoted in Shackford, *Man and Legend*, 184–86. Crockett to Carey & Hart, January 22, 1835, Rosenbach Museum and Library.

22. Derr, *Frontiersman*, 218.

23. Crockett to John P. Ash, December 27, 1834, University of the South.

24. Quoted in Davis, *Three Roads*, 397. Crockett to Charles Schultz, December 25, 1834, Gilder-Lehrman Collection, Pierpont Morgan Library.

25. Arpad, *Original Legendary*, 192–93.

26. Ibid, 192.

27. Davis, *Three Roads*, 396.

28. Crockett to John P. Ash, December 27, 1834.

29. Quoted in Shackford, *Man and Legend*, 183.

30. Davis, *Three Roads*, 399.

31. Crockett to John P. Ash, December 27, 1834.

32. Adam Huntsman to James Polk, January 1, 1835, quoted in Weaver and Hall, *Correspondence of James K. Polk*, vol. 3, 1835–1836 (Nashville, 1975), 3.

33. *Congressional Debates* 11: 1,191–92.

34. Shackford, *Man and Legend*, 193.

35. Crockett, *Col. Crockett's Tour*, 173.

36. Shackford, *Man and Legend*, 196.

37. Davis, *Three Roads*, 402. Shackford, *Man and Legend*, 196.

38. Folmsbee and Catron, "David Crockett: Congressman," 75. Shackford, *Man and Legend*, 200–2.

39. Derr, *Frontiersman*, 221. Shackford, *Man and Legend*, 119, 188–89.

40. David Crockett, *The Life of Martin Van Buren* (New York, 1835), 80–81.

41. Davis, *Three Roads*, 403–5. Folmsbee and Catron, "David Crockett and West Tennessee," 23.

42. Davis, *History of Memphis*, 151–52.

43. Quoted in Shackford, *Man and Legend*, 204.

44. Crockett to Carey and Hart, July 8, 1835, quoted in Shackford, *Man and Legend*, 204.

45. Crockett to Carey and Hart, August 11, 1835, Crockett Vertical File, Maryland Historical Society.

46. Shackford 206–9. Davis, *Three Roads*, 407. In the end, nothing came of these charges.

47. William Armour to James K. Polk, September 7, 1835, in Weaver and Hall, *Correspondence of James K. Polk*, vol. 3, 286.

48. Joel R. Smith to James K. Polk, August 9, 1835, in ibid, 261.

49. Quoted in Cobia, *Crockett's Expedition to the Alamo*, 24. *Charleston Courier*, August 31, 1835.

Chapter 14: Lone Star on the Horizon

1. Landon Y. Jones, *William Clark and the Shaping of the West* (New York, 2004), 109–12. Derr, *Frontiersman*, 229.
2. Brands, *Lone Star Nation*, 24.
3. Ibid, 24–25. William C. Davis, *Lone Star Rising* (New York, 2004), 57.
4. Davis, *Lone Star Rising*, 89. Derr, *Frontiersman*, 229.
5. Stephen L. Hardin, *Texian Iliad* (Austin, 1994), 5.
6. Ibid, 6.
7. Ibid.
8. Ibid. Brands, *Lone Star Nation*, 220–21.
9. Brands, *Lone Star Nation*, 224.
10. Randy Roberts and James S. Olson, *A Line in the Sand* (New York, 2001), 91.
11. Brazos, *The Life of Robert Hall*, Reprint. (Austin, 1992), 19. Davis, *Three Roads*, 408, 692n. Roberts and Olson, *A Line in the Sand*, 91.
12. Cooper, "Crockett Firearms," 67.
13. Crockett to George Patton, October 31, 1835, in Shackford, *Man and Legend*, 210.
14. Ibid, 212.
15. Quoted in Haley, *Sam Houston*, page 110, *Red River Herald*, October 7, 1835.
16. Quoted in Haley, *Sam Houston*, 109. Houston to Isaac Parker, 5 October 1835, in Williams and Barker, *Writings of Sam Houston*, vol. 1, 302.
17. Quoted in Cobia, *Crockett's Expedition to the Alamo*, 28. Atlas Jones to Calvin Jones, November 13, 1835, Southern Historical Collection, University of North Carolina, Chapel Hill (SHC-UNC).
18. Davis, *Three Roads*, 409.
19. Quoted in Cobia, *Crockett's Expedition to the Alamo*, 29.
20. Calvin Jones to Edmund Jarvis, December 2, 1835, Jones Papers SHC-UNC. Also quoted in Cobia, *Crockett's Expedition to the Alamo*, 29, and Davis, *Three Roads*, 409.
21. Davis, *History of Memphis*, 141.
22. Ibid.
23. Ibid, 143.
24. Ibid, 144–45.
25. Ibid, 146.
26. Ibid, 140.
27. Hardin, *Texian Illiad*, 118. Stephen L. Hardin, "Gallery: David Crockett," *Military Illustrated* 23 (February-March, 1990): 28–30.
28. Bernard DeVoto, *Mark Twain's America* (Boston, 1932), 3–4.
29. Cobia, *Crockett's Expedition to the Alamo*, 36.

30. William F. Pope, *Early Days in Arkansas* (Little Rock, 1895), 183–84. Also quoted in Cobia, *Crockett's Expedition to the Alamo*, 42.

31. Pope, *Early Days in Arkansas*, 185. Cobia, *Crockett's Expedition to the Alamo*, 44–46. *Arkansas Gazette*, November 17, 1835.

32. *Arkansas Gazette*, November 17, 1835. Quoted in Cobia, *Crockett's Expedition to the Alamo*, 44.

33. Quoted in Cobia, *Crockett's Expedition to the Alamo*, 50. Vance Randolph, *We Always Lie to Strangers: Tall Tales from the Ozarks* (Westport, CT, 1951), 160.

34. David Crockett, *Davy Crockett's Own Story, as Written by Himself* (New York, 1955), 255–58.

35. *New York Sun*, January 12, 1836. *Arkansas Gazette*, May 15, 1955. Also in Davis, *Three Roads*, 411.

36. *Arkansas Gazette*, November 17, 1835. Also in Gary S. Zaboly, "Crockett Goes to Texas: A Newspaper Chronology," *Journal of the Alamo Battlefield Association* 1 (Summer, 1995): 7–8.

37. Derr, *Frontiersman*, 227. Davis, *Three Roads*, 412. Folmsbee and Catron, "David Crockett in Texas," *East Tennessee Historical Society Publications* 30 (1958), 50–51.

38. Shackford, *Man and Legend*, 214. Cobia, *Crockett's Expedition to the Alamo*, 77.

39. Quoted in Shackford, *Man and Legend*, 214, republished in *Niles Register*, L, 432–33, for August 27, 1836, from the Jackson, Tennessee, *Truth Teller*.

40. Quoted in Cobia, *Crockett's Expedition to the Alamo*, 71. Pat B. Clark, *The History of Clarksville and Old Red River Country, Texas* (Dallas, 1937), 5.

41. Claude V. Hall, "Early Days in the Red River Country," *Bulletin of East Texas State Teacher's College*, 14: 49–70.

42. Cobia, *Crockett's Expedition to the Alamo*, 70–71. Davis, *Three Roads*, 412.

43. Crockett to Wiley and Margaret Flowers, January 9, 1836, quoted in Shackford, *Man and Legend*, 214–15.

44. Cobia, *Crockett's Expedition to the Alamo*, 72–73.

45. Davis, *Three Roads*, 413.

46. Cobia, *Crockett's Expedition to the Alamo*, 94.

47. Derr, *Frontiersman*, 227.

48. Davis, *Three Roads*, 413, 694n. Cobia, *Crockett's Expedition to the Alamo*, 122.

49. Cobia, *Crockett's Expedition to the Alamo*, 100.

50. Ibid, 101. James Gaines to James W. Robinson, January 9, 1836, in William C. Binkley, *Official Correspondence of the Texan Revolution, 1835–1836*, 2 vols. (New York, 1936).

51. Cobia, *Crockett's Expedition to the Alamo*, 100; *Galveston* [Texas] *News*, January 9, 1898.

52. *Morning Courier and New York Enquirer*, March 26, 1836.

53. Crockett to Margaret and Wiley Flowers, January 9, 1836. Quoted in Shackford, *Man and Legend*, 216.

54. The shrewd and perceptive historian William C. Davis makes an observation that no other researcher, including Shackford, has: simply that the discrepancy in the date of the letter

may be the result of Crockett having written it in at least two sittings over a few-day period. See Davis, *Three Roads*, 695n.

55. Shackford, *Man and Legend*, 217–19.
56. Crockett to Margaret and Wiley Flowers, January 9, 1836.

Chapter 15: "Victory or Death"

1. Houston to Jackson, February 13, 1833, in Williams and Barker, *Writings of Sam Houston*, vol. 1, 274–76.
2. Statement of Enlistments, January 14, 1836, in John H. Jenkins, *Papers of the Texas Revolution 1835–1836* (Austin, TX, 1973), vol. 4, 13. Amelia Williams, "A Critical Study of the Siege of the Alamo and the Personnel of Its Defenders, Chapter IV," *Southern Historical Quarterly* 37 (January 1934): 167. Folmsbee and Catron, "David Crockett in Texas," 54.
3. Committee of Vigilance and Safety, January 18, 1836, in Jenkins, *Papers of the Texas Revolution*, vol. 4, 66. Quoted in Cobia, *Crockett's Expedition to the Alamo*, 130.
4. Cobia, *Crockett's Expedition to the Alamo*, 130.
5. Ibid, 130, 247n. Audited Military Claims, Republic of Texas, Texas State Library and Archives, Austin. Also in Davis, *Three Roads*, 416. Shackford, *Man and Legend*, 222.
6. Crockett to Flowers, January 9, 1836, Asbury Papers. Quoted in Shackford, *Man and Legend*, 216.
7. Cobia, *Crockett's Expedition to the Alamo*, 139. From Herbert Simms Kimble Letter, September 5, 1836, William Irving Lewis File, Daughters of the Texas Revolution Library, San Antonio.
8. Cobia, *Crockett's Expedition to the Alamo*, 139.
9. Ibid.
10. Derr, *Frontiersman*, 228.
11. Marques James, *The Raven* (Indianapolis, 1929), 224.
12. James C. Neill to Sam Houston, January 14, 1836, in Binkley, *Official Correspondence*, vol. 1, 295. Davis, *Lone Star Rising*, 205.
13. Davis, *Lone Star Rising*, 205.
14. Brands, *Lone Star Nation*, 338. Davis, *Lone Star Rising*, 205.
15. John M. Swisher, *The Swisher Memoirs* (San Antonio, 1932): 18–19.
16. Ibid, 18.
17. Ibid.
18. Ibid.
19. Ibid.
20. Davis, *Lone Star Rising*, 209–10. Hardin, *Texian Iliad*, 22–23.
21. Hardin, "Gallery: David Crockett," 30–31.
22. Cobia, *Crockett's Expedition to the Alamo*, 161.

23. Ibid, 158.

24. Davis, *Three Roads*, 524; see his note on arrival dates, 717–718n. Folmsbee and Catron, "David Crockett in Texas," 60. Also see Todd Hansen, *The Alamo Reader* (Mechanicsburg, PA, 2003), 504–6.

25. Antonio Menchacha, *Memoirs* (San Antonio, 1937), 22. *San Antonio Daily Express*, February 12, 1905. Hansen, *Alamo Reader*, 504–5.

26. Cobia, *Crockett's Expedition to the Alamo*, 167.

27. Davis, *Three Roads*, 516.

28. Quoted in Cobia, *Crockett's Expedition to the Alamo*, 171, from John Sutherland, *The Fall of the Alamo* (San Antonio, 1936) 11–12. Davis cites a shorter version, and Cobia points out some discrepancies, including Lindley, in the Sutherland source.

29. Quoted in Cobia, *Crockett's Expedition to the Alamo*, 173. Davis, *Three Roads*, 516, 718–719n. Sutherland, *Fall of the Alamo*, 11–12. Hansen, *Alamo Reader*, 140.

30. Quoted in Jeff Long, *Duel of Eagles* (New York, 1990), 132.

31. Cobia, *Crockett's Expedition to the Alamo*, 175.

32. Long, *Duel of Eagles*, 132. Menchacha, *Memoirs*, 22–23.

33. Ibid, both sources.

34. Quoted in Hardin, *Texian Iliad*, 111. James Bowie to Henry Smith, February 2, 1836, in Jenkins, ed., *Papers of the Texas Revolution*, 4: 236–38.

35. Walter Lord, *A Time to Stand* (New York, 1961), 84.

36. Long, *Duel of Eagles*, 31.

37. Davis, *Three Roads*, 519, 719n. Sutherland, *Fall of the Alamo*, 11. Long, *Duel of Eagles*, 131.

38. Long, *Duel of Eagles*, 126. Hansen, *Alamo Reader*, 673.

39. Quoted in Long, *Duel of Eagles*, 127; John Baugh, letter to Henry Smith, February 13, 1836, in Jenkins, *Papers of the Texas Revolution*, #2076. Hansen, *Alamo Reader*, 674.

40. William B. Travis, letter to Henry Smith, in Jenkins, *Papers of the Texas Revolution*, #2094. Hansen, *Alamo Reader*, 22–23.

41. Long, *Duel of Eagles*, 127.

42. William B. Travis and James Bowie to Henry Smith, February 14, 1836, in Jenkins, *Papers of the Texas Revolution*, #2094; Hansen, *Alamo Reader*, 24–25.

43. Quoted in Lord, *A Time to Stand*, 85, 232n. Hansen, *Alamo Reader*, 25.

44. Hardin, *Texian Iliad*, 120.

45. Long, *Duel of Eagles*, 149.

46. Hardin, *Texian Iliad*, 120.

47. Jose Enrique de la Pena, *With Santa Anna in Texas* (College Station, TX, 1975), 27.

48. Ibid.

49. Roberts and Olson, *A Line in the Sand*, 119.

50. Quoted in Hansen, *Alamo Reader*, 142.

51. Long, *Duel of Eagles*, 156. Roberts and Olson, *A Line in the Sand*, 121.

52. Roberts and Olson, *A Line in the Sand*, 121.

53. Quoted in Hansen, *Alamo Reader*, 143. Also quoted in Long, *Duel of Eagles*, 157.

54. Hansen, *Alamo Reader*, 144. Lord, *A Time to Stand*, 94. Sutherland, *Fall of the Alamo*, 18–19.

55. Long, *Duel of Eagles*, 158. Roberts and Olson, *A Line in the Sand*, 122.

56. Long, *Duel of Eagles*, 158; Lord, *A Time to Stand*, 94.

57. Quoted in Long, *Duel of Eagles*, 158. Vincente Filisola, *The History of the War in Texas* (Austin, 1985–1987), vol. 2, 150. Hansen, *Alamo Reader*, 144.

58. Quoted in Hansen, *Alamo Reader*, 144.

59. Quoted in Lord, *A Time to Stand*, 97. Hardin, *Texian Iliad*, 121.

60. Quoted in Long, *Duel of Eagles*, 159, and Hansen, *Alamo Reader*, 31–32. William B. Travis and James Bowie letter to James Fannin, February 23, 1836, in Jenkins, *Papers of the Texas Revolution*, #2161.

61. Quoted in Cobia, *Crockett's Expedition to the Alamo*, 193. Sutherland, *Fall of the Alamo*, 20.

62. Ibid, both sources.

63. Davis, *Three Roads*, 536. Samuel E. Asbury, "The Private Journal of Juan Nepomuceno Almonte," *Southwestern Historical Quarterly* 48 (July 1944): 10–32. Roberts and Olson, *A Line in the Sand*, 124.

64. Sutherland, in Hansen, *Alamo Reader*, 146–47.

65. Hardin, *Texian Iliad*, 127. Roberts and Olson, *A Line in the Sand*, 124.

66. Long, *Duel of Eagles*, 162–163. Lord, *A Time to Stand*, 102.

67. Roberts and Olson, *A Line in the Sand*, 124–25.

68. Quoted in Roberts and Olson, *A Line in the Sand*, 125. Jose Batres to James Bowie, February 23, 1836, in Jenkins, *Papers of the Texas Revolution* 4: 44. Lord, *A Time to Stand*, 102.

69. Davis, *Three Roads*, 537.

70. Roberts and Olson, *A Line in the Sand*, 125–26.

71. Davis, *Three Roads*, 537. Roberts and Olson, *A Line in the Sand*, 126.

72. William Travis to the People of Texas, February 24, 1836, Army Papers, Record Group 401, Texas State Library and Archives, Austin. Hansen, *Alamo Reader*, 32.

73. Brands, *Lone Star Nation*, 356.

Chapter 16: Smoke from a Funeral Pyre

1. Davis, *Three Roads*, 541. Cobia, *Crockett's Expedition to the Alamo*, 196–98.

2. William Travis to Sam Houston, quoted in Cobia, *Crockett's Expedition to the Alamo*, 197. Also quoted in Hansen, *Alamo Reader*, 34.

3. Long, *Duel of Eagles*, 190. Davis, *Three Roads*, 542.

4. Quoted in Long, *Duel of Eagles*, 191. Lord, *A Time To Stand*, 109. Letter from William Travis to Sam Houston. Hansen, *Alamo Reader*, 34.

5. Brands, *Lone Star Nation*, 357.

6. Quoted in Ibid.

7. Ibid, 358. Long, *Duel of Eagles*, 200.

8. Joseph Field, *Three Years in Texas* (Boston, 1836), 17. Asbury, "Almonte Journal," 19. Davis, *Three Roads*, 545. Hansen, *Alamo Reader*, 686.

9. Brands, *Lone Star Nation*, 359.

10. Hardin, *Texian Iliad*, 133.

11. Ibid, 133–34. Lord, *A Time to Stand*, 117; Albert A. Nofi, *The Alamo and the Texas War of Independence* (Conshohocken, PA, 1992), 68–70, 74. Harden, *Texian Illiad*, 133–34.

12. Hardin, *Texian Iliad*, 134. Asbury, "Almonte Journal," 19, March 1, 1836.

13. Quoted in Thomas Ricks Lindley, "Drawing Truthful Deductions," *Journal of the Alamo Battlefield Association* I (September, 1995): 31–33.

14. Hardin, *Texian Iliad*, 134.

15. Roberts and Olson, *A Line in the Sand*, 148–49. It was actually the arrival of General Antonio Gaona's First Brigade and Cavalry Regiment.

16. Lord, *A Time To Stand*, 137. Roberts and Olson, *A Line in the Sand*, 149. Hansen, *Alamo Reader*, 683, 716–17.

17. Quoted in Hansen, *Alamo Reader*, 601, Robert McAlpin Williamson letter to William B. Travis, March 1, 1836.

18. Quoted in Hansen, *Alamo Reader*, 35–36.

19. Quoted in Hansen, *Alamo Reader*, 35–36. William Travis to President of the Convention, March 3, 1836, *San Felipe Telegraph* and *Texas Register*, March 12, 1836.

20. Ibid, 36.

21. Ibid, 37–38.

22. Travis to David Ayers, March 3, 1836, *Texas Monument* [La Grange, TX, newspaper], March 31, 1852. Hansen, *Alamo Reader*, 38.

23. Long, *Duel of Eagles*, 209.

24. Davis, *Three Roads*, 556.

25. Quoted in Cobia, *Crockett's Expedition to the Alamo*, 208. J. M. Morphis, *History of Texas* (New York, 1875), 175. There exists some compelling speculation and evidence that Crockett may have gone outside the Alamo on a mission to gather reinforcements during the siege. See Thomas Ricks Lindley, *Alamo Traces* (Plano, TX, 2003), 140–42. Cobia, *Crockett's Expedition to the Alamo*, 203–13.

26. Brands, *Lone Star Nation*, 365.

27. Antonio Lopez de Santa Anna, "Manifesto," in *The Mexican Side of the Texas Revolution*, translated by Carlos Castaneda (Dallas, 1928), 13.

28. Antonio Lopez de Santa Anna, Military Order, March 3, 1836, *United States Magazine and Democratic Review* (October, 1838): 143, quoted in Hansen, *Alamo Reader*, 336–37.

29. De la Pena, *With Santa Anna in Texas*, 43–44. Hansen, *Alamo Reader*, 335.

30. Davis, *Three Roads*, 556.

31. Ibid, 557. Brands, *Lone Star Nation*, 369.

32. Hardin, *Texian Iliad*, 138.

33. Ibid. De la Pena, *With Santa Anna in Texas*, 46. Roberts and Olson, *A Line in the Sand*, 160.

34. Roberts and Olson, *A Line in the Sand*, 159. De la Pena, *With Santa Anna in Texas*, 47.

35. De la Pena, *With Santa Anna in Texas*, 46–47. Long, *Duel of Eagles*, 241. Roberts and Olson, *A Line in the Sand*, 161.

36. De la Pena, *With Santa Anna in Texas*, 47.

37. Davis, *Three Roads*, 559. Lord, *A Time to Stand*, 155; Roberts and Olson, *A Line in the Sand*, 162.

38. Hardin, *Texian Iliad*, 139.

39. Davis, *Three Roads*, 560, 732–33n. Joe, Travis's slave, quoted in *Alamo Reader*, 77–82. Hardin, *Texian Iliad*, 139. Bruce Winders, *Sacrificed at the Alamo: Tragedy and Triumph in the Texas Revolution* (Abilene, TX, 2004), 126.

40. Hardin, *Texian Iliad*, 146.

41. Lord, *A Time to Stand*, 156–57.

42. Hardin, *Texian Iliad*, 146. De la Pena, *With Santa Anna in Texas*, 48–50.

43. De la Pena, *With Santa Anna in Texas*, 48–49.

44. Davis, *Three Roads*, 562. Hardin, *Texian Iliad*, 147. Roberts and Olson, *A Line in the Sand*, 165–68. Lord, *A Time to Stand*, 161.

45. Roberts and Olson, *A Line in the Sand*, 168. Davis, *Three Roads*, 562.

46. Quoted in Hardin, *Texian Iliad*, 147. Pohl and Hardin, "Military History of the Texas Revolution," 294, 296. Glaser, "Victory and Death," in Schoelwer with Glaser, *Alamo Images*, 85.

47. Roberts and Olson, *A Line in the Sand*, 168. Sutherland, *Fall of the Alamo*, 40. Davis, *Three Roads*, 561, 734n. Hardin, *Texian Iliad*, 148. Long, *Duel of Eagles*, 253.

48. Hardin, *Texian Iliad*, 148. De la Pena, *With Santa Anna in Texas*, 53. Filisola, *History of the War in Texas*, 2, 179.

49. De la Pena, *With Santa Anna in Texas*, 53. The exact nature of Crockett's death remains unknown, mired in speculation and multiple supposed firsthand "eyewitness" accounts, and the controversy and debate surrounding his demise at the Alamo, like Crockett's own legend, will likely never die. Thousands and thousands of pages and a number of books are devoted to that subject alone. The bibliography at the end of this work delineates most of the significant texts and authors who have participated in the ongoing discussion.

50. Davis, *Lone Star Rising*, 234–35.

51. Brands, *Lone Star Nation*, 389.

52. Ibid, 394–97. Davis, *Lone Star Rising*, 237–38.

53. Hardin, *Texian Iliad*, 173–74. Davis, *Lone Star Rising*, 238. De la Pena, *With Santa Anna in Texas*, 88–90.

54. Brands, *Lone Star Nation*, 451.

55. Ibid.

56. Quoted in Brands, *Lone Star Nation*, 453–54.

57. Lord, *A Time to Stand*, 193–96. Davis, *Lone Star Rising*, 269–71. Brands, *Lone Star Nation*, 450–55.

58. Derr, *Frontiersman*, 253.

59. Quoted in Shackford, *Man and Legend*, 235, *Niles Weekly Register*, L, 121–22, April 16, 1836. Lists of slain at Alamo do not include Jesse Benton.

60. Quoted in Shackford, *Man and Legend*, 236.

61. Mary Daggett Lake, "David Crockett's Widow, the Pioneer Wife and Mother Who Was Widowed by the Fall of the Alamo," *Texas Monthly* 2 (December 1928): 703–8; Shackford, *Man and Legend*, 236.

62. Lake, "David Crockett's Widow" 706.

63. Derr, *Frontiersman*, 251. Shackford, *Man and Legend*, 239.

64. De la Pena, *With Santa Anna in Texas*, 52.

65. Davis, *Three Roads*, 566, 739n. Long, *Duel of Eagles*, 266, 387n. Pablo Diaz, *Tejano Accounts*, 44, 76. Hanson, *Alamo Reader*, 527–32.

66. Hansen, *Alamo Reader*, 530. Long, *Duel of Eagles*, 266. Davis, *Three Roads*, 566. Pablo Diaz, "The Alamo Bones," *San Antonio Express*, July 1, 1906.

67. Quoted in Hansen, *Alamo Reader*, 530–31, and Long, *Duel of Eagles*, 266. Interview by Charles M. Barnes.

Epilogue

1. Gary L. Foreman, *Crockett: The Gentleman from the Cane* (Dallas, 1986), 57.

2. John Seelye, *"On to the Alamo": Colonel Crockett's Exploits and Adventures in Texas* (New York, 2003), xi. Crockett, *Narrative*, xviii–xix.

3. Seelye, *"On to the Alamo,"* xi. Crockett, *Narrative*, xix. Foreman, *Gentleman from the Cane*, 57.

4. Arpad, *Original Legendary*, 187–88.

5. Ibid, 188.

6. Foreman, *Gentleman from the Cane*, 57. Seelye, *"On to the Alamo,"* xii.

7. Michael A. Lofaro, *Davy Crockett: The Man, the Legend, the Legacy 1786–1986* (Knoxville, TN, 1985), 106–7.

8. Quoted in Lofaro, *Crockett: The Man*, 111, from Isaac Goldberg and Hubert Heffner, eds., *America's Lost Plays* (Bloomington, IN, 1963), vol. 4.

9. Lofaro, *Crockett: The Man*, 112.

10. Ibid, xxi–xxii.

11. Seelye, *"On to the Alamo,"* xii.

12. Roberts and Olson, *A Line in the Sand*, 240.

13. Derr, *Frontiersman*, 23–24. See also Richard Boyd Hauck, "Making It All Up," in Lofaro, *Crockett: The Man*, 116–18.

14. Roberts and Olson, *A Line in the Sand*, 243–44. Paul F. Anderson, *The Davy Crockett Craze: A Look at the 1950s Phenomenon and the Davy Crockett Collectibles* (Hillside, IL, 1996), 49. For a detailed consideration of the 1950s Crockett craze and merchandising, also see Margaret Jane King, "The Davy Crockett Craze: A Case Study in Popular Culture" (Ph.D dissertation, University of Hawaii, 1976).

15. Roberts and Olson, *A Line in the Sand*, 244. Anderson, *The Davy Crockett Craze*, 87–160. King, "The Davy Crockett Craze," 8–17.

16. Gordon Wood, *The Americanization of Benjamin Franklin* (New York, 2004) 176. Roberts and Olson, *A Line in the Sand*, 244.

17. Roberts and Olson, *A Line in the Sand*, 245.

18. Ibid. Anderson, *The Davy Crockett Craze*, 49–73. Final sales figures are not yet in for merchandise attendant to *Spider-Man* and *Spider-Man 2*, so the wiry web shooter may one day outstrip Crockett.

19. Ibid, 247.

20. Derr, *Frontiersman*, 268.

21. Ibid, 267.

22. Hauck, *Bio-Bibliography*, 95.

23. Ibid, 95–96. See also Roberts and Olson, *A Line in the Sand*, 257–76, and Hauck, "Making It All Up," in Lofaro, *Crockett: The Man*, 118–20.

24. Wood, *Benjamin Franklin*, 2.

25. Ibid, 3.

BIBLIOGRAPHY

The literature on David Crockett is substantive and can be overwhelming, especially when including the works that focus on the Crockett legend and the attendant mythology. For those wishing to embark on further Crockett reading and study, the best place to commence is certainly David Crockett's own work, *A Narrative of the Life of David Crockett of the State of Tennessee.* The standard is edited by James A. Shackford and Stanley J. Folmsbee, published in 1973, and includes extensive annotations that are useful and interesting. Another good one is the 1987 version edited by Paul Andrew Hutton, which includes an excellent and extensive introduction.

Of the biographies, since 1956 the definitive work has been James A. Shackford's *David Crockett, The Man and the Legend.* The groundbreaking study, which was originally a dissertation presented by Shackford to the Graduate School of Vanderbilt University and was subsequently published by the University of North Carolina Press, remains essential to the Crockett canon. To date, the most authoritative and thorough treatment of Crockett's life is William C. Davis's 1998 *Three Roads to the Alamo: The Lives and Fortunes of David Crockett, James Bowie, and William Barret Travis.* The book is a monumental volume, masterfully crafted and researched, with an extensive (nearly book-length itself) notes section. Professor Davis, a noted historian, brilliantly and seamlessly interweaves what could effectively be three stand-alone biographies into one tome, and the result is an impressive volume that promises to stand the test of time and be the standard by which others are measured. Mark Derr's 1993 biography *The Frontiersman: The Real Life and Many Legends of Davy Crockett* is also very good.

Numerous scholars have contributed richly to the ongoing Crockett study, and some are particularly worthy of mention. Joseph Arpad's 1970 Ph.D. dissertation for Duke University's Department of English, entitled "David Crockett: An Original Legendary Eccentricity and Early American Character," is a fascinating study dealing with Crockett's relative "originality" and the shape and formation of the United States' national identity. Richard Boyd Hauck's 1982 *Crockett: A Bio-Bibliography* is an excellent and comprehensive (yet economical) treatment of Crockett's life, legend, fictions, and folklore. A series of articles by Stanley J. Folmsbee and Anna Grace Catron in the *East Tennessee Historical Society Publications* and *West Tennessee Historical Society Papers*, written over nearly twenty years spanning 1956 to 1974, provide augmentations and revisions to the Shackford biography. The articles to note are: "The Early Career of David Crockett," "David Crockett, Congressman," "David Crockett in Texas," and "David Crockett and West Tennessee."

Two scholarly collections are fundamental to an overall understanding of both David and "Davy" Crockett. Michael A. Lofaro's 1986 *Davy Crockett: The Man, the Legend, the Legacy* is a first-rate anthology with a well-considered chronology and interesting essays by the finest Crockett scholars. Another collection, published in 1989, is *Crockett at Two Hundred*, edited by Michael A. Lofaro and Joe Cummings. The work commemorates the two-hundredth birthday of David Crockett and offers significant insight into Crockett's place in American culture.

Finally, Manley F. Cobia Jr.'s 2003 *Journey into the Land of Trials: The Story of Davy Crockett's Expedition to the Alamo* presents a compelling itinerary of Crockett's journey from Tennessee to the Alamo, which is to my knowledge the only book-length work to focus primarily on that expedition.

The sheer volume of works dedicated to the Alamo precludes detailed commentary here, with a few notable exceptions. Todd Hansen's 2003 *The Alamo Reader: A Study in History* has been called the "definitive Alamo resource," and indeed it places, for the first time, many of the existing Alamo-related documents under one cover (adding up to nearly 800 pages). It is a worthwhile and long overdue collection.

Two excellent and highly readable studies of the Texas Revolution were published in 2004. The first is William C. Davis's *Lone Star Rising*, which is a necessary supplement and companion to his *Three Roads to the Alamo*. *Lone Star Rising* delivers exquisite detail of the political and social situation in Texas leading up to the siege, and the work is especially interesting in its illumination of Sam Houston and Stephen F. Austin, two significant architects of Texas. Also fine is H. W. Brand's 2004 *Lone Star Nation*, which reads like a good novel while delivering strong history of the fight for an independent Texas.

Thomas Ricks Lindley's 2003 *Alamo Traces* is a fine forensic study of the Alamo's most perplexing problems, and his careful research and severe scrutiny of facts (he's a former detective) yield new evidence and conclusions, making the work essential for any serious further study of the Alamo. Also superlative is Stephen L. Hardin's 1994 *Texian Iliad: A Military History of the Texas Revolution*, a fabulous military account of the entire revolution, exquisitely illustrated by Gary S. Zaboly. The most engaging and readable rendition of the Alamo story is Walter Lord's timeless 1961 *A Time to Stand*. Lord employs spare and unadorned prose to create a deeply enjoyable narrative account.

A few fictionalized versions of the story are worth reading. Of these, Stephen Harrigan's 2000 *The Gates of the Alamo* is the most fulfilling. Dee Brown's classic 1942 *Wave High the Banner: A Novel Based on the Life of Davy Crockett* is also quite enjoyable.

Literature devoted to the controversial death of David Crockett forms a monstrous and unwieldy subcategory of Texana and Alamo writing, and the arguments will no doubt continue on into perpetuity, mostly because there remains insufficient conclusive evidence to allow us to know definitively how he perished. Supposition and speculation based on the various "eyewitness" accounts form the central list of possibilities. The discussion (in many cases a very heated argument) can be addressed by perusing the following works: William C. Davis, *Three Roads to the Alamo*, 737n; William C. Davis, "How Davy Probably Didn't Die," *Journal of the Alamo Battlefield Association* 2 (Fall 1997): 11–37; Dan Kilgore, *How Did Davy Die?* (Texas A&M Press, 1978); Bill Groneman's following books and articles—*Eyewitness to the Alamo: Revised Edition* (Republic of Texas Press, 2001); *Death of a Legend: The Myth and Mystery Surrounding the Death of Davy Crockett* (Republic of Texas Press, 1999); *Defense of a Legend* (Republic of Texas Press, 1994); "The Controversial Alleged Account of José Enrique de la Peña," *Military History of the West* (Fall 1995); and "A Rejoinder: Publish Rather Than Perish—Regardless—Jim Crisp and the de la Peña Diary," *Military History of the West* (Fall 1995). For some time now, a vigorous repartee has raged between Bill Groneman and antagonist James Crisp, whose essays on the subject of Crockett's death include the following: "The Little Book That Wasn't There: The Myth and the Mystery of the de la Peña Diary," *Southwestern Historical Quarterly* 98 (October 1994): 260–96; "Texas History—Texas Mystery," *Sallyport—The Magazine of Rice University* (February/March 1995): 13–21; "When Revision Becomes Obsession: Bill Groneman and the de la Peña Diary," *Military History of the West* (Fall 1995). Finally, Todd Hansen's 2003 *Alamo Handbook* (791–98) itemizes sources and supposed firsthand accounts and provides an interesting ranking system of their relative reliability.

Some very useful resources exist in the form of Crockett chronologies and bibliographies, and to date the best of these are as follows: *Crockett at Two Hundred: New Perspectives on the Man and the Myth*, edited by Michael A. Lofaro and Joe Cummings, 1989. Within this work exists an exhaustive bibliography that is cleverly arranged, in the form of Miles Tanenbaum's "Following Davy's Trail: A Crockett Bibliography" (192–241). Richard Boyd Hauck's previously mentioned *Crockett: A Bio-Bibliography* (1982) also presents a concise chronology as well as an incisive bibliography and discussion of the Crockett record.

Two recent books worth noting include a very interesting overview and contextual primer called *Sacrificed at the Alamo: Tragedy and Triumph in the Texas Revolution* (Abilene, TX, 2004). This study is written by Richard Bruce Winders, noted historian and curator of the Alamo, and is part of the Military History of Texas series. The book does a nice job of establishing historical background and context for why the siege at the Alamo took place at all. Finally, James E. Crisp's newest effort, *Sleuthing the Alamo: Davy Crockett's Last Stand and Other Mysteries of the*

Texas Revolution (New York, 2005), condenses more than a decade of scholarly research on the Alamo and the Texas Revolution into one tidy and very personal volume, along the way peeling off some cherished layers of mythology that have long threatened to obfuscate "truths" about the Texas Revolution.

Selected Works

THESES AND DISSERTATIONS

Arpad, Joseph. "David Crockett, An Original Legendary Eccentricity and Early American Character." Ph.D. dissertation, Duke University, 1970.

Catron, Anna Grace. "The Public Career of David Crockett." Master's thesis, University of Tennessee, 1955.

King, Margaret Jane. "The Davy Crockett Craze: A Case Study in Popular Culture." Ph.D. dissertation, University of Hawaii, 1976.

Shackford, James A. "The Autobiography of David Crockett: An Annotated Edition." Ph.D. dissertation, Vanderbilt University, 1948.

GOVERNMENT DOCUMENTS

American State Papers, Indian Affairs, Library of Congress, Washington DC, 1832–1834.

BOOKS

Abbott, John S. C. *David Crockett.* New York, 1874.

Alderman, Ralph M., ed. *The Letters of James Kirke Paulding.* Wisconsin, 1962.

Anderson, Paul F. *The Davy Crockett Craze: A Look at the 1950's Phenomenon and the Davy Crockett Collectibles.* Hillside, IL, 1996.

Audubon, John James. *Writings and Drawings.* New York, 1999.

———. *Treasury of Audubon Birds.* New York, 1993.

Bagnall, Norma Hayes. *On Shaky Ground: The New Madrid Earthquakes of 1811–1812.* Columbia, MO, 1996.

Barker, Eugene C. *The Austin Papers.* 3 vols. Washington, DC, 1919–1926.

Bartram, William. *Travels and Other Writings.* New York, 1996.

Bercovitch, Sacvan. *The Puritan Origins of the American Self.* New Haven, CT, 1975.

Binkley, William C. *Official Correspondence of the Texan Revolution, 1835–1836.* 2 vols. New York, 1936.

Brands, H. W. *Lone Star Nation: How a Ragged Army of Volunteers Won the Battle for Texas Independence—and Changed America.* New York, 2004.

———. *The First American: The Life and Times of Benjamin Franklin.* New York, 2000.

Brazos. *Life of Robert Hall.* Reprint. Austin, 1992.

Brown, Peter Lancaster. *Halley's Comet and the Principia.* Suffolk, UK, 1986.

Buchanan, John. *Jackson's Way: Andrew Jackson and the People of the Western Waters.* New York, 2001.

Burstein, Andrew. *The Passions of Andrew Jackson.* New York, 2003.

Burke, James Wakefield. *David Crockett: The Man Behind the Myth.* Austin, 1984.

Campbell, Randolph B. *Gone to Texas: A History of the Lone Star State.* New York, 2003.

Cantrell, Gregg. *Stephen F. Austin: Empresario of Texas.* New Haven, CT, 2001.

Catlin, George. *North American Indians.* Edited by Peter Matthiessen. New York, 1989.

Chernow, Ron. *Alexander Hamilton.* New York, 2004.

Cobia, Manley F. *Journey into the Land of Trials: The Story of Davy Crockett's Expedition to the Alamo.* Franklin, TN, 2003.

Crisp, James E. *Sleuthing the Alamo: Davy Crockett's Last Stand and Other Mysteries of the Texas Revolution.* New York, 2005.

Crockett, David. *A Narrative of the Life of David Crockett of the State of Tennessee.* Introduction by Paul Andrew Hutton. Lincoln, NE, 1987.

———. *A Narrative of the Life of David Crockett of the State of Tennessee.* Edited by James A. Shackford and Stanley J. Folmsbee. Knoxville, 1973.

———. *A Narrative of the Life of David Crockett of the State of Tennessee.* Edited by John J. Arpad. New Haven, CT, 1972.

———. *An Account of Col. Crockett's Tour to the North and Down East, in the Year of Our Lord One Thousand Eight Hundred and Thirty-Four.* Philadelphia, Carey & Hart, 1835.

———. *The Life of Martin Van Buren: Hair-Apparent to the "Government," and the Appointed Successor of General Jackson.* Philadelphia, 1834.

Cutrer, Thomas W. *Ben McCulloch and the Frontier Military Tradition.* Chapel Hill, NC, 1993.

Davis, James D. *History of the City of Memphis.* Memphis, 1873.

Davis, William C. *Lone Star Rising: The Revolutionary Birth of the Texas Republic.* New York, 2004.

———. *Three Roads to the Alamo: The Lives and Fortunes of David Crockett, James Bowie, and William Barret Travis.* New York, 1998.

de la Peña, Enriqué. *With Santa Anna in Texas, A Personal Narrative of the Revolution.* Edited by Carmen Perry. College Station, TX, 1975.

Derr, Mark. *The Frontiersman: The Real Life and Many Legends of Davy Crockett.* New York, 1993.

de Tocqueville, Alexis. *Journey to America.* New York, 1971.

———. *Democracy in America.* New York, 1969.

DeVoto, Bernard. *Mark Twain's America.* Boston, 1932.

Dorson, Richard M. *Folklore and Fakelore.* Boston, 1976.

————. *American Folklore*. Chicago, 1959.

————. *Davy Crockett: American Comic Legend*. New York, 1939.

Eckert, Allan W. *The Frontiersman: A Narrative*. Ashland, KY, 2001.

Field, Joseph. *Three Years in Texas*. Boston, 1836.

Filisola, Vincente. *Memoirs for the History of the War in Texas*. 2 vols. Austin, 1986–1987.

Flannery, Tim. *The Eternal Frontier: An Ecological History of North America and Its Peoples*. New York, 2001.

Flores, Richard R. *Remembering the Alamo: Memory, Modernity, and the Master Symbol*. Austin, 2002.

Ford, Alice. *Audubon's Animals: The Quadrupeds of North America*. New York, 1951.

Foreman, Gary L. *Crockett: The Gentleman from the Cane*. Dallas, 1986.

Franklin, Benjamin. *Autobiography*. Leonard W. Labaree et al, eds. New Haven, CT, 1964.

Gaddis, John Lewis. *The Landscape of History: How Historians Map the Past*. New York, 2002.

Garland, Hamlin, ed. *The Autobiography of David Crockett*. New York, 1923.

Graves, John. *Goodbye to a River*. Houston, 1959.

Gregory, Jack, and Strickland, Rennard. *Sam Houston with the Cherokees 1829–1833*. Austin, 1967.

Groneman, William. *Eyewitness to the Alamo*. Plano, TX, 2001.

————. *Death of a Legend: The Myth and Mystery Surrounding the Death of Davy Crockett*. Plano, TX, 1999.

————. *Defense of a Legend. Crockett and the de la Peña Diary*. Plano, TX, 1994.

Halbert, H. S., and T. H. Ball. *The Creek War of 1813 and 1814*. Chicago, 1895.

————. *The Creek War of 1813 and 1814*. Edited by Frank L. Owsley, Jr. Tuscaloosa, AL, 1995.

Haley, James L. *Sam Houston*. Norman, OK, 2002.

Hansen, Todd. *The Alamo Reader*. Mechanicsburg, PA, 2003.

Hardin, Stephen L. *Texian Iliad: A Military History of the Texas Revolution, 1835–1836*. Austin, 1994.

Harrigan, Stephen. *The Gates of the Alamo*. New York, 2000.

Hauck, Richard Boyd. *Crockett: A Bio-Bibliography*. Westport, CT, 1982.

Hoffer, Peter Charles. *Sensory Worlds in Early America*. Baltimore, 2003.

Jackson, Andrew. *The Correspondence of Andrew Jackson*. Edited by John Spencer Bassett and J. Franklin Jameson. 7 vols. Washington, DC, 1926–1935.

Jahoda, Gloria. *The Trail of Tears*. New York, 1975.

James, Marquis. *The Raven: A Biography of Sam Houston*. Indianapolis, 1929.

Jenkins, John H., ed. and trans. *Papers of the Texan Revolution, 1835–1836*. 10 vols. Austin, TX, 1973.

Jones, Landon Y. *William Clark and the Shaping of the West*. New York, 2004.

Kilgore, Dan. *How Did Davy Die?* College Station, TX, 1978.

Lawrence, Bill. *The Early American Wilderness as the Explorers Saw It*. New York, 1991.

Lindley, Thomas Ricks. *Alamo Traces: New Evidence, New Conclusions*. Plano, TX, 2003.

Lofaro, Michael. *Daniel Boone: An American Life.* Lexington, KY, 2003.

———. *Davy Crockett: The Man, the Myth, the Legacy, 1786–1986.* Knoxville, 1985.

Lofaro, Michael, and Joe Cummings, eds. *Crockett at Two Hundred.* Knoxville, 1989.

Long, Jeff. *Duel of Eagles.* New York, 1990.

Lord, Walter. *A Time to Stand.* New York, 1960.

Meine, Franklin J. *Tall Tales of the Southwest: An Anthology of Southern and Southwestern Humor, 1830–1860.* New York, 1933.

Mintz, Steven. *Huck's Raft: A History of American Childhood.* Cambridge, MA, 2004.

Nabokov, Peter, ed. *Native American Testimony: A Chronicle of Indian-White Relations From Prophecy to the Present, 1492–2000.* New York, 1999.

Nevins, Alan, ed., *The Diary of John Quincy Adams, 1794–1845.* New York, 1928.

Nofi, Albert A. *The Alamo and the Texas War of Independence, September 30, 1835, to April 21, 1836.* Conshohocken, PA, 1992.

O'Brien, Sean Michael. *In Bitterness and in Tears: Andrew Jackson's Destruction of the Creeks and Seminoles.* Westport, CT, 2003.

Parrington, Vernon Louis. *Main Currents in American Thought.* New York, 1927.

Parton, James. *General Jackson.* New York, 1892.

———. *Life of Andrew Jackson: In Three Volumes.* New York, 1860.

Paulding, James K. *Westward Ho! A Tale.* 2 vols. New York, 1832.

Paulding, William I. *Literary Life of James K. Paulding.* New York, 1867.

Peterson, Roger Tory, and Fisher, James. *Wild America.* New York, 1955.

Potter, R. M. *The Fall of the Alamo.* San Antonio, TX, 1860.

Ratner, Lorman A. *Andrew Jackson and His Tennessee Lieutenants.* Westport, CT, 1997.

Register of Debates in Congress. vols. 3–11. Washington, DC, 1827–1835.

Reid, John, and Eaton, Henry. *The Life of Andrew Jackson.* 1817. Tuscaloosa, AL, 1974.

Reid, Samuel C., Jr. *The Scouting Expeditions of McCulloch's Texas Rangers.* New York, 1847.

Remini, Robert. *Andrew Jackson and His Indian Wars.* New York, 2001.

———. *The Battle of New Orleans: Andrew Jackson and America's First Military Victory.* New York, 1999.

———. *Daniel Webster: The Man and His Times.* New York, 1997.

Roberts, Randy, and James S. Olson. *A Line in the Sand.* New York, 2001.

———. *John Wayne: American.* New York, 1995.

Rourke, Constance. *Davy Crockett.* New York, 1934.

———. *American Humor: A Study of the National Character.* New York, 1931.

Santa Anna, Antonio Lopez de. *The Mexican Side of the Texan Revolution.* Translated by Carlos Castañeda. Dallas, 1928.

Schlesinger, Arthur. *The Age of Jackson.* New York, 1945.

Schoelwer, Susan P., and Tom Glaser. *Alamo Images: Changing Perceptions of a Texas Experience.* Dallas, 1985.

Shackford, James A. *David Crockett: The Man and the Legend.* Chapel Hill, NC, 1956.

Shapiro, Irwin. *Yankee Thunder: The Legendary Life of Davy Crockett.* New York, 1944.

Slotkin, Richard. *Regeneration Through Violence: The Mythology of the American Frontier, 1600–1860.* Middletown, CT, 1973.

Smith, Richard Penn. *On to the Alamo: Colonel Crockett's Exploits and Adventures in Texas.* Edited by John Seeyle. New York, 2003.

Smith, Seba. *The Life and Writings of Major Jack Downing, of Downingsville, Away Down East in the State of Maine, Written by Himself.* Boston, 1833. Reprint New York, 1973.

———. *My Thirty Years Out of the Senate.* New York, 1859.

Sterling, Keir B. *Selected Works by Eighteenth Century Naturalists and Travel Writers.* New York, 1974.

Sugden, John. *Tecumseh: A Life.* New York, 1997.

Sutherland, John. *The Fall of the Alamo.* San Antonio, TX, 1936.

Swisher, John M. *The Swisher Memoirs.* San Antonio, TX, 1932.

Tinkle, Lon. *Thirteen Days to Glory.* New York, 1958.

Torrence, Robert M., and Robert L. Whittenburg. *Colonel Davy Crockett, A Genealogy.* Washington, DC, 1956.

Weaver, Herbert, and Kermit L. Hall, eds. *Correspondence of James K. Polk.* Vol. 3, 1835–1836. Nashville, 1975.

Weaver, Herbert, and Paul H. Bergeron, eds. *Correspondence of James K. Polk.* Vol. 1, 1817–1833. Nashville, 1969.

———. *Correspondence of James K. Polk.* Vol. 2, 1833–1834. Nashville, 1972.

Williams, Amelia, and Eugene C. Barker, eds. *Writings of Sam Houston,* 8 Vols. Austin, 1938–1943.

Williams, Emma Inman. *Historic Madison, The Story of Jackson, and Madison County, Tennessee, from the Prehistoric Moundbuilders to 1917.* Jackson, TN, 1946.

Winders, Richard Bruce. *Sacrificed at the Alamo: Tragedy and Triumph in the Texas Revolution.* Abilene, TX, 2004.

Wood, Gordon S. *The Americanization of Benjamin Franklin.* New York, 2004.

Young, James Sterling. *The Washington Community, 1800–1828.* New York, 1966.

ARTICLES

Albanese, Catherine. "Citizen Crockett: Myth History, and Nature Religion." *Soundings: An Interdisciplinary Journal* 61 (1978): 87–104.

Almonte, Juan Nepomuceno. "The Private Journal of Juan Nepomuceno Almonte." Introduction by Samuel E. Asbury. *Southwestern Historical Quarterly* 48 (July 1944): 10–32.

Arpad, Joseph J. "John Wesley Jarvis, James Kirk Paulding, and Colonel Nimrod Wildfire." *New York Folklore Quarterly* 21 (1965): 92–106.

Bishop, H. O. "Colonel Crockett in New York." *National Republic* 17 (November 1929): 28–29, 39.

———. "Colonel Crockett Goes Visiting." *National Republic* 17 (October 1929): 24–25, 39.

———. "Davy Crockett—Bear Hunter." *National Republic* 17 (August 1929): 31–37.

B.J.J. "Davy Crockett's Electioneering Tour." *Harper's New Monthly Magazine* 35 (April 1867): 606–11.

Blair, Walter. "Six Davy Crocketts." *Southwest Review* 25 (July 1940): 443–62.

Cooper, Jim. "A Study of Some David Crockett Firearms." *East Tennessee Historical Society Papers* 8 (1966): 62–69.

Crisp, James E. "Crockett's Height." *Alamo Journal* 102 (September 1996): 13.

———. "Texas History—Texas Mystery." *Sallyport—The Magazine of Rice University* (February/March 1995): 13–21.

———. "A Reply: When Revision Becomes Obsession. Bill Groneman and the de la Peña Diary." *Military History of the West* 25 (Fall 1995): 143–56.

———. "The Little Book That Wasn't There: The Myth and Mystery of the de la Peña Diary." *Southern Historical Quarterly* 98 (October 1994): 259–96.

Davis, Curtis Carroll. "A Legend at Full Length: Mr. Chapman Paints Colonel Crockett—and Tells About It." *Proceeding of the American Antiquarian Society* 69 (October 1959): 155–74.

Davis, William C. "How Davy Probably Didn't Die." *Journal of the Alamo Battlefield Association* 2 (Fall 1997): 11–37.

"Fall of the Alamo." *The Knickerbocker* 8 (September 1836): 295–98. Author unknown.

Folmsbee, Stanley J. "David Crockett and West Tennessee." *West Tennessee Historical Society Publications* 28 (1974): 5–24.

Folmsbee, Stanley J., and Anna Grace Catron. "David Crockett in Texas." *East Tennessee Historical Society Publications* 30 (1958): 48–74.

———. "David Crockett, Congressman." *East Tennessee Historical Society Publications* 29 (1957): 40–78.

———. "The Early Career of David Crockett." *East Tennessee Historical Society Publications* 28 (1956): 58–85.

Groneman, William. "A Rejoinder: Publish Rather Than Perish—Regardless; Jim Crisp and the de la Peña Diary." *Military History of the West* 25 (Fall 1995): 157–66.

———. "The Controversial Alleged Account of José Enrique de la Peña," *Military History of the West* (Fall 1995).

Hall, Claude V. "Early Days in the Red River Country." *Bulletin of the East Texas State Teachers College* 14 (June 1931): 49–79.

Hardin, Stephen L. "Gallery: David Crockett." *Military Illustrated* 23 (February-March 1990): 28–35.

Hauck, Richard Boyd. "The Man in the Buckskin Hunting Shirt: Fact and Fiction in the Crockett Story." In *Davy Crockett: The Man, the Legend, the Legacy,* edited by Michael A. Lofaro. Knoxville, 1985, 3–20.

———. "The Real Davy Crockett: Creative Autobiography and the Invention of His Legend." *Crockett at Two Hundred,* edited by Michael A. Lofaro and Joe Cummings. Knoxville, 1989.

Heale, M. J. "The Role of the Frontier in Jacksonian Politics: David Crockett and the Myth Of the Self-Made Man." *Western Historical Quarterly* 4 (October 1973): 405–23.

Henderson, Jessie A. "Unmarked Historic Spots of Franklin County." *East Tennessee Historical Magazine,* 2d s., 3 (January 1935) 111:20.

Hicklin, J. R. "The Carson-Vance Duel." *The State* [North Carolina] 6 (December 10, 1938): 9.

Hunter, Marvin. "Crockett's Colorful Career Ended in Texas." *Frontier Times* 15 (1938): 139–40.

Hunter, Mary Kate. "David Crockett of Tennessee and Texas." *East Texas Magazine* 2 23, 39.

Hutson, James A. "Benjamin Franklin and the West." *Western Historical Quarterly* (October 1973): 425–34.

Hutton, Paul Andrew. "Mr. Crockett Goes to Washington." *American History* (April 2000): 20–28.

———. "The Alamo: An American Epic." *American History Illustrated* 20 (March 1986): 12–26, 35–37.

———. "A Tale of Two Alamos." *SMU Mustang* 36 (Spring 1986): 16–27.

Lake, Mary Daggett. "David Crockett's Widow: The Pioneer Wife and Mother Who Was Widowed by the Fall of the Alamo." *Texas Monthly* 2 (December 1938): 703–8.

———. "The Family of David Crockett in Texas." *Tennessee Historical Magazine* series 2, 3 (1935): 174–78.

Lindley, Thomas Ricks. "Alamo Artillery: Number, Type, Caliber and Concussion." *Alamo Journal* 82 (July 1992).

———. "Drawing Truthful Deductions." *Journal of the Alamo Battlefield Association* 1 (September 1995): 19–42.

———. "Killing Crockett: It's All in the Execution." *Alamo Journal* 96 (May 1995): 3–12.

———. "Killing Crockett, II: Theory Paraded as Fact." *Alamo Journal* 97 (July 1995): 3–16.

———. "Killing Crockett: Lindley's Opinion." *Alamo Journal* 98 (October 1995): 9–24.

Lofaro, Michael A. "From Boone to Crockett: The Beginnings of Frontier Humor." *Mississippi Folklore Register* 14 (1980): 57–74.

Miles, Guy S. "David Crockett Evolves, 1821–1824." *American Quarterly* 8 (1956): 53–60.

Palmquist, Robert F. "High Private: David Crockett at the Alamo." *Real West: True Tales of the American Frontier* (December 1981): 12–15, 41–43.

Pearson, Josephine A. "The Tennessee Woman Trecker—Elizabeth—Widow of David Crockett." *Tennessee Historical Magazine* series 2, 3 (1935), 169–73.

Pohl, James W., and Steven L. Hardin. "The Military of the Texas Revolution: An Overview," *Southwest Historical Quarterly* 89 (January 1986): 269–308.

Richardson, T. C. "The Girl Davy Left Behind." *Farm and Ranch* 25 (June 1927): 3, 11.

Shackford, James. "David Crockett: The Legend and the Symbol." In *The Frontier Humorists: Critical Views*, edited by M. Thomas Inge (1975): 208–18.

Seeyle, John. "The Well-Wrought Crockett: Or, How the Fakelorists Passed through the Credibility Gap and Discovered Kentucky." In *Toward a New American Literary History: Essays in Honor of Arlin Turner*, edited by Louis J. Budd et al. Durham, NC, 1980: 91–110. Also in Lofaro, *Davy Crockett*, 21–45.

Stout, Dr. S. H. "David Crockett." *American Historical Magazine* 7 (January 1902): 3–21.

Tanenbaum, Miles. "Following Davy's Trail: A Crockett Bibliography." In Lofaro and Cummings, *Crockett at Two Hundred*, 192–241.

Turner, H. S. "Andrew Jackson and David Crockett: Reminiscences of Colonel Chester." *Magazine of American History* 27 (May 1892): 385–87.

Worner, William Frederick. "David Crockett in Columbia." *Lancaster County* [Pennsylvania] *Historical Society Papers* 27 (December 1923): 176–77.

Wright, Marcus J. "Colonel David Crockett of Tennessee." *Magazine of American History* 10 (December 1883): 484–89.

Zaboly, Gary S. "Crockett Goes to Texas: A Newspaper Chronology," *Journal of Alamo Battlefield Association* I (Summer, 1995): 5–18.

INDEX

Page references that are italicized refer to illustrations.

ABOUT THE AUTHOR

Buddy Levy is the author of *Echoes on Rimrock: In Pursuit of the Chukar Partridge*. As a free-lance journalist he has covered adventure sports and lifestyle around the world, including several Eco-Challenges and other adventure expeditions in Morocco, Borneo, Argentina, Europe, and the Philippines. His magazine articles have appeared in *Shooting Sportsman*, *Big Sky Journal*, the *Utne Reader*, *Backpacker*, *Trail Runner*, *Ski*, and *Couloir*. He is clinical assistant professor of English at Washington State University, and lives in northern Idaho with his wife, two children, and two black Labs.

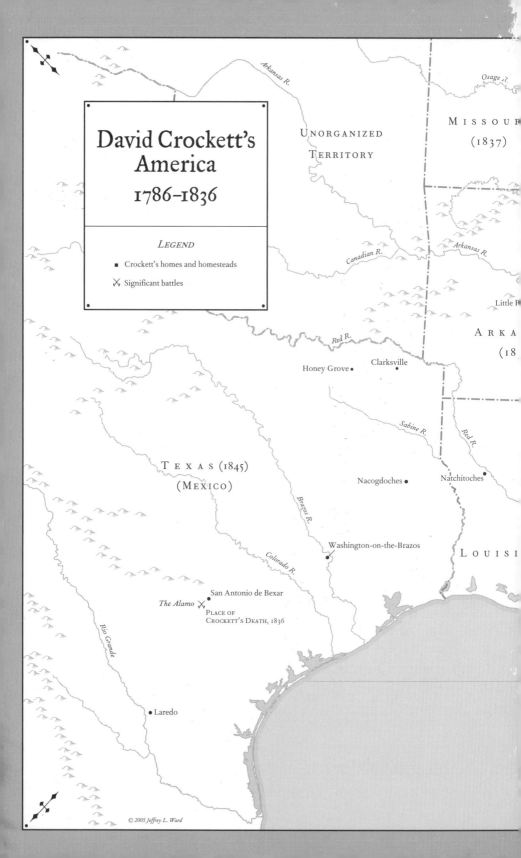

David Crockett's America
1786–1836

LEGEND

■ Crockett's homes and homesteads

✕ Significant battles

Arkansas R.

UNORGANIZED
TERRITORY

Osage R.

MISSOUR

(1837)

Canadian R.

Arkansas R.

Little F

Red R.

Honey Grove ●   Clarksville ●

ARKA

(18

Sabine R.

Red R.

TEXAS (1845)

(MEXICO)

Nacogdoches ●   Natchitoches ●

Brazos R.

Washington-on-the-Brazos ●

LOUISI

Colorado R.

San Antonio de Bexar
The Alamo ✕
PLACE OF
CROCKETT'S DEATH, 1836

Rio Grande

● Laredo

© 2005 Jeffrey L. Ward